W9-AEC-711

A GRAPHIC ADAPTATION

THE GETTYSBURG ADDRESS

WRITTEN BY **JONATHAN HENNESSEY** ART BY **AARON MCCONNELL**

LETTERING BY **TOM ORZECHOWSKI**

wm

WILLIAM MORROW
An Imprint of HarperCollins*Publishers*

PSST!
TILLIE...!
≑gasp≑ WHATISIT?!
...IT'S QUIET NOW.
THE SHELLING AND GUNFIRE OUT THERE SEEM TO HAVE... DIED DOWN.
WE ARE THINKING OF GOING BACK TO CHECK ON THE FARM.
MAMA! THE SMELL...!
OH! TRY NOT TO LOOK.

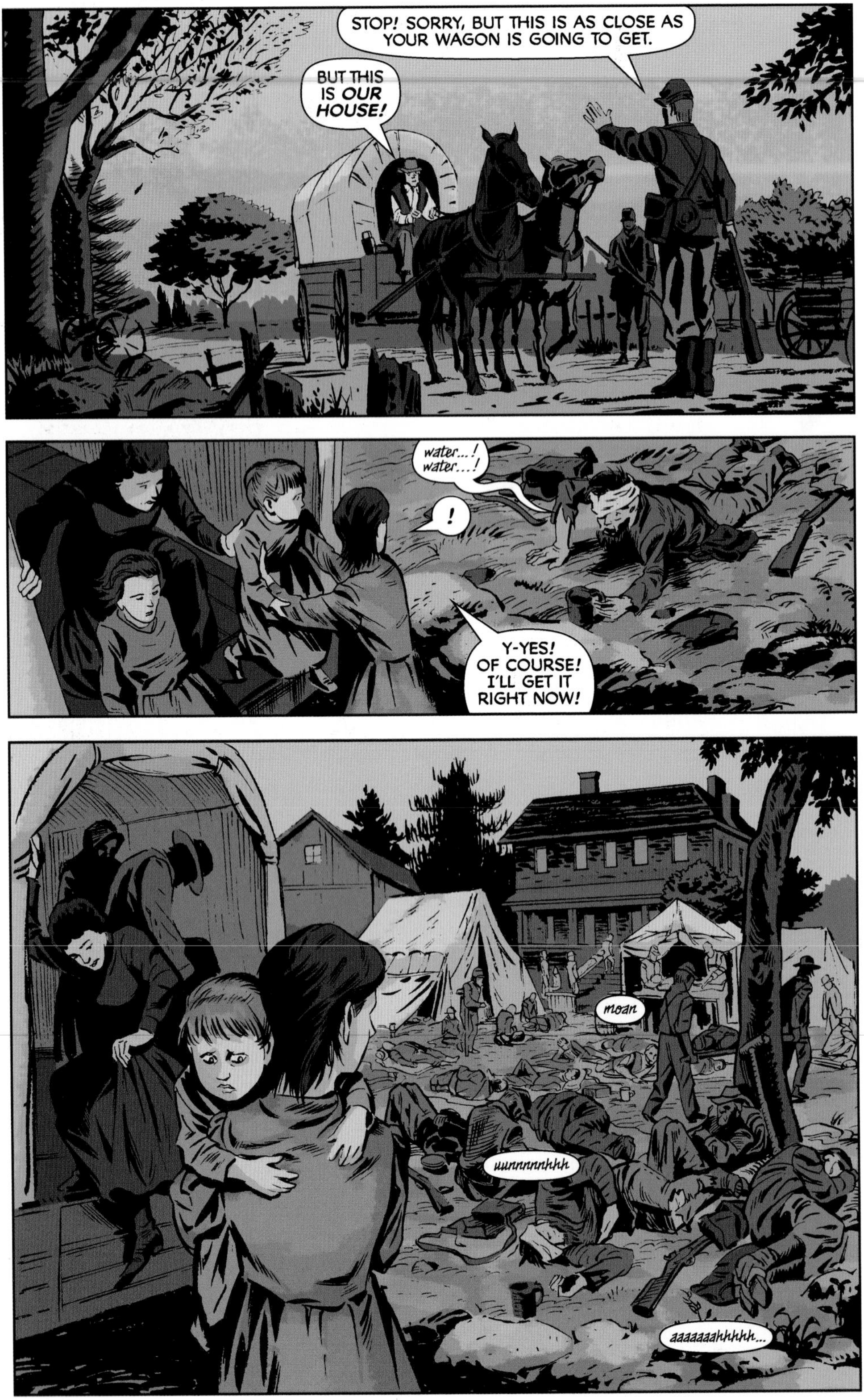
STOP! SORRY, BUT THIS IS AS CLOSE AS YOUR WAGON IS GOING TO GET.
BUT THIS IS OUR HOUSE!
water...! water...!
!
Y-YES! OF COURSE! I'LL GET IT RIGHT NOW!
moan
uunnnnnhhh
aaaaaaahhhhh...

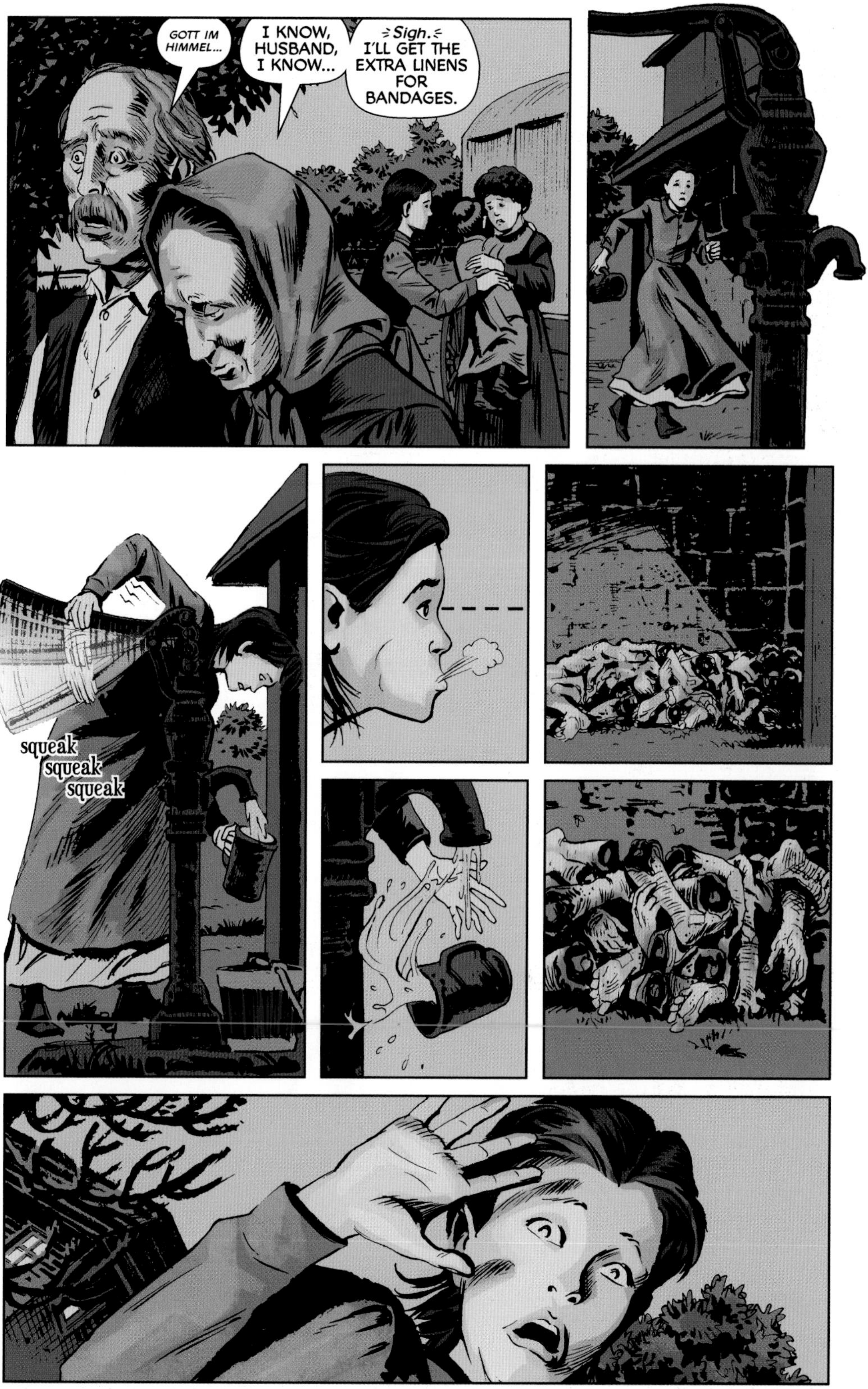
GOTT IM HIMMEL...
I KNOW, HUSBAND, I KNOW...
Sigh. I'LL GET THE EXTRA LINENS FOR BANDAGES.
squeak squeak squeak

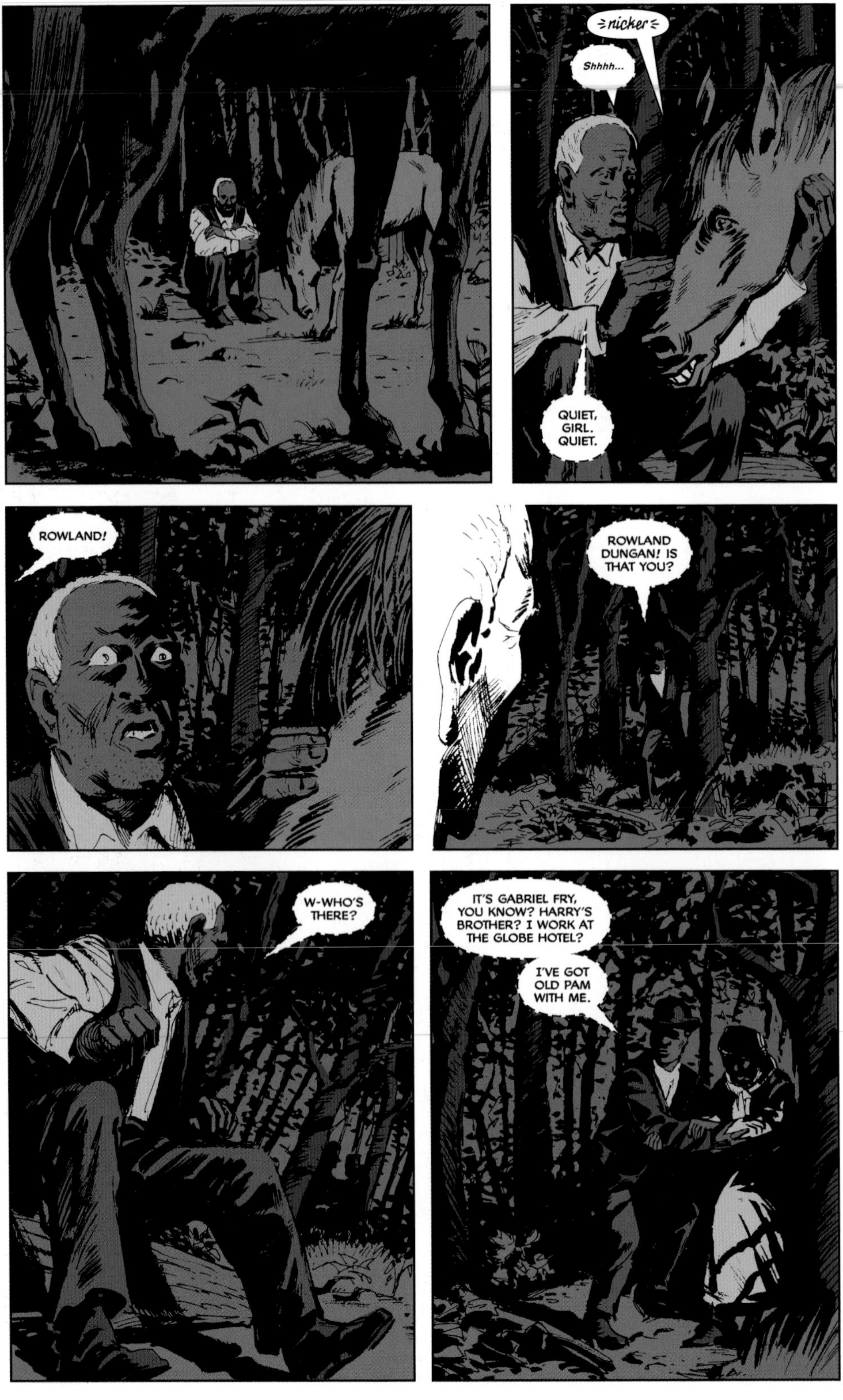

nicker
Shhhh...
QUIET, GIRL. QUIET.
ROWLAND!
ROWLAND DUNGAN! IS THAT YOU?
W-WHO'S THERE?
IT'S GABRIEL FRY, YOU KNOW? HARRY'S BROTHER? I WORK AT THE GLOBE HOTEL?
I'VE GOT OLD PAM WITH ME.

I SAW THE HORSES AND GOT SCARED FOR A MINUTE IT WAS CAVALRY.

WHAT ARE YOU DOING HERE?

MR. LAMBETH-- YOU KNOW, LIVES OUT ON HANOVER ROAD? HE PAID ME TO HIDE HIS LIVESTOCK AND VALUABLES FROM THE REBELS. I BEEN HERE FOR...I DON'T KNOW. *DAYS.*

SO YOU TWO CAME FROM *TOWN?* WHAT HAPPENED?

WE DON'T KNOW FOR SURE YET. BUT THERE WAS SUCH A FIGHT, *ROWLAND. SUCH A FIGHT...!*

≷sniff≷

SHE'S BEEN MIGHTY SCARED, GABRIEL. AFRAID OF GETTING *TAKEN BACK.*

HUH. AND YOU THINK I'M NOT? YOU WERE BORN *FREE.* IN *PENNSYLVANIA.*

THAT'S NOT HOW IT WAS FOR ME AND OLD PAM.

WELL... YOU TWO BEST STAY HERE WITH ME.

I *THOUGHT* THIS WAS A DECENT SPOT TO HIDE, BUT... IF *YOU ALL* FOUND ME, WHO'S TO SAY THE REBELS WON'T?

FAIR QUESTION, THERE, BOY.

WHO *IS* TO SAY THEY WON'T...?

CREEE-
EEAK

CRACK!

AND FROM WHAT I HEAR, NOT A SINGLE ONE OF PICKETT'S *COLONELS* EVEN SURVIVED THE...

...*LOOK OUT!*

YAARRGH!!

THIS IS NO RETREAT. THIS IS A DOWNRIGHT *DEBACLE,* I TELL YOU.

ENGINEERS! WE GOT A BUSTED WHEEL DOWN HERE!

groan

COME ON. WE'LL SWAP YOU INTO ANOTHER AMBULANCE.

HALF OF US IN HERE ARE ALREADY DEAD. JUST LEAVE ME BY THE ROAD. I CAN ≷COUGH≷ TAKE NO MORE.

HEY, TARHEEL...?

MAYBE THE KIND THING TO DO IS JUST TAKE THE MAN AT HIS WORD...

WHAT? NO! WE'VE LOST FAR TOO MANY THESE PAST THREE DAYS!

DAMN IT ALL!

CLEAR IT UP THROUGH HERE, OR WE'LL ROLL RIGHT OVER YOU!

IT'S NO USE... ≷COUGH≷

THE YANKEES TOOK OUT OUR BRIDGE OVER THE ≷HACK≷ POTOMAC SOMETIME YESTERDAY.

...AND WITH ALL THIS RAIN... THE RIVER RISING...

...WE'LL BE TRAPPED. TRAPPED.

IT'S ALL OVER.

7

TRAP-T-T-TRAP-TRAP-T-RAP...

...T-T-T-TRAP-TRAP...

...TRAP—TRAP—T—T...

MR. PRESIDENT! DO YOU HEAR THAT?

NEWS... AT LAST.

WHAT HAVE WE? IF THERE IS MERCY IN THIS WORLD, IT WILL BE A DISPATCH FROM GENERAL MEADE.

IT'S... IT'S VERY STRANGE, MR. PRESIDENT. THIS MESSAGE ISN'T EVEN IN MILITARY CIPHER.

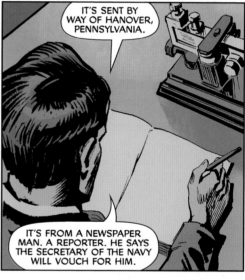

IT'S SENT BY WAY OF HANOVER, PENNSYLVANIA.

IT'S FROM A NEWSPAPER MAN. A REPORTER. HE SAYS THE SECRETARY OF THE NAVY WILL VOUCH FOR HIM.

AND WHAT DOES THIS MAN SAY?

ACCORDING TO HIM, A GREAT BATTLE HAS BEEN FOUGHT AT GETTYSBURG...

...AND THAT WHEN HE LEFT THE FIELD, AT HALF PAST SIX THIS EVENING, "EVERYTHING LOOKED HOPEFUL."

Gettysburg

...GETTYSBURG...

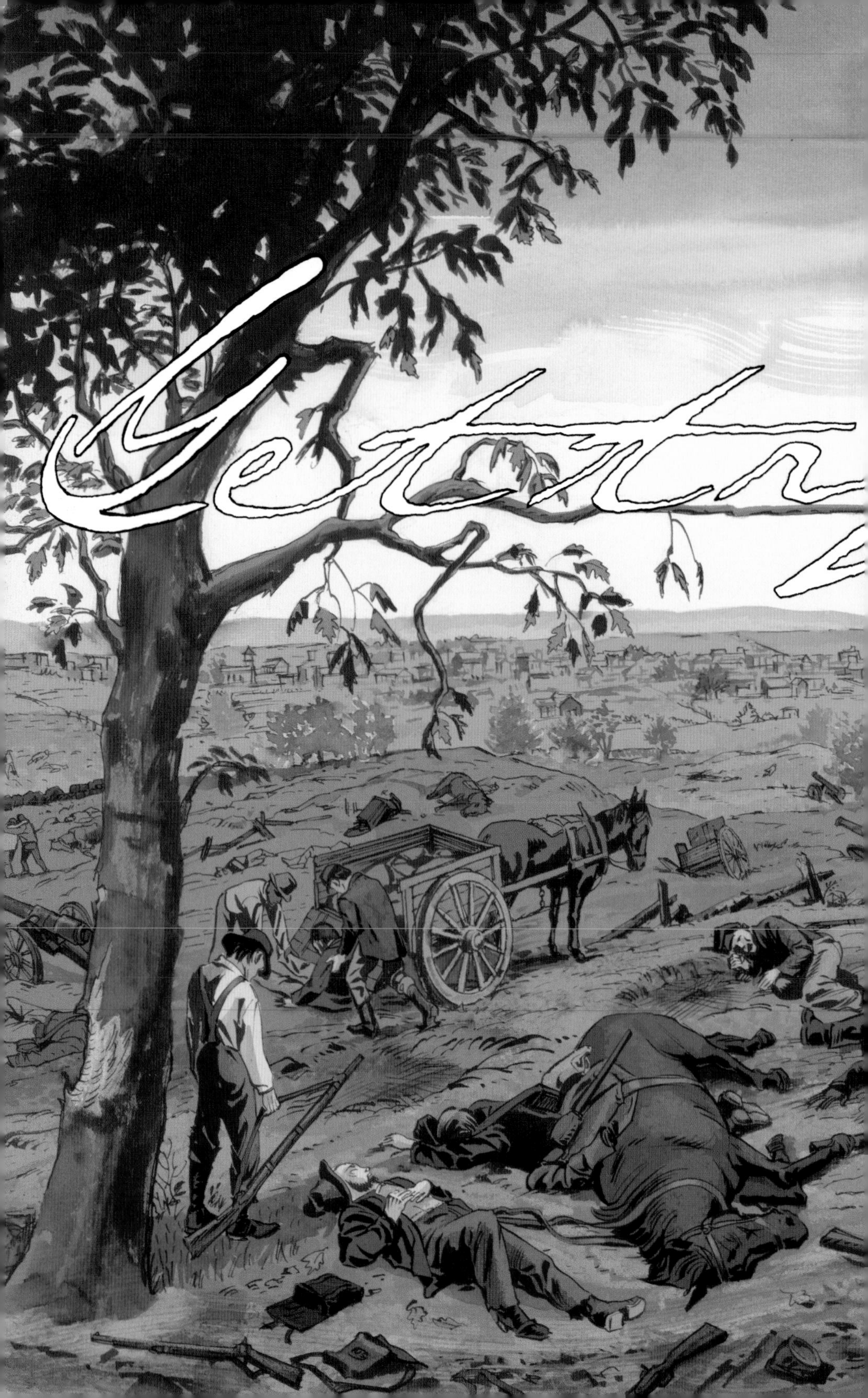

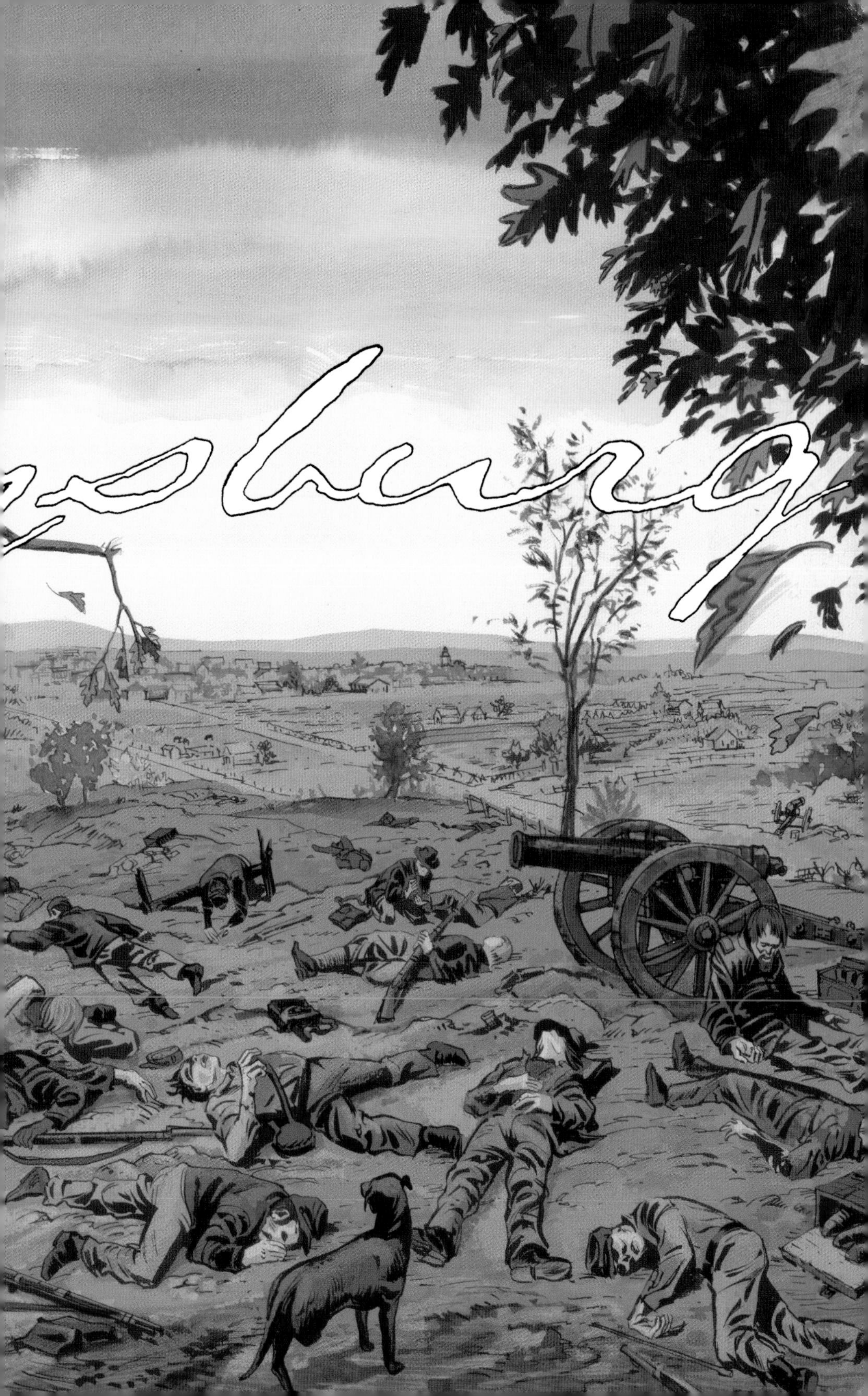
sburg

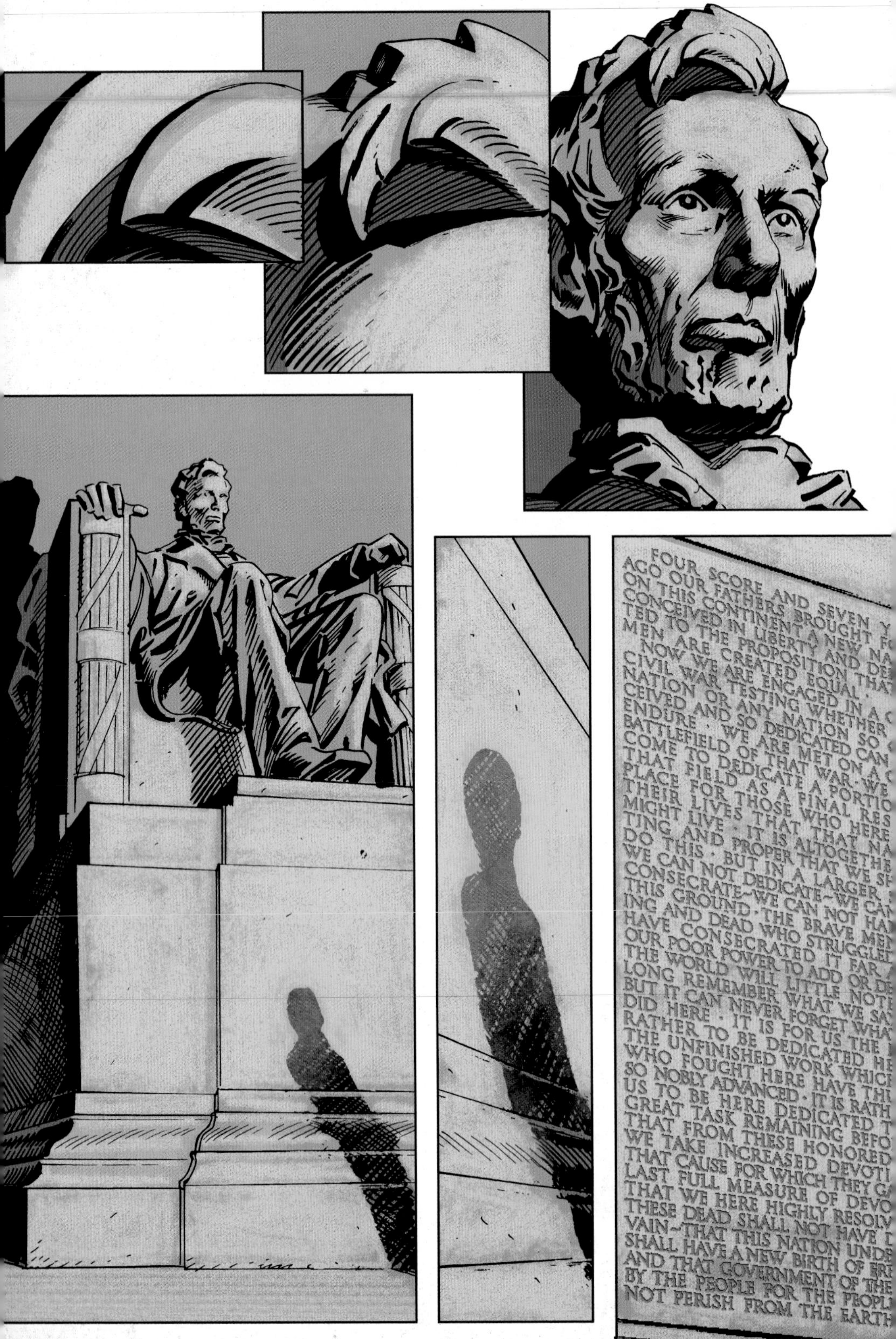

FOUR SCORE AND SEVEN Y
AGO OUR FATHERS BROUGHT F
ON THIS CONTINENT A NEW NA
CONCEIVED IN LIBERTY AND DE
TED TO THE PROPOSITION THA
MEN ARE CREATED EQUAL
NOW WE ARE ENGAGED IN A G
CIVIL WAR TESTING WHETHER
NATION OR ANY NATION SO
CEIVED AND SO DEDICATED CAN
ENDURE · WE ARE MET ON A G
BATTLEFIELD OF THAT WAR · WE
COME TO DEDICATE A PORTIO
THAT FIELD AS A FINAL RES
PLACE FOR THOSE WHO HERE
THEIR LIVES THAT THAT NA
MIGHT LIVE · IT IS ALTOGETHE
TING AND PROPER THAT WE SH
DO THIS · BUT IN A LARGER
WE CAN NOT DEDICATE ~ WE CA
CONSECRATE ~ WE CAN NOT HA
THIS GROUND · THE BRAVE ME
ING AND DEAD WHO STRUGGLE
HAVE CONSECRATED IT FAR
OUR POOR POWER TO ADD OR DE
THE WORLD WILL LITTLE NOT
LONG REMEMBER WHAT WE SA
BUT IT CAN NEVER FORGET WHA
DID HERE · IT IS FOR US THE
RATHER TO BE DEDICATED HE
THE UNFINISHED WORK WHICH
WHO FOUGHT HERE HAVE TH
SO NOBLY ADVANCED · IT IS RATH
US TO BE HERE DEDICATED T
GREAT TASK REMAINING BEFO
THAT FROM THESE HONORED
WE TAKE INCREASED DEVOTI
THAT CAUSE FOR WHICH THEY GA
LAST FULL MEASURE OF DEVO
THAT WE HERE HIGHLY RESOLV
THESE DEAD SHALL NOT HAVE
VAIN ~ THAT THIS NATION UNDE
SHALL HAVE A NEW BIRTH OF FR
AND THAT GOVERNMENT OF THE
BY THE PEOPLE FOR THE PEOPL
NOT PERISH FROM THE EARTH

IT IS PROBABLY THE MOST **FAMOUS AND** INFLUENTIAL SPEECH IN AMERICAN HISTORY.

ITS WORDS, OVER TIME, HAVE DONE NO LESS THAN TRANSFORM THE COUNTRY...

...OR SO IT HAS BEEN CLAIMED.

THE SPEECH OPENS WITH THE NOW ICONIC PHRASE:

"FOUR SCORE AND SEVEN YEARS AGO."

THOSE SIX WORDS ARE UNDENIABLY FAMILIAR TO AMERICANS. NEARLY ALL OF US HAVE HEARD THEM SO MANY TIMES, WE REMEMBER THEM--AND CAN QUOTE THEM BACK--EFFORTLESSLY.

BY ITS SHEER REPETITION, THE PHRASE "FOUR SCORE AND SEVEN YEARS AGO" OFTEN CARRIES NO MORE WEIGHT THAN AN ADVERTISING JINGLE, A TIRED LINE FROM AN OLD MOVIE, OR A SHOPWORN PLATITUDE ABOUT THE WEATHER.

BUT THE MAN WHO WROTE THOSE WORDS CHOSE THEM JUDICIOUSLY. IN FACT HE STAKED HUNDREDS OF THOUSANDS OF AMERICAN LIVES ON WHAT HE THOUGHT THEY MEANT.

FOR THEIR AUTHOR, THOSE SIX WORDS DID NOT SIMPLY REFER TO A SPECIFIC DATE IN HISTORY. NOR EVEN JUST TO THE MOMENTOUS EVENTS THAT OCCURRED THAT YEAR.

INSTEAD, THOSE WORDS ANSWERED THE QUESTION OF WHAT THE UNITED STATES OF AMERICA REALLY IS.

THAT QUESTION, WHICH HAD ONCE BEEN A MATTER FOR CIVILIZED DEBATE...

...HAD BY THE TIME OF THE GETTYSBURG ADDRESS DEGENERATED INTO A REASON FOR MEN TO KILL ONE ANOTHER.

TO THE MAN WHO WROTE AND SPOKE THE WORDS "FOUR SCORE AND SEVEN YEARS AGO"...

...THEY MEANT EVERYTHING.

DC TOURS
ARCHIVES OF THE UNITED STATES OF AMERICA
CHARTERS OF FREEDOM

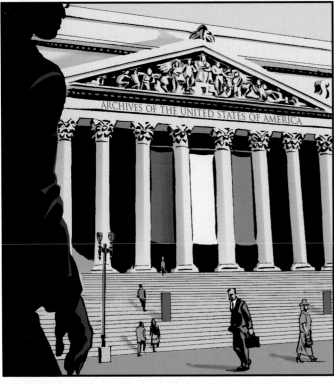

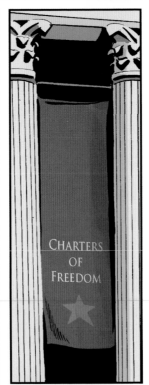

TODAY, THE ROTUNDA OF THE CHARTERS OF FREEDOM AT THE NATIONAL ARCHIVES BUILDING IN WASHINGTON, D.C., DISPLAYS TWO OF OUR COUNTRY'S FOUNDING DOCUMENTS.

THE CONSTITUTION OF THE UNITED STATES: A PLAN FOR A FEDERAL GOVERNMENT.

THE DECLARATION OF INDEPENDENCE: A 1776 PROCLAMATION BY THE CITIZENS OF THIRTEEN COLONIES IN AMERICA.

THOSE CITIZENS WERE DECLARING THAT THEIR MOTHER COUNTRY-- GREAT BRITAIN-- HAD VIOLATED THEIR ESSENTIAL HUMAN RIGHTS. CITING THOSE INJUSTICES, THE DECLARATION DARED TRY TO LEGALLY AND MORALLY JUSTIFY THE UNTHINKABLE...

...THE PERMANENT SEVERANCE OF THE COLONIES FROM THEIR GOVERNMENT...

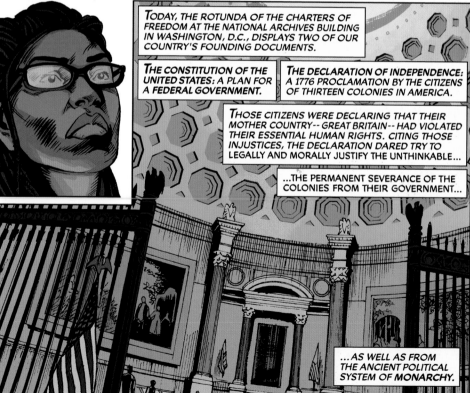

...AS WELL AS FROM THE ANCIENT POLITICAL SYSTEM OF MONARCHY.

THE TWO DOCUMENTS ARE DISPLAYED SIDE BY SIDE.

THE SANCTITY OF THEIR SETTING SUGGESTS THAT THEY ARE IN HARMONY. THAT THE DOCUMENTS ESSENTIALLY STAND FOR THE SAME IDEAS.

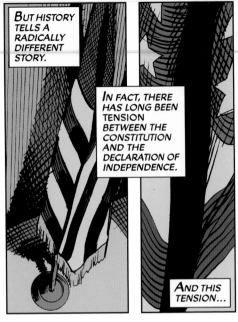

BUT HISTORY TELLS A RADICALLY DIFFERENT STORY.

IN FACT, THERE HAS LONG BEEN TENSION BETWEEN THE CONSTITUTION AND THE DECLARATION OF INDEPENDENCE.

AND THIS TENSION...

...DETONATED INTO A DISASTROUS **CIVIL WAR** THAT RAGED FOR MORE THAN FOUR YEARS.

SPLLISHH

Billy & Johnny's
BATTLEFIELD
Antiques & Collectibles

THE CIVIL WAR
TOOK PLACE FROM
1861 TO 1865.

DURING THAT PERIOD IN HISTORY...

...THE UNITED STATES WAS ONE OF THE LAST COUNTRIES WHERE SLAVERY REMAINED LEGAL...

... AND IT HAD MORE SLAVES THAN ANY OTHER COUNTRY ON EARTH.

THE CIVIL WAR WAS AN OFTEN DESPERATE, BLOODY STRUGGLE BETWEEN TWO COMBATANTS.

UNIONISTS: MEMBERS AND SUPPORTERS OF THE UNION-- THE FEDERAL GOVERNMENT OF THE UNITED STATES ITSELF. THE UNION WAS THEN JUST 73 YEARS OLD.

SECESSIONISTS: THOSE LOYAL TO ELEVEN SOUTHERN STATES THAT HAD REJECTED THE FEDERAL GOVERNMENT. THEY CLAIMED TO HAVE LEGALLY SEPARATED OR SECEDED FROM THE UNION. THOSE STATES ORGANIZED THEIR OWN ALLIANCE, WHICH THEY CHRISTENED THE CONFEDERATE STATES OF AMERICA.

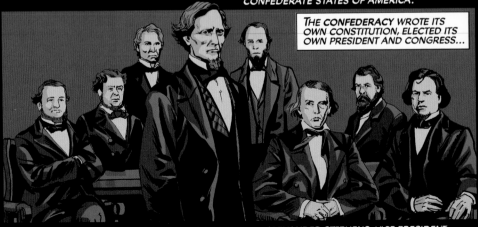

THE CONFEDERACY WROTE ITS OWN CONSTITUTION, ELECTED ITS OWN PRESIDENT AND CONGRESS...

JEFFERSON DAVIS, PRESIDENT OF THE CONFEDERACY.

ALEXANDER STEPHENS, VICE PRESIDENT OF THE CONFEDERACY.

...AND SOON ESTABLISHED ITS CAPITAL AT RICHMOND, VIRGINIA.

...LESS THAN 100 MILES FROM THE SEAT OF THE U.S. GOVERNMENT IN WASHINGTON, D.C.

AT THE OUTSET OF THE CIVIL WAR AND FOR ITS ENTIRE FIRST YEAR, SLAVERY WAS A LEGAL AND LONG-STANDING INSTITUTION *IN* BOTH CAPITAL CITIES.

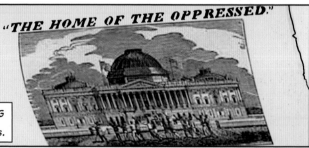

"THE HOME OF THE OPPRESSED."

SLAVE LABOR WAS USED DURING THE U.S. CAPITOL BUILDING'S MAJOR EXPANSION IN THE 1850s.

THE NUMBER OF AMERICAN SOLDIERS WHO LOST THEIR LIVES IN THE CIVIL WAR RIVALS THE TOTAL FROM ALL OTHER **AMERICAN** WARS COMBINED.

ADJUSTED FOR POPULATION *GROWTH*, THIS WOULD BE LIKE 5 1/2 MILLION SOLDIERS DYING IN A WAR TODAY.

REVOLUTIONARY WAR: 4,435

WAR OF 1812: 2,260

WAR WITH MEXICO: 13,283

SPANISH-AMERICAN WAR: 2,446

PHILIPPINE INSURGENCY: 4,196

WORLD WAR I: 116,516

WORLD WAR II: 405,399

KOREAN CONFLICT: 36,574

VIETNAM CONFLICT: 58,209

PERSIAN GULF CONFLICT: 382

OPERATION IRAQI FREEDOM: 4,326

OPERATION ENDURING FREEDOM (AFGHANISTAN): 2,124

OTHERS (INCLUDING INDIAN WARS): 4,846

TOTAL SOULS LOST: 655,144

CIVIL WAR MILITARY DEATHS (COMBINED UNION AND CONFEDERATE) 622,511.

A PERSUASIVE 2011 STUDY PUT THE NUMBER OF CIVIL WAR DEAD EVEN HIGHER-- TO 750,000.

IN THESE EARLIER TIMES, THE OFFICE OF THE PRESIDENCY WAS CONSIDERED SO DISTINGUISHED...

...THAT THE MEN WHO HELD IT RARELY APPEARED TO THE PUBLIC OUTSIDE WASHINGTON.

IN FACT, TO THE PRESIDENTS OF THE 18th, 19th, AND EARLY 20th CENTURIES, THE MODERN TRADITION OF PRESIDENTIAL ELECTION CAMPAIGNING WOULD BE ODIOUS...

...FAR BENEATH THEIR SENSE OF DIGNITY.

SOCK IT TO ME?!

THE VIEW

ABRAHAM LINCOLN, FOR EXAMPLE, CHOSE NOT TO APPEAR AT THE NATIONAL CONVENTION OF THE POLITICAL PARTY THAT NOMINATED HIM: THE REPUBLICAN PARTY. LINCOLN MADE ONLY ONE APPEARANCE DURING THE ENTIRE CAMPAIGN. AND TO AVOID THE "EMBARRASS-MENT" OF BEING SEEN VOTING FOR HIMSELF, HE REMOVED HIS OWN NAME FROM HIS BALLOT!

THIS SPIRIT OF HIGH PRESIDENTIAL STATURE AFFECTED EVERYTHING ABOUT THE OFFICE. AND IT WAS RARE FOR THE PRESIDENT TO MAKE A SPEECH AFTER A MILITARY ENGAGEMENT, EVEN DURING THE CIVIL WAR.

THE BATTLE OF GETTYSBURG, HOWEVER, WAS A DIFFERENT STORY.

THE BATTLE OF GETTYSBURG LASTED FOR THREE DAYS: JULY 1-3, 1863.

MUCH OF THAT YEAR HAD BEEN AN EXCRUCIATING TIME FOR THOSE WHO SUPPORTED THE GOVERNMENT.

PATRIOTIC ZEAL FOR THE UNION HAD SURGED EARLY IN THE WAR.

BUT BY 1863, REUNITING ALL THE STATES-- THEN NUMBERING 36*-- SEEMED INCREASINGLY FUTILE.

*THE BREAKUP OF VIRGINIA AND WEST VIRGINIA-- PREVIOUSLY ONE LARGE STATE-- HAD TAKEN PLACE DURING THE WAR. WEST VIRGINIA OFFICIALLY ENTERED THE UNION JUST A FEW WEEKS BEFORE THE BATTLE OF GETTYSBURG.

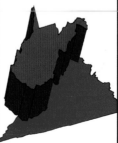

NEVADA WOULD BECOME A STATE LATER IN THE CIVIL WAR, BRINGING THE TOTAL, IN 1864, TO 37.

BY THE SUMMER OF 1863, UNIONISTS HAD BEEN DEALT CRUSHING BLOWS: **THE BATTLE OF FREDERICKSBURG** AND **THE BATTLE OF CHANCELLORSVILLE**, BOTH IN VIRGINIA.

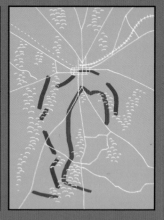

MAY 31, 1863

Why are we Defeated?

The Springfield (Mass.) *Republican* has of late been exploiting the theory that the reason the Army of the Potomac was defeated at Chancellorsville, and the reason it has been defeated in so many campaigns, is that the soldiers *do not fight* as well as the rebels. It has recently been backed up in its position by the opinion of a Massachusetts officer who was taken prisoner at Chancellorsville, carried to Richmond, and has recently been exchanged. It is rather a curious theory certainly to preach in New-England; after that we have seen and heard of the ...

AND NEARLY A THOUSAND MILES AWAY...

...UNION FORCES WERE STRIVING TO TAKE THE CRITICAL RIVER STRONGHOLD OF VICKSBURG, MISSISSIPPI.

BUT THEY WERE STALLED IN A BITTER SIEGE OF THAT CITY.

PRESIDENT ABRAHAM LINCOLN HAD MORE PROBLEMS.

OF ALL THE GENERALS ELEVATED TO LEAD THE UNION ARMIES, NOT A SINGLE ONE HAD LIVED UP TO EXPECTATIONS.

AFTER COMMITTING BLUNDERS OR FAILING TO TAKE THE OFFENSIVE, ONE COMMANDER AFTER ANOTHER HAD COME AND GONE.

ONE UNION GENERAL CALLED FOR LINCOLN TO BE REPLACED WITH A DICTATOR.

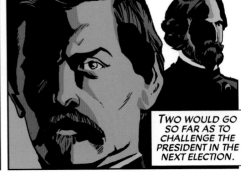

TWO WOULD GO SO FAR AS TO CHALLENGE THE PRESIDENT IN THE NEXT ELECTION.

SEGMENTS OF THE UNION ARMY WERE BADLY DEMORALIZED.

...AND EVEN RUMORED TO BE NEAR MUTINY.

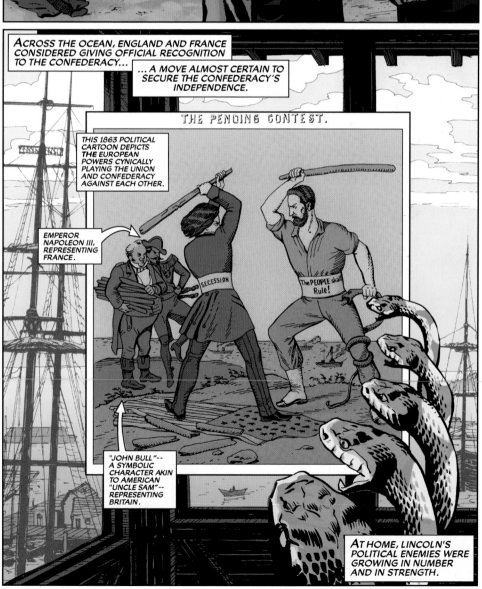

ACROSS THE OCEAN, ENGLAND AND FRANCE CONSIDERED GIVING OFFICIAL RECOGNITION TO THE CONFEDERACY...

...A MOVE ALMOST CERTAIN TO SECURE THE CONFEDERACY'S INDEPENDENCE.

THE PENDING CONTEST.

THIS 1863 POLITICAL CARTOON DEPICTS THE EUROPEAN POWERS CYNICALLY PLAYING THE UNION AND CONFEDERACY AGAINST EACH OTHER.

EMPEROR NAPOLEON III, REPRESENTING FRANCE.

SECESSION

The PEOPLE shall Rule!

"JOHN BULL"-- A SYMBOLIC CHARACTER AKIN TO AMERICAN "UNCLE SAM"-- REPRESENTING BRITAIN.

AT HOME, LINCOLN'S POLITICAL ENEMIES WERE GROWING IN NUMBER AND IN STRENGTH.

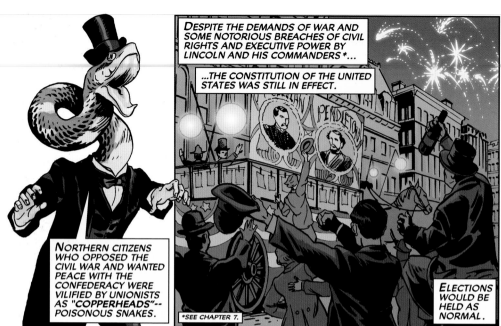

DESPITE THE DEMANDS OF WAR AND SOME NOTORIOUS BREACHES OF CIVIL RIGHTS AND EXECUTIVE POWER BY LINCOLN AND HIS COMMANDERS *...

...THE CONSTITUTION OF THE UNITED STATES WAS STILL IN EFFECT.

NORTHERN CITIZENS WHO OPPOSED THE CIVIL WAR AND WANTED PEACE WITH THE CONFEDERACY WERE VILIFIED BY UNIONISTS AS "COPPERHEADS"-- POISONOUS SNAKES.

*SEE CHAPTER 7.

ELECTIONS WOULD BE HELD AS NORMAL.

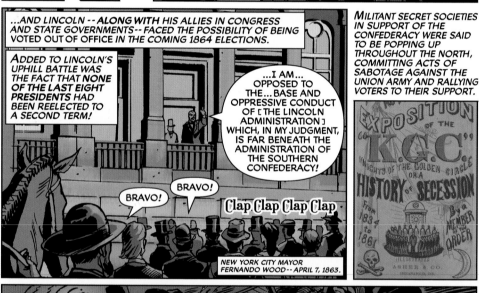

...AND LINCOLN -- ALONG WITH HIS ALLIES IN CONGRESS AND STATE GOVERNMENTS-- FACED THE POSSIBILITY OF BEING VOTED OUT OF OFFICE IN THE COMING 1864 ELECTIONS.

ADDED TO LINCOLN'S UPHILL BATTLE WAS THE FACT THAT NONE OF THE LAST EIGHT PRESIDENTS HAD BEEN REELECTED TO A SECOND TERM!

...I AM... OPPOSED TO THE... BASE AND OPPRESSIVE CONDUCT OF [THE LINCOLN ADMINISTRATION] WHICH, IN MY JUDGMENT, IS FAR BENEATH THE ADMINISTRATION OF THE SOUTHERN CONFEDERACY!

BRAVO!

BRAVO!

Clap Clap Clap Clap

NEW YORK CITY MAYOR FERNANDO WOOD-- APRIL 7, 1863.

MILITANT SECRET SOCIETIES IN SUPPORT OF THE CONFEDERACY WERE SAID TO BE POPPING UP THROUGHOUT THE NORTH, COMMITTING ACTS OF SABOTAGE AGAINST THE UNION ARMY AND RALLYING VOTERS TO THEIR SUPPORT.

EXPOSITION OF THE "K.G.C." KNIGHTS OF THE GOLDEN CIRCLE OR A HISTORY OF SECESSION From 1834 to 1861 By A MEMBER OF THE ORDER ILLUSTRATED ASHER & CO. INDIANAPOLIS, IND.

W. REYNOLDS COOPER SHOP

SOME NORTHERN WHITES BLAMED BLACKS FOR THE WAR. RACE RIOTS HAD BROKEN OUT IN U.S. CITIES.

DETROIT RACE RIOT, MARCH 6, 1863.

MANY OF THE TOUGH POLICY CHOICES LINCOLN HAD MADE WERE GRIEVOUSLY UNPOPULAR, EVEN AMONG THOSE STILL LOYAL TO THE UNION.

I PROTEST AGAINST [THE EMANCIPATION PROCLAMATION] AS A VIOLATION OF THE CONSTITUTION AND THE LIBERTIES OF MY COUNTRY...

I PROTEST AGAINST IT AS BEING AS MUCH A *SIN* AGAINST THE *RELIGION OF CHRIST* AS IT IS TO THE MORAL SENTIMENT OF MANKIND.

GEORGE HELM YEAMAN, CONGRESSMAN FROM KENTUCKY, DECEMBER 18, 1862.

EVEN SOME MEMBERS OF LINCOLN'S OWN CABINET WERE ANGLING TO SUCCEED HIM AS PRESIDENT.

BUT THE MOST PRESSING DANGER WAS YET TO COME.

THE COMMANDER OF THE CONFEDERATE MILITARY FORCES IN THE EAST WAS GENERAL ROBERT E. LEE.

LEE HAD SERVED, WITH CONSIDERABLE SUCCESS, ALL OF HIS ADULT LIFE IN THE U.S. ARMY...

...AGAINST WHOSE GOVERNMENT HE HAD NOW TAKEN ARMS.

CAPTAIN ROBERT E. LEE ON A SCOUTING MISSION BEFORE THE BATTLE OF CONTRERAS -- MEXICAN-AMERICAN WAR, AUGUST 1847.

WINFIELD SCOTT, THE U.S. ARMY GENERAL IN CHIEF AT THE OUTSET OF THE CIVIL WAR, WANTED LEE TO FIGHT FOR THE SIDE OF THE UNION. SCOTT EVEN PLANNED TO ASSIGN LEE TO A TOP COMMAND. BUT WHEN LEE'S BELOVED HOME STATE OF VIRGINIA DECLARED ITS SECESSION, LEE TURNED THE PROMOTION DOWN. HE LEFT THE U.S. ARMY ALTOGETHER.

With all my devotion to the Union, and the feeling of loyalty and duty of an American citizen, I have not been able to make up my mind to raise my hand against my relatives, my children, my home. I have, therefore, resigned my commission in the army, and, save in defence of my native state, with the sincere hope that my poor services may never be needed, I hope I may never be called on to draw my sword.

AFTER OUTFIGHTING, OUTSMARTING, AND OUT-MANEUVERING THE UNION ARMY AGAIN AND AGAIN, LEE UNDERTOOK A SINGULARLY BOLD MOVE.

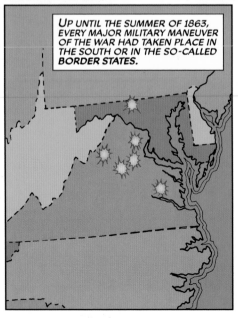

UP UNTIL THE SUMMER OF 1863, EVERY MAJOR MILITARY MANEUVER OF THE WAR HAD TAKEN PLACE IN THE SOUTH OR IN THE SO-CALLED BORDER STATES.

BUT NOW, SEIZING HIS MOMENTUM, LEE DECIDED TO INVADE THE NORTH.

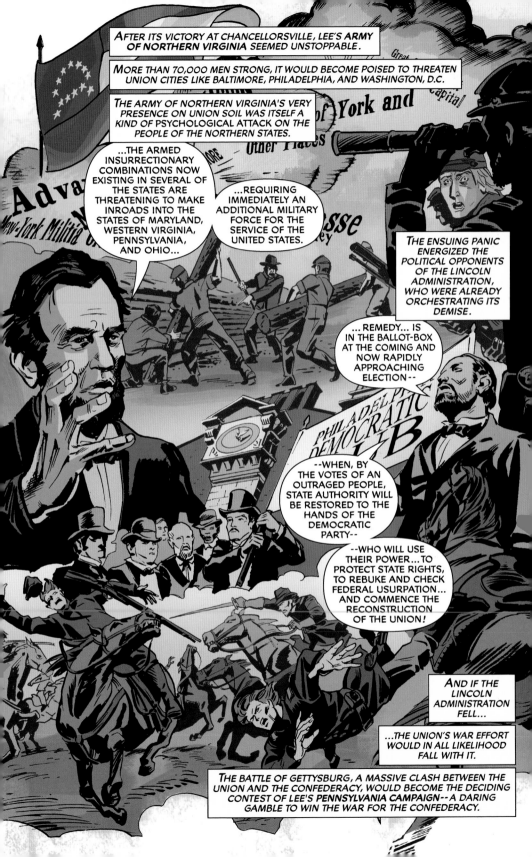

AFTER ITS VICTORY AT CHANCELLORSVILLE, LEE'S ARMY OF NORTHERN VIRGINIA SEEMED UNSTOPPABLE.

MORE THAN 70,000 MEN STRONG, IT WOULD BECOME POISED TO THREATEN UNION CITIES LIKE BALTIMORE, PHILADELPHIA, AND WASHINGTON, D.C.

THE ARMY OF NORTHERN VIRGINIA'S VERY PRESENCE ON UNION SOIL WAS ITSELF A KIND OF PSYCHOLOGICAL ATTACK ON THE PEOPLE OF THE NORTHERN STATES.

...THE ARMED INSURRECTIONARY COMBINATIONS NOW EXISTING IN SEVERAL OF THE STATES ARE THREATENING TO MAKE INROADS INTO THE STATES OF MARYLAND, WESTERN VIRGINIA, PENNSYLVANIA, AND OHIO...

...REQUIRING IMMEDIATELY AN ADDITIONAL MILITARY FORCE FOR THE SERVICE OF THE UNITED STATES.

THE ENSUING PANIC ENERGIZED THE POLITICAL OPPONENTS OF THE LINCOLN ADMINISTRATION, WHO WERE ALREADY ORCHESTRATING ITS DEMISE.

...REMEDY... IS IN THE BALLOT-BOX AT THE COMING AND NOW RAPIDLY APPROACHING ELECTION--

--WHEN, BY THE VOTES OF AN OUTRAGED PEOPLE, STATE AUTHORITY WILL BE RESTORED TO THE HANDS OF THE DEMOCRATIC PARTY--

--WHO WILL USE THEIR POWER...TO PROTECT STATE RIGHTS, TO REBUKE AND CHECK FEDERAL USURPATION... AND COMMENCE THE RECONSTRUCTION OF THE UNION!

AND IF THE LINCOLN ADMINISTRATION FELL...

...THE UNION'S WAR EFFORT WOULD IN ALL LIKELIHOOD FALL WITH IT.

THE BATTLE OF GETTYSBURG, A MASSIVE CLASH BETWEEN THE UNION AND THE CONFEDERACY, WOULD BECOME THE DECIDING CONTEST OF LEE'S PENNSYLVANIA CAMPAIGN-- A DARING GAMBLE TO WIN THE WAR FOR THE CONFEDERACY.

THE AFTERMATH OF THE BATTLE OF GETTYSBURG...

...AND THE MOUNTING DEVASTATION OF THE ENTIRE CIVIL WAR...

...FORCED ABRAHAM LINCOLN'S HAND.

WHEN THE BATTLE WAS OVER, HE FACED THE DAUNTING TASK OF CONVINCING THE WAR-WEARY AMERICAN PEOPLE THAT THE COSTLY, PUNISHING CONFLICT HAD TO GO ON.

IN NOVEMBER, 1863, LINCOLN WAS INVITED TO APPEAR AT A MILITARY CEMETERY BEING ERECTED AT THE SITE OF THE BATTLE OF GETTYSBURG.

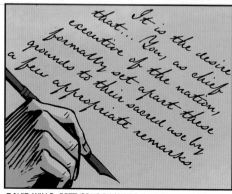

UNKNOWN, 425 BODIES

THE CEMETERY'S DEDICATION CEREMONY CAME AT A TIME WHEN THE JOB OF BURYING THE BATTLE DEAD WAS STILL ONLY ABOUT 1/3 COMPLETE.

It is the desire that... You, as chief executive of the nation, formally set apart these grounds to their sacred use by a few appropriate remarks.

DAVID WILLS, GETTYSBURG LAWYER AND OFFICIAL AGENT OF PENNSYLVANIA GOVERNOR CURTIN, 1863.

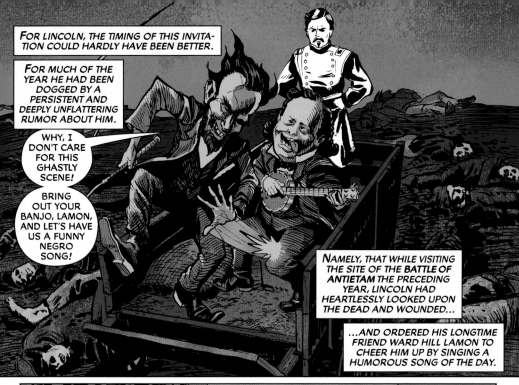

FOR LINCOLN, THE TIMING OF THIS INVITATION COULD HARDLY HAVE BEEN BETTER.

FOR MUCH OF THE YEAR HE HAD BEEN DOGGED BY A PERSISTENT AND DEEPLY UNFLATTERING RUMOR ABOUT HIM.

WHY, I DON'T CARE FOR THIS GHASTLY SCENE!

BRING OUT YOUR BANJO, LAMON, AND LET'S HAVE US A FUNNY NEGRO SONG!

NAMELY, THAT WHILE VISITING THE SITE OF THE **BATTLE OF ANTIETAM** THE PRECEDING YEAR, LINCOLN HAD HEARTLESSLY LOOKED UPON THE DEAD AND WOUNDED...

...AND ORDERED HIS LONGTIME FRIEND WARD HILL LAMON TO CHEER HIM UP BY SINGING A HUMOROUS SONG OF THE DAY.

THOSE WHO OPPOSED LINCOLN RAKED HIM OVER THE COALS FOR THIS ALLEGED OUTRAGE, EVEN WRITING SONGS AND POEMS ABOUT IT.

Abe may crack his jolly jokes
o'er bloody fields of sthricken battle,
while yet the ebbin' life-tide shmokes
from men that died like butchered cattle.

AND NOW HERE WAS AN OPPORTUNITY TO TRAVEL TO A DIFFERENT BATTLEFIELD...

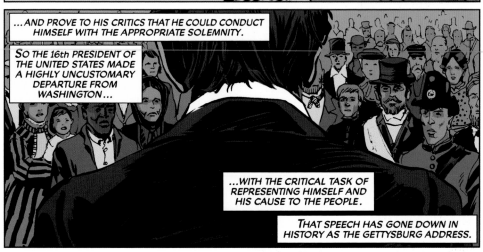

...AND PROVE TO HIS CRITICS THAT HE COULD CONDUCT HIMSELF WITH THE APPROPRIATE SOLEMNITY.

SO THE 16th PRESIDENT OF THE UNITED STATES MADE A HIGHLY UNCUSTOMARY DEPARTURE FROM WASHINGTON...

...WITH THE CRITICAL TASK OF REPRESENTING HIMSELF AND HIS CAUSE TO THE PEOPLE.

THAT SPEECH HAS GONE DOWN IN HISTORY AS THE GETTYSBURG ADDRESS.

JUST 271 WORDS IN LENGTH AND REQUIRING NO MORE THAN A FEW MINUTES TO RECITE OUT LOUD...

...THE GETTYSBURG ADDRESS IS A SYNTHESIS OF TWO OF ABRAHAM LINCOLN'S DEAREST BELIEFS:

HIS VISION OF THE MEANING OF THE CIVIL WAR...

THESE DEAD SHALL NOT HAVE DIED IN VAIN

E WHO HERE GAVE THEIR LIVES

FOR WHICH T

...AND THE VERY NATURE OF THE AMERICAN UNION.

BOUND UP WITHIN ITS WORDS, ONE MAY SEE AN EXPRESSION OF THE MOST CRUCIAL-- YET OFTEN CONFLICTING-- IDEAS IN AMERICAN HISTORY:

THAT THAT NATION MIGHT LIVE

AMERICAN GOVERNMENT...

ANY NATION SO CONCEIVED

...AND AMERICAN PHILOSOPHY.

A FINAL RESTING PLACE

THE GETTYSBURG ADDRESS IS, POINTEDLY, ONE MAN'S ATTEMPT TO RESOLVE WHAT HAD PROVED TO BE SEVERAL NEARLY FATAL CONTRADICTIONS...

THE BRAVE MEN LIVIN AND DEAD WHO STRUGGLE HERE

A NEW BIRTH OF FREEDOM.

...BETWEEN THE DECLARATION OF INDEPENDENCE AND THE U. S. CONSTITUTION.

BY HOLDING UP A MAGNIFYING GLASS TO THE WORDS OF THE GETTYSBURG ADDRESS, THEN, WE CAN ALSO HOLD UP A MAGNIFYING GLASS TO THE CIVIL WAR...

A NEW BIRTH OF FREEDOM

...AND TO THE ENTIRE SWEEP OF AMERICAN HISTORY.

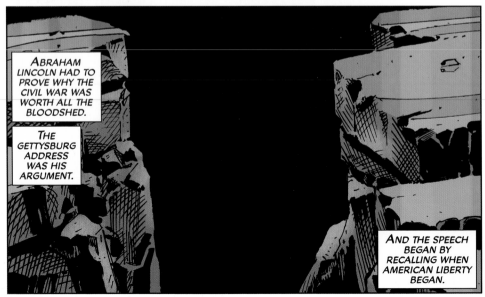

ABRAHAM LINCOLN HAD TO PROVE WHY THE CIVIL WAR WAS WORTH ALL THE BLOODSHED.

THE GETTYSBURG ADDRESS WAS HIS ARGUMENT.

AND THE SPEECH BEGAN BY RECALLING WHEN AMERICAN LIBERTY BEGAN.

FOUR SCORE AND SEVEN YEARS AGO

DID THE CONFEDERACY HAVE THE RIGHT TO SECEDE?

DID THE U.S. GOVERNMENT HAVE THE RIGHT TO ESSENTIALLY FORCE IT AT GUNPOINT TO REMAIN?

A DEEPER ISSUE MUST FIRST BE EXAMINED.

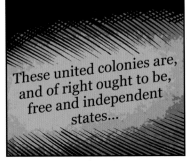

These united colonies are, and of right ought to be, free and independent states...

IMAGINE A SHORT QUIZ ON THE VITAL **FACTS** OF THE UNITED STATES.

WHAT IS ITS CAPITAL? WHAT OCEANS BORDER IT? HOW MANY STATES MAKE IT UP?

THESE QUESTIONS HAVE SIMPLE AND DEFINITE ANSWERS.

SPLISH

BUT WHAT ABOUT THIS QUESTION?

WHEN, PRECISELY, WAS THE UNITED STATES FOUNDED?

OR TO PHRASE IT IN A MORE REVEALING WAY...

WHEN, PRECISELY, WAS THE UNION FOUNDED?

PROFOUND CONSEQUENCES HINGE ON THE ANSWER TO THIS SURPRISINGLY THORNY QUESTION.

THE FOUNDING DATE DETERMINES THE TRUE NATURE OF JUST WHAT THE UNITED STATES-- THE UNION-- REALLY IS.

...AND WHETHER OR NOT SECESSION MIGHT HAVE BEEN JUSTIFIABLE.

THE OPENING PHRASE OF THE GETTYSBURG ADDRESS IS LINCOLN'S ANSWER TO THE QUESTION OF THE UNION'S FOUNDING DATE.

AND WITH THAT ANSWER, LINCOLN ALSO SETS OUT AN EXPLICIT PERSONAL VISION OF THE NATURE OF THE UNION.

"FOUR SCORE AND SEVEN YEARS AGO" REFERS TO 1776: THE YEAR THE DECLARATION OF INDEPENDENCE WAS SIGNED.

SIGNING THE DECLARATION MIGHT WELL HAVE BEEN SIGNING A DEATH WARRANT. FOR ANY MAN PUTTING HIS NAME ON THE DOCUMENT RISKED EXECUTION AS A TRAITOR TO THE BRITISH CROWN.

BUT THE PATRIOTS OF 1776 WERE WILLING TO STAKE THEIR LIVES ON THEIR BELIEF IN POPULAR SOVEREIGNTY.

SOVEREIGNTY. IT IS THE ISSUE OF WHOM A CIVILIZATION SEES AS ITS SUPREME EARTHLY AUTHORITY.

THE SOVEREIGN WIELDS POWER TO RULE THE REST.

WHILE THE AMERICAN PEOPLE WERE UNDER BRITISH RULE, THE MONARCH-- THE KING OR QUEEN-- WAS THE SOVEREIGN.

WHAT WAS THE PLACE OF THE PEOPLE IN THIS MONARCHY SYSTEM? THEY WERE BRITISH "SUBJECTS."

...AS IN "SUBJECT TO" THE MONARCH'S WILL.

BUT BY THE 1770s, A CRITICAL MASS OF AMERICANS HAD COME TO BELIEVE THAT THIS ANCIENT MONARCHY SYSTEM WAS CORRUPT.

UNJUST.

UNSUPPORTABLE.

THESE DEFIANT COLONISTS RENOUNCED THE RULE OF KINGS. THEY INSTEAD EMBRACED THE PEOPLE AS THE RIGHTFUL SOURCE OF SOVEREIGNTY.

THIS CONVICTION INSPIRED THE AMERICAN REVOLUTION.

37

THE DECLARATION OF INDEPENDENCE IS THE FULLEST EXPRESSION OF THE REVOLUTION'S IDEAS.

IT REJECTS MONARCHY AND ENSHRINES POPULAR SOVEREIGNTY WITH THE WORDS:

"...GOVERNMENTS ARE INSTITUTED AMONG MEN, DERIVING THEIR JUST POWERS FROM THE CONSENT OF THE GOVERNED."

OR PUT ANOTHER WAY, ONLY THE PEOPLE *HAVE* THE AUTHORITY TO CREATE GOVERNMENT AND LAWS. NO SUPPOSEDLY "HIGHER" POWER-- LIKE A KING, DICTATOR, OR SOME RELIGIOUS FIGURE-- CAN RIGHTLY IMPOSE A GOVERNMENT ON THE PEOPLE WITHOUT THEIR CONSENT.

TO ABRAHAM LINCOLN, THE AMERICAN PEOPLE-- VERY DIFFERENT GROUPS OF MEN SCATTERED AMONG VERY DIFFERENT COLONIES-- WERE FIRST AND FOREMOST UNITED BY THEIR DEVOTION TO THESE GREAT PRINCIPLES.

THAT MEN ARE CAPABLE OF GOVERNING THEMSELVES *THROUGH THE POWER OF REASON.*

THAT MEN HAVE ESSENTIAL HUMAN RIGHTS.

THAT MEN MUST BE FREE FROM ARBITRARY GOVERNMENT POWER.

IN LINCOLN'S MIND, THEN, THAT IS WHAT THE UNITED STATES-- "THE UNION"-- REALLY IS.

IT IS THE WHOLE OF THE AMERICAN PEOPLE AND THEIR SACRED BOND TO THESE PRINCIPLES, THIS VISION OF HUMANITY.

THE UNION WAS THEREFORE CREATED IN 1776-- AT THE MOMENT AMERICANS ANNOUNCED TO THE WORLD THEIR REVOLUTIONARY VISION.

EVERY TIME LINCOLN USED THE WORD "UNION," HE WAS REFERRING TO THESE SHARED BELIEFS. ANYTHING POLITICAL -- A GOVERNMENT, AN ALLIANCE OF STATES, EVEN THE CONSTITUTION-- WAS BESIDE THE POINT.

THE SIGNERS OF THE DECLARATION OF INDEPENDENCE DID NOT CLAIM TO REPRESENT THE WHOLE OF THE AMERICAN PEOPLE. THEY CLAIMED INSTEAD TO REPRESENT THE PEOPLE OF THE INDIVIDUAL STATES.

YET LINCOLN WOULD STILL ARGUE THAT THE CREATION OF THE UNION WAS STILL AN ACT OF THE WHOLE OF THE AMERICAN PEOPLE...

...BECAUSE THE BELIEFS THEY HELD IN COMMON TRANSCENDED STATE BOUNDARIES.

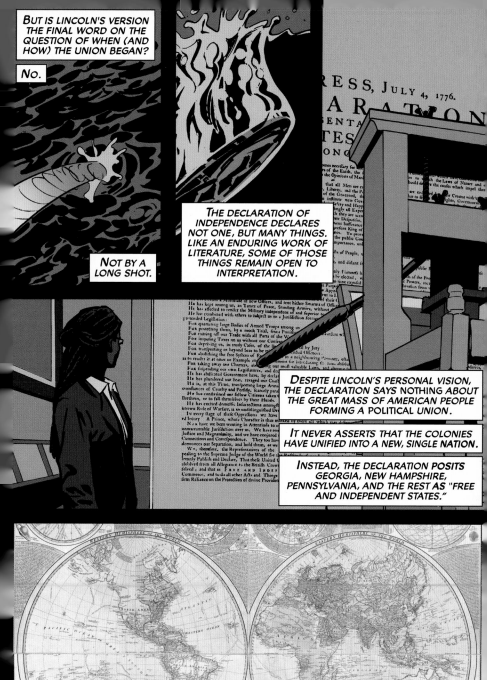

BUT IS LINCOLN'S VERSION THE FINAL WORD ON THE QUESTION OF WHEN (AND HOW) THE UNION BEGAN?

NO.

NOT BY A LONG SHOT.

THE DECLARATION OF INDEPENDENCE DECLARES NOT ONE, BUT MANY THINGS. LIKE AN ENDURING WORK OF LITERATURE, SOME OF THOSE THINGS REMAIN OPEN TO INTERPRETATION.

DESPITE LINCOLN'S PERSONAL VISION, THE DECLARATION SAYS NOTHING ABOUT THE GREAT MASS OF AMERICAN PEOPLE FORMING A POLITICAL UNION.

IT NEVER ASSERTS THAT THE COLONIES HAVE UNIFIED INTO A NEW, SINGLE NATION.

INSTEAD, THE DECLARATION POSITS GEORGIA, NEW HAMPSHIRE, PENNSYLVANIA, AND THE REST AS "FREE AND INDEPENDENT STATES."

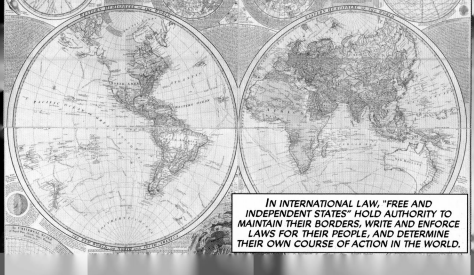

IN INTERNATIONAL LAW, "FREE AND INDEPENDENT STATES" HOLD AUTHORITY TO MAINTAIN THEIR BORDERS, WRITE AND ENFORCE LAWS FOR THEIR PEOPLE, AND DETERMINE THEIR OWN COURSE OF ACTION IN THE WORLD.

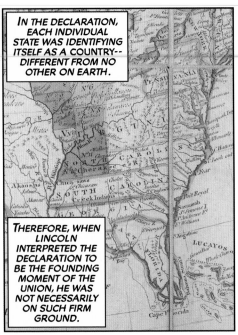

IN THE DECLARATION, EACH INDIVIDUAL STATE WAS IDENTIFYING ITSELF AS A COUNTRY-- DIFFERENT FROM NO OTHER ON EARTH.

THEREFORE, WHEN LINCOLN INTERPRETED THE DECLARATION TO BE THE FOUNDING MOMENT OF THE UNION, HE WAS NOT NECESSARILY ON SUCH FIRM GROUND.

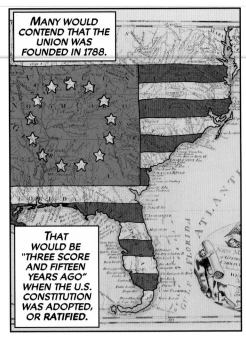

MANY WOULD CONTEND THAT THE UNION WAS FOUNDED IN 1788.

THAT WOULD BE "THREE SCORE AND FIFTEEN YEARS AGO" WHEN THE U.S. CONSTITUTION WAS ADOPTED, OR RATIFIED.

FOR ONLY BY ADOPTING THE CONSTITUTION...

...DID THE STATES CREATE ANYTHING LIKE AN ACTUAL NATIONAL GOVERNMENT.

THE CONSTITUTION WAS DRAFTED BY A SMALL NUMBER OF REPRESENTATIVES FROM THE STATES.

AND THE DOCUMENT WAS NOT RATIFIED IN ONE BIG NATIONAL VOTE. INSTEAD, IT BECAME LAW ONLY AFTER 13 SEPARATE ELECTIONS HELD IN THE STATES.

SO THIS IDEA OF A 1788 FOUNDING DATE GIVES US A RADICALLY DIFFERENT ANSWER TO THE QUESTION OF JUST WHAT THE UNITED STATES-- THE UNION-- REALLY IS.

THE UNION *IS* THE STATES. A MUTUAL, POLITICAL AGREEMENT. NOTHING MORE, NOTHING LESS.

...AND CERTAINLY NOT LINCOLN'S MYSTICAL SENSE OF A BOND BETWEEN PEOPLE AND PHILOSOPHY.

NEW YORK CITY'S FEDERAL HALL, FIRST CAPITOL OF THE UNITED STATES.

THE NOTION OF A 1788 FOUNDING DATE LEADS TO A PERPLEXING QUESTION.

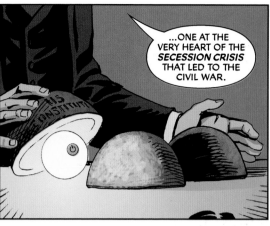

...ONE AT THE VERY HEART OF THE *SECESSION CRISIS* THAT LED TO THE CIVIL WAR.

SLIDE

FLIP

SLIDE

FLIP

FLIP

HERE IS THE CONUNDRUM.

AFTER THEY FORMED THE UNION, *WHAT EXACTLY "HAPPENED TO"* THE STATES' SOVEREIGNTY?

WHEN THEY RATIFIED THE CONSTITUTION, DID THE STATES SIGN THEIR SOVEREIGNTY AWAY?

DID THEY REALLY AGREE TO *GIVE UP* THE INDEPENDENCE THEY HAD SO GRANDLY AND SO RECENTLY CLAIMED IN THE DECLARATION?

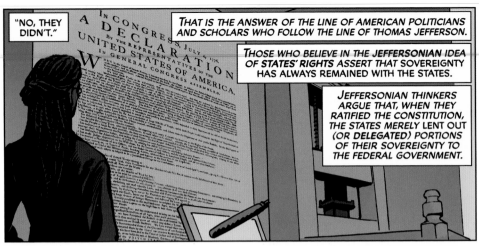

"NO, THEY DIDN'T."

THAT IS THE ANSWER OF THE LINE OF AMERICAN POLITICIANS AND SCHOLARS WHO FOLLOW THE LINE OF THOMAS JEFFERSON.

THOSE WHO BELIEVE IN THE JEFFERSONIAN IDEA OF STATES' RIGHTS ASSERT THAT SOVEREIGNTY HAS ALWAYS REMAINED WITH THE STATES.

JEFFERSONIAN THINKERS ARGUE THAT, WHEN THEY RATIFIED THE CONSTITUTION, THE STATES MERELY LENT OUT (OR DELEGATED) PORTIONS OF THEIR SOVEREIGNTY TO THE FEDERAL GOVERNMENT.

I GO ON THE GROUND THAT THIS CONSTITUTION WAS MADE BY THE STATES; THAT IT IS A FEDERAL UNION OF THE STATES, IN WHICH THE SEVERAL STATES STILL RETAIN THEIR SOVEREIGNTY.

PROMINENT STATES' RIGHTS ADVOCATE JOHN C. CALHOUN, 7th VICE PRESIDENT OF THE U.S. (1825-1832) AND SENATOR FROM SOUTH CAROLINA (1832-1843; 1845-1850).

WHY WOULD THE SOVEREIGN STATES DELEGATE ANY OF THEIR SOVEREIGNTY? SO THAT THEY COULD ALL HAVE THE BENEFIT AND CONVENIENCE OF SHARING A FEDERAL GOVERNMENT.

...AN ENTITY TO RUN A POST OFFICE, HELP RESOLVE CONFLICTS AMONG THE STATES, AND REPRESENT THEM AROUND THE GLOBE WITH BOTH DIPLOMACY AND MILITARY MIGHT.*

*AMONG OTHER FUNCTIONS.

SOME TOOK THIS JEFFERSONIAN-STATES' RIGHTS LINE OF THINKING EVEN FURTHER.

THEY CONSTRUED THAT IN RATIFYING THE CONSTITUTION, THE STATES WERE MAKING A SIMPLE, LEGAL AGREEMENT: A CONTRACT OR A COMPACT.

ACCORDING TO THIS **COMPACT THEORY**, THEN, THE UNION IS A "CREATURE" OR "PUPPET" OF THE STATES.

[GOVERNMENTS] ARE MERE REVOCABLE PROCURATIONS, SIMPLE DELEGATIONS OF LIMITED AND TEMPORARY AUTHORITY, EXECUTED BY THE SOVEREIGN PEOPLE... TO ACCOMPLISH CERTAIN PURPOSES, BY CERTAIN DEFINED MEANS... ...NOTHING ELSE.

...THE PEOPLE CREATED [OUR FEDERAL GOVERNMENT], AND THE CREATOR MUST BE SUPERIOR TO HIS CREATURE.

LITTLETON TAZEWELL, U.S. SENATOR FROM VIRGINIA (1824-1832).

SO UNDER THE COMPACT THEORY, STATES CREATING THE FEDERAL GOVERNMENT IS BASICALLY LIKE AN INDIVIDUAL HIRING A LAWYER, A BANKER, A PUBLIC RELATIONS REP, AND A BODYGUARD-- "AGENTS" TO PERFORM CERTAIN TASKS.

EMPLOYMENT ICE

FEDERAL GOVERNMENT WANTED-- APPLY WITHIN

AND IF THESE AGENTS MAY BE HIRED, THEY LOGICALLY CAN BE FIRED.

IF A STATE HAS THE POWER TO JOIN *THE UNION* AND ENJOY BENEFITS BY MEMBERSHIP IN IT...

...THAT STATE MUST ALSO HAVE THE POWER TO SECEDE FROM IT *IF IT DECIDES THOSE BENEFITS HAVE LOW VALUE.*

IT IS THE INHERENT RIGHT OF NATIONS... TO DISREGARD THE OBLIGATIONS OF COMPACTS OF ALL SORTS--

--BY DECLARING THEMSELVES NO LONGER BOUND IN ANY WAY BY THEM.

ALEXANDER STEPHENS

THIS IS AMONG THE SEVERAL WAYS THE SOUTH JUSTIFIED SECESSION.

AMONG THE DELEGATED POWERS [OF THE U.S. CONSTITUTION] THERE IS NONE WHICH INTERFERES WITH THE EXERCISE OF THE RIGHT OF SECESSION BY A STATE.

JEFFERSON DAVIS

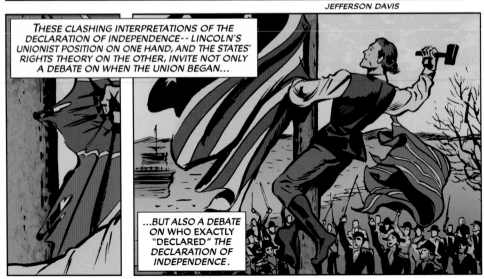

THESE CLASHING INTERPRETATIONS OF THE DECLARATION OF INDEPENDENCE-- LINCOLN'S UNIONIST POSITION ON ONE HAND, AND THE STATES' RIGHTS THEORY ON THE OTHER, INVITE NOT ONLY A DEBATE ON WHEN THE UNION BEGAN...

...BUT ALSO A DEBATE ON WHO EXACTLY "DECLARED" THE DECLARATION OF INDEPENDENCE.

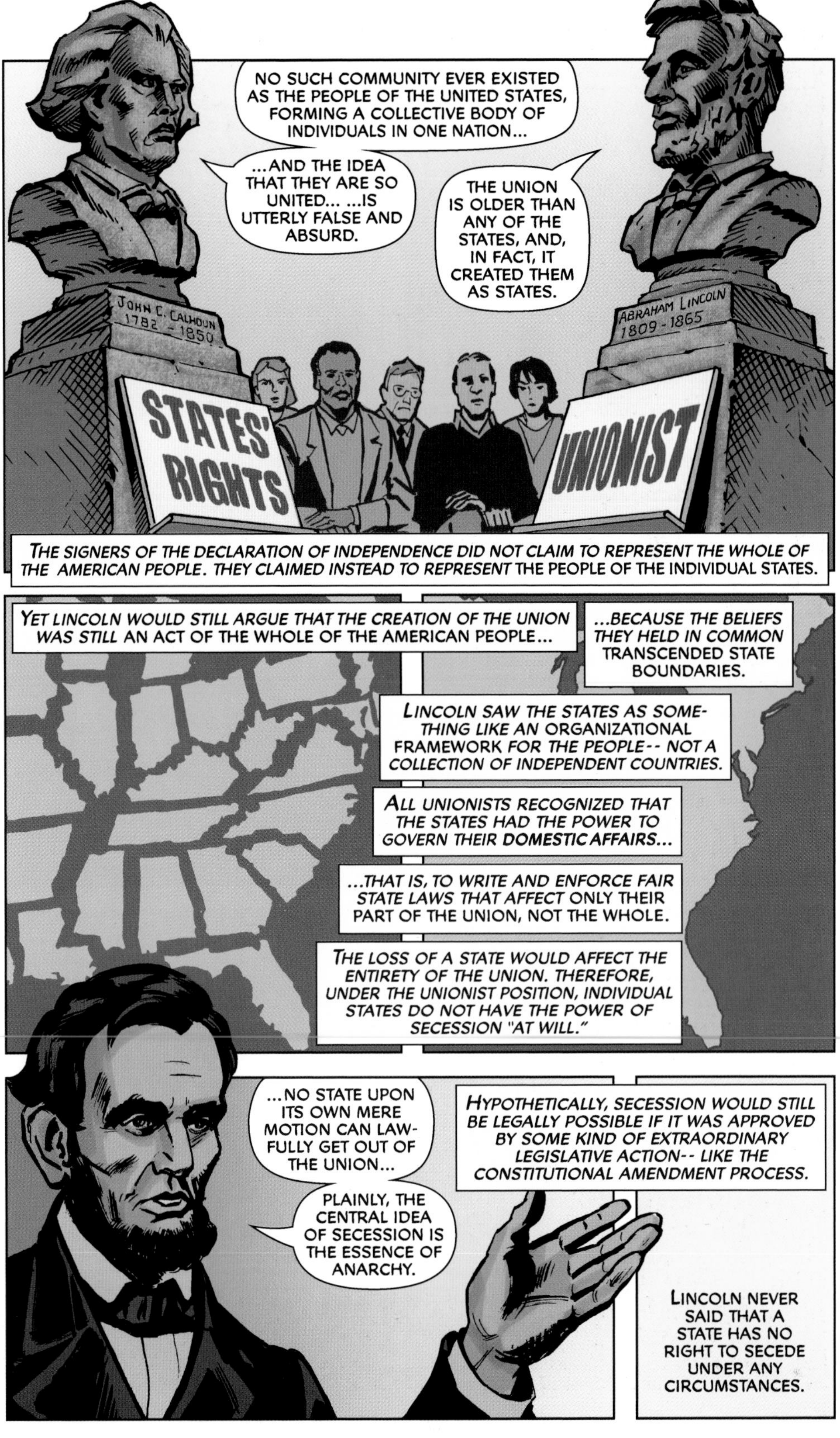
NO SUCH COMMUNITY EVER EXISTED AS THE PEOPLE OF THE UNITED STATES, FORMING A COLLECTIVE BODY OF INDIVIDUALS IN ONE NATION...
...AND THE IDEA THAT THEY ARE SO UNITED... ...IS UTTERLY FALSE AND ABSURD.
THE UNION IS OLDER THAN ANY OF THE STATES, AND, IN FACT, IT CREATED THEM AS STATES.
JOHN C. CALHOUN 1782 - 1850
ABRAHAM LINCOLN 1809 - 1865
STATES' RIGHTS
UNIONIST
THE SIGNERS OF THE DECLARATION OF INDEPENDENCE DID NOT CLAIM TO REPRESENT THE WHOLE OF THE AMERICAN PEOPLE. THEY CLAIMED INSTEAD TO REPRESENT THE PEOPLE OF THE INDIVIDUAL STATES.
YET LINCOLN WOULD STILL ARGUE THAT THE CREATION OF THE UNION WAS STILL AN ACT OF THE WHOLE OF THE AMERICAN PEOPLE...
...BECAUSE THE BELIEFS THEY HELD IN COMMON TRANSCENDED STATE BOUNDARIES.
LINCOLN SAW THE STATES AS SOMETHING LIKE AN ORGANIZATIONAL FRAMEWORK FOR THE PEOPLE-- NOT A COLLECTION OF INDEPENDENT COUNTRIES.
ALL UNIONISTS RECOGNIZED THAT THE STATES HAD THE POWER TO GOVERN THEIR DOMESTIC AFFAIRS...
...THAT IS, TO WRITE AND ENFORCE FAIR STATE LAWS THAT AFFECT ONLY THEIR PART OF THE UNION, NOT THE WHOLE.
THE LOSS OF A STATE WOULD AFFECT THE ENTIRETY OF THE UNION. THEREFORE, UNDER THE UNIONIST POSITION, INDIVIDUAL STATES DO NOT HAVE THE POWER OF SECESSION "AT WILL."
...NO STATE UPON ITS OWN MERE MOTION CAN LAWFULLY GET OUT OF THE UNION...
PLAINLY, THE CENTRAL IDEA OF SECESSION IS THE ESSENCE OF ANARCHY.
HYPOTHETICALLY, SECESSION WOULD STILL BE LEGALLY POSSIBLE IF IT WAS APPROVED BY SOME KIND OF EXTRAORDINARY LEGISLATIVE ACTION-- LIKE THE CONSTITUTIONAL AMENDMENT PROCESS.
LINCOLN NEVER SAID THAT A STATE HAS NO RIGHT TO SECEDE UNDER ANY CIRCUMSTANCES.

ADDING TO THE CONTROVERSY (AS JEFFERSON DAVIS POINTED OUT) IS THE FACT THAT THE CONSTITUTION...

...IS UTTERLY SILENT ON THE SUBJECT OF SECESSION.

ON THE FLIP SIDE, THE DECLARATION OF INDEPENDENCE IS, BY ITS VERY NATURE, AN ARGUMENT IN FAVOR OF SECESSION...

...OR PERHAPS MORE TO THE POINT...

...REBELLION.

WHY? GREAT BRITAIN DID NOT RECOGNIZE ANY LEGAL METHOD FOR THE AMERICAN COLONIES TO BREAK AWAY.

THE REBELLING COLONISTS CALLED ON PRINCIPLES THEY CONSIDERED HIGHER THAN THE LAWS OF MAN.

PIVOTAL TO ALL THE RIGHTS THAT THE DECLARATION AFFIRMS IS THE RIGHT OF REVOLUTION.

IN THE WORDS OF THE DECLARATION ITSELF, WHEN ANY GOVERNMENT "BECOMES DESTRUCTIVE OF" ESSENTIAL HUMAN RIGHTS, THE PEOPLE HAVE THE AUTHORITY "TO ALTER OR TO ABOLISH" THAT GOVERNMENT AND CREATE A NEW ONE.

EVEN LINCOLN FIRMLY BELIEVED THIS.

SECESSION WAS CONSTANTLY DEFENDED BY VIRTUE OF THE RIGHT OF REVOLUTION.

DID THE UNITED STATES SO PERSECUTE THE SOUTH THAT THE CONFEDERATE STATES FAIRLY EXERCISED THEIR RIGHT OF REVOLUTION?

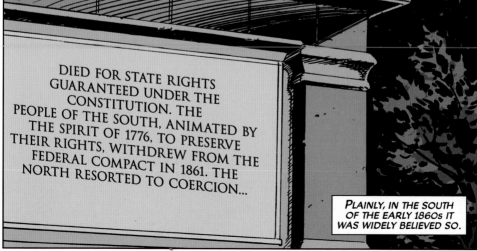

DIED FOR STATE RIGHTS GUARANTEED UNDER THE CONSTITUTION. THE PEOPLE OF THE SOUTH, ANIMATED BY THE SPIRIT OF 1776, TO PRESERVE THEIR RIGHTS, WITHDREW FROM THE FEDERAL COMPACT IN 1861. THE NORTH RESORTED TO COERCION...

PLAINLY, IN THE SOUTH OF THE EARLY 1860s IT WAS WIDELY BELIEVED SO.

CONFEDERATE SOLDIERS' MONUMENT, ERECTED 1903. GROUNDS OF THE TEXAS STATE CAPITOL BUILDING, AUSTIN, TEXAS.

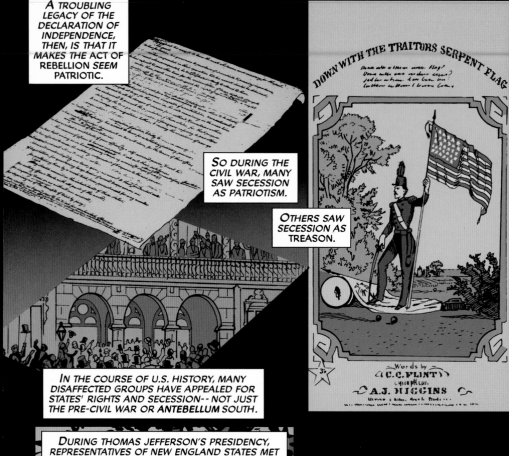

A TROUBLING LEGACY OF THE DECLARATION OF INDEPENDENCE, THEN, IS THAT IT MAKES THE ACT OF REBELLION *SEEM* PATRIOTIC.

SO DURING THE CIVIL WAR, MANY SAW SECESSION AS PATRIOTISM.

OTHERS SAW SECESSION AS TREASON.

DOWN WITH THE TRAITORS SERPENT FLAG

Words by
C.C. FLINT
A.J. HIGGINS

IN THE COURSE OF U.S. HISTORY, MANY DISAFFECTED GROUPS HAVE APPEALED FOR STATES' RIGHTS AND SECESSION-- NOT JUST THE PRE-CIVIL WAR OR *ANTEBELLUM* SOUTH.

DURING THOMAS JEFFERSON'S PRESIDENCY, REPRESENTATIVES OF NEW ENGLAND STATES MET TO CONSIDER SECEDING FROM THE UNION. THEY WERE UPSET ABOUT JEFFERSON'S POLICIES AND THE CONSTITUTION'S PROTECTIONS FOR SLAVERY.

WHERE ONE STANDS ON THESE CONTENTIOUS ISSUES COMES DOWN TO WHETHER THE UNION WAS FORMED IN 1776 WITH THE DECLARATION OF INDEPENDENCE-- OR IN 1788 WITH THE CONSTITUTION.

THE TWO DOCUMENTS INSEPARABLY MAKE UP THE INTELLECTUAL FOUNDATION OF THE UNITED STATES. YET IN MEANINGFUL WAYS THEY ARE POLAR OPPOSITES.

THOSE CONTRADICTIONS ARE LIKE SELF-DESTRUCTIVE FLAWS ENCODED INTO THE "IDEOLOGICAL DNA" OF THE UNITED STATES.

WHO IS TO BLAME FOR THIS? FOR MAKING THE CARNAGE AND UPHEAVAL OF 1861-1865 INEVITABLE?

BLAME MUST BE LAID AT THE FEET OF THE MEN ABRAHAM LINCOLN REFERS TO IN THE NEXT PASSAGE OF THE GETTYSBURG ADDRESS.

STATE SOVEREIGNTY.

SECESSION.

STATES' RIGHTS.

REBELLION.

HARTFORD CONVENTION-- CONNECTICUT, 1814-1815.

OUR FATHERS

"...WE MUTUALLY PLEDGE TO EACH OTHER OUR LIVES, OUR FORTUNES AND OUR SACRED HONOR."

HURRAH!

HURRAH!

CLANG! CLANG!

"OUR FATHERS"-- THE SIGNERS OF THE DECLARATION OF INDEPENDENCE, AND THOSE WHO FOUGHT AND DIED TO SUPPORT THEM IN THE AMERICAN REVOLUTION-- SHARED MANY FUNDAMENTAL BELIEFS.

FIRST PUBLIC READING OF THE DECLARATION OF INDEPENDENCE: PHILADELPHIA, JULY 8, 1776.

CLANG! CLANG!

AMERICANS PROUDLY IMAGINE THESE "FATHERS" AS A UNITED PEOPLE.

BUT THAT VISION IS NOT AN HONEST-- OR ACCURATE-- ONE.

"OUR FATHERS" SHARPLY DIFFERED ON HOW POWERFUL GOVERNMENT SHOULD BE, HOW "BIG" OR HOW "SMALL."

THE DECLARATION AND THE CONSTITUTION MIRROR THE DIVERSE CIVILIZATION THAT CREATED THEM. JUST AS THE DOCUMENTS ARE ON THE ISSUE OF STATE SOVEREIGNTY, THEY ARE ALSO AT ODDS ON GOVERNMENT POWER.

THE DECLARATION LEANS TOWARD "SMALL GOVERNMENT," THE CONSTITUTION TOWARD "BIG GOVERNMENT."

THIS IS ANOTHER CONTRADICTION THAT SET THE STAGE FOR CIVIL WAR.

AMERICANS AND THEIR SECTIONS

WHAT ACCOUNTED FOR OUR FOUNDING FATHERS' MOTLEY ATTITUDES TOWARD GOVERNMENT POWER?

IT CAN IN PART BE EXPLAINED BY THE CULTURAL AND CHARACTER TRAITS OF AMERICA'S REGIONS OR SECTIONS.

EVEN WHEN THE U.S. WAS JUST STARTING OUT, THERE WERE ALREADY TROUBLING SECTIONAL RIFTS BETWEEN NORTH AND SOUTH.

THE FIRST YEAR OF THE REVOLUTIONARY WAR, A MASSACHUSETTS SOLDIER REPORTED IN A LETTER THAT SOUTHERN TROOPS REFERRED TO NORTHERNERS AS "DAMN'D YANKEES."

THOMAS JEFFERSON CHARACTERIZED HIS COUNTRYMEN THIS WAY.

IN THE NORTH [MEN] ARE...

COOL

SOBER

LABORIOUS

PERSEVERING...

IN THE SOUTH THEY ARE...

FIERY

VOLUPTUARY

INDOLENT

UNSTEADY...

IN 1787, PIERCE BUTLER-- DELEGATE FROM SOUTH CAROLINA TO THE U.S. CONSTITUTIONAL CONVENTION-- CALLED THE INTERESTS OF SOUTH AND NORTH...

...AS DIFFERENT AS THE INTERESTS OF RUSSIA AND TURKEY.

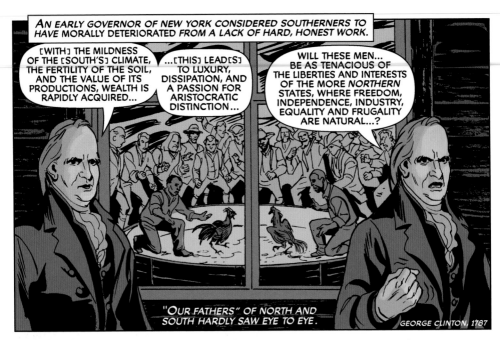

AN EARLY GOVERNOR OF NEW YORK CONSIDERED SOUTHERNERS TO HAVE MORALLY DETERIORATED *FROM A LACK OF HARD, HONEST WORK.*

[WITH] THE MILDNESS OF THE [SOUTH'S] CLIMATE, THE FERTILITY OF THE SOIL, AND THE VALUE OF ITS PRODUCTIONS, WEALTH IS RAPIDLY ACQUIRED...

...[THIS] LEAD[S] TO LUXURY, DISSIPATION, AND A PASSION FOR ARISTOCRATIC DISTINCTION...

WILL THESE MEN... BE AS TENACIOUS OF THE LIBERTIES AND INTERESTS OF THE MORE *NORTHERN* STATES, WHERE FREEDOM, INDEPENDENCE, INDUSTRY, EQUALITY AND FRUGALITY ARE NATURAL...?

"OUR FATHERS" OF NORTH AND SOUTH HARDLY SAW EYE TO EYE.

GEORGE CLINTON, 1787

THE "SMALL GOVERNMENT" EXPERIMENT

THE COSTLY 1776-1781 WAR WITH GREAT BRITAIN LEFT MOST AMERICANS WITH TWO THINGS ON WHICH THEY COULD AGREE.

PATRIOTS BURY AN EFFIGY OF KING GEORGE III, SAVANNAH, GEORGIA, AUGUST 1776.

CONSIDER: WHAT WERE TWO OF THE GRAVEST OBJECTIONS AMERICANS HAD TO *THE BRITISH MONARCHY'S* RULE?

FIRST: GOVERNMENT WIELDED TOO MUCH POWER-- A KIND OF CONTROL OVER THEIR AFFAIRS THAT AMERICANS BELIEVED ROBBED THEM OF LIBERTY.

SECOND: GREAT BRITAIN DIRECTED ITS POWER FROM A GREAT DISTANCE. *THIS* DEPRIVED AMERICANS OF INFLUENCE IN GOVERNMENT.

THEREFORE, "OUR FATHERS" AGREED THAT GOVERNMENT SHOULD BE NOT DISTANT BUT *LOCAL*...

...AND NOT POWERFUL BUT *WEAK.*

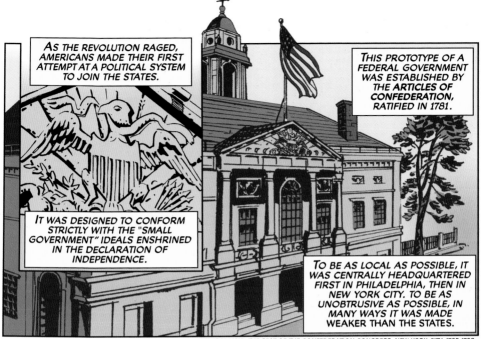

AS THE REVOLUTION RAGED, AMERICANS MADE THEIR FIRST ATTEMPT AT A POLITICAL SYSTEM TO JOIN THE STATES.

THIS PROTOTYPE OF A FEDERAL GOVERNMENT WAS ESTABLISHED BY THE *ARTICLES OF CONFEDERATION,* RATIFIED IN 1781.

IT WAS DESIGNED TO CONFORM STRICTLY WITH THE "SMALL GOVERNMENT" IDEALS ENSHRINED IN THE DECLARATION OF INDEPENDENCE.

TO BE AS LOCAL AS POSSIBLE, IT WAS CENTRALLY HEADQUARTERED FIRST IN PHILADELPHIA, THEN IN NEW YORK CITY. TO BE AS UNOBTRUSIVE AS POSSIBLE, IN MANY WAYS IT WAS MADE WEAKER THAN THE STATES.

FEDERAL HALL, THE SEAT OF THE CONFEDERATION CONGRESS, NEW YORK CITY, 1785-1789.

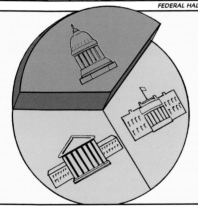

THIS PURPOSEFULLY SMALL GOVERNMENT HAD ONLY ONE BRANCH: THE CONFEDERATION CONGRESS.

IT HAD NO EXECUTIVE AND NO SUPREME COURT.

"OUR FATHERS" EVEN DENIED THIS CONGRESS THE AUTHORITY TO COLLECT TAXES OR RAISE A MILITARY.

THIS GOVERNMENT WAS NOT EVEN EMPOWERED TO MAKE LAWS COVERING INDIVIDUALS' BEHAVIOR, SUCH AS MODERN FEDERAL LAWS AGAINST DEALING ILLEGAL FIREARMS OR DRUGS.

TRULY A PUPPET OF THE STATES, THE CONFEDERATION CONGRESS PROVED FEEBLE. IT COULD NOT PREVENT THE NEWLY FREE AMERICA FROM SLIPPING TOWARD DISORDER AND DISGRACE.

THE CONFEDERATION CONGRESS COULD NOT PAY THE STAGGERING DEBT FROM THE REVOLUTIONARY WAR, AND THE ECONOMY FOUNDERED.

...VERMONT DOES NOT WISH TO ENTER INTO A WAR WITH THE STATE OF NEW YORK, BUT SHE WILL ACT ON THE DEFENSIVE...

...AND EXPECT THAT CONGRESS... LET THE TWO CONTENDING STATES SETTLE THEIR OWN CONTROVERSY.

AN AREA CALLING ITSELF "VERMONT" HAD DECLARED ITS INDEPENDENCE FROM NEW YORK STATE. CONGRESS, UNABLE TO RESOLVE THE DISPUTE, THREW UP ITS HANDS.

THOMAS CHITTENDEN, GOVERNOR OF THE "REPUBLIC OF VERMONT," 1783.

CITIZENS OF CONNECTICUT AND PENNSYLVANIA TOOK UP ARMS AGAINST EACH OTHER IN A BLOODY BORDER SKIRMISH.

SPAIN SEIZED CONTROL OF THE MISSISSIPPI RIVER.

FORT ROSALIE-- SITE OF MODERN NATCHEZ, MISSISSIPPI.

AND BRITISH SOLDIERS LURKED ON THE FRONTIER, POISED TO GO ON THE ATTACK NOT IF THE UNION FELL APART BUT, AS THEY SAW IT, WHEN.

AS TO THE FUTURE GRANDEUR OF AMERICA...

...THE [AMERICANS'] MUTUAL ANTIPATHIES AND CLASHING INTERESTS, THEIR DIFFERENCE OF GOVERNMENTS, HABITUDES, AND MANNERS, -- PLAINLY INDICATES, THAT THE AMERICANS WILL HAVE NO CENTER OF UNION... AND NO COMMON INTEREST...

THEIR FATE SEEMS TO BE, -- A DISUNITED PEOPLE, 'TILL THE END OF TIME.

SOMETHING HAD TO BE DONE BEFORE IT WAS TOO LATE. OTHERWISE, THE REVOLUTION WOULD HAVE BEEN FOR NOTHING.

JOSIAH TUCKER, BRITISH WRITER AND ECONOMIST, 1781.

THE "BIG GOVERNMENT" REMEDY

TO COPE WITH ALL THESE CRISES, THE GOVERNMENT HAD TO BE MADE STRONGER.

BUT IN THE POLITICAL CLIMATE OF THE 1780s, THAT IDEA WAS TABOO.

ONLY A SMALL NUMBER DARED CONSIDER SUCH A THING.

THE PROPOSAL WAS SO INFLAMMATORY THAT IT COULD ONLY BE DISCUSSED IN SECRET MEETINGS.

PATRICK HENRY, THE FORMER GOVERNOR OF VIRGINIA, HEARD ABOUT THESE MEETINGS AND SAID...

I SMELL A RAT!

...A REVEALING INDICATOR OF PUBLIC OPINION AT THE TIME.

NEVERTHELESS, DISCUSSIONS CONTINUED BEHIND CLOSED DOORS.

THE CONSTITUTION WAS THE PRODUCT OF THIS ACTIVIST MINORITY.

BUT THE JOB OF GETTING THE PEOPLE TO ADOPT THE CONSTITUTION'S STRONGER AND MORE CENTRAL GOVERNMENT WOULD REQUIRE A MASSIVE FEAT OF PERSUASION...

...AND SUPPORTERS HAD TO WORK FOR RATIFICATION WHILE THE CRISES FACING THE STATES KEPT GETTING WORSE.

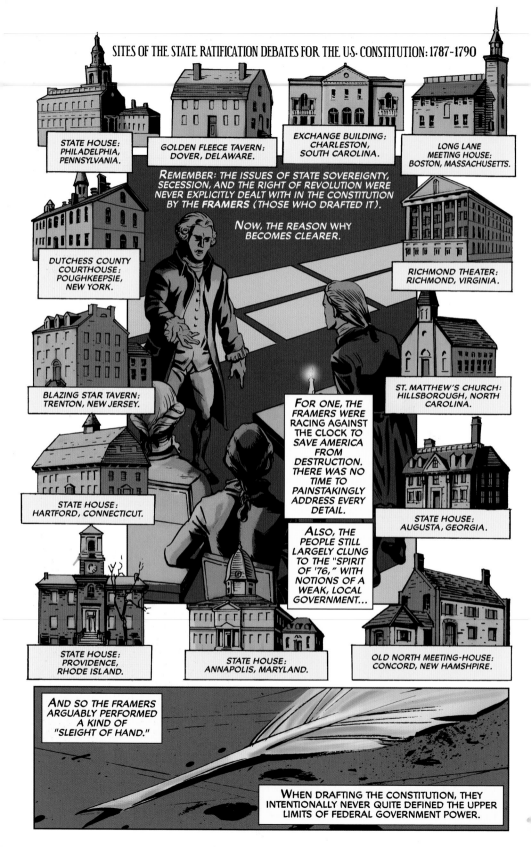

SITES OF THE STATE RATIFICATION DEBATES FOR THE U.S. CONSTITUTION: 1787-1790

STATE HOUSE: PHILADELPHIA, PENNSYLVANIA.

GOLDEN FLEECE TAVERN: DOVER, DELAWARE.

EXCHANGE BUILDING: CHARLESTON, SOUTH CAROLINA.

LONG LANE MEETING HOUSE: BOSTON, MASSACHUSETTS.

REMEMBER: THE ISSUES OF STATE SOVEREIGNTY, SECESSION, AND THE RIGHT OF REVOLUTION WERE NEVER EXPLICITLY DEALT WITH IN THE CONSTITUTION BY THE FRAMERS (THOSE WHO DRAFTED IT).

NOW, THE REASON WHY BECOMES CLEARER.

DUTCHESS COUNTY COURTHOUSE: POUGHKEEPSIE, NEW YORK.

RICHMOND THEATER: RICHMOND, VIRGINIA.

BLAZING STAR TAVERN: TRENTON, NEW JERSEY.

ST. MATTHEW'S CHURCH: HILLSBOROUGH, NORTH CAROLINA.

FOR ONE, THE FRAMERS WERE RACING AGAINST THE CLOCK TO SAVE AMERICA FROM DESTRUCTION. THERE WAS NO TIME TO PAINSTAKINGLY ADDRESS EVERY DETAIL.

STATE HOUSE: HARTFORD, CONNECTICUT.

STATE HOUSE: AUGUSTA, GEORGIA.

ALSO, THE PEOPLE STILL LARGELY CLUNG TO THE "SPIRIT OF '76," WITH NOTIONS OF A WEAK, LOCAL GOVERNMENT...

STATE HOUSE: PROVIDENCE, RHODE ISLAND.

STATE HOUSE: ANNAPOLIS, MARYLAND.

OLD NORTH MEETING-HOUSE: CONCORD, NEW HAMSHPIRE.

AND SO THE FRAMERS ARGUABLY PERFORMED A KIND OF "SLEIGHT OF HAND."

WHEN DRAFTING THE CONSTITUTION, THEY INTENTIONALLY NEVER QUITE DEFINED THE UPPER LIMITS OF FEDERAL GOVERNMENT POWER.

PERHAPS THE FRAMERS WERE BETTING THAT MOST WHO WOULD VOTE TO RATIFY THE CONSTITUTION WOULD NOT, IN EFFECT, "READ THE FINE PRINT."

THE CONSTITUTION'S VAGUE DEFINITION OF GOVERNMENT POWER MIGHT ALSO BE BECAUSE...

...THEY THEMSELVES WERE NOT OF ONE MIND ON THE SUBJECT.

ONE FRAMER IN PARTICULAR HAD FEW RESERVATIONS ABOUT "BIG GOVERNMENT."

ALEXANDER HAMILTON WAS NOT SUCH A DISCIPLE OF THE "SPIRIT OF '76" IDEALS OF WEAK AND LOCAL GOVERNMENT.

HAMILTON, A HUGELY AMBITIOUS MAN, GREW UP AS A CHILD GENIUS ON THE CARIBBEAN ISLAND OF NEVIS. HE LATER BECAME A SOLDIER IN THE REVOLUTIONARY WAR.

THIS FIRSTHAND EXPERIENCE STRENGTHENED WHAT HAMILTON ALREADY BELIEVED: THAT A "SMALL GOVERNMENT," STATES' RIGHTS SYSTEM COULD BE DISASTROUSLY IMPOTENT.

IN THE WAR, HE SAW HOW POORLY THE CONTINENTAL CONGRESS PROVIDED FOR AMERICAN SOLDIERS. LATER, AS A DELEGATE TO THE CONFEDERATION CONGRESS, HAMILTON STRUGGLED IN VAIN TO GET MEMBER STATES TO PAY THE UNITED STATES' MANY DEBTS.

HAMILTON WANTED THE CONSTITUTION TO ESTABLISH A GOVERNMENT THAT WOULD BE CENTRAL AND STRONG, WITH A WIDE SCOPE OF POWERS.

A FIRM UNION WILL BE OF THE UTMOST MOMENT TO THE PEACE AND LIBERTY OF THE STATES...

HE AT ONE POINT SHOCKED DELEGATES AT THE CONSTITUTIONAL CONVENTION BY PROPOSING THAT THE PRESIDENT AND SENATORS BE ELECTED FOR LIFE!

ALEXANDER HAMILTON, 1787.

IN CONTRAST WITH "JEFFERSONIAN" THINKERS WHO FAVOR STATES' RIGHTS, THOSE WHO ESPOUSE "HAMILTONIAN" IDEAS ESSENTIALLY FAVOR "BIG GOVERNMENT."

IN THE END, THE CONSTITUTION WAS RATIFIED.

GEORGE WASHINGTON, SO DEARLY BELOVED BY THE AMERICAN PEOPLE THAT HE COULD UNITE THEM LIKE NO OTHER, WAS MADE PRESIDENT WITH 100% OF THE VOTE.

WASHINGTON WAS LARGELY A "HAMILTONIAN." HE WAS IN FAVOR OF A FORCEFUL FEDERAL GOVERNMENT. EVEN THOSE WHO DISAGREED WITH WASHINGTON TENDED TO BE WON OVER BY HIS SHEER POPULARITY.

THERE ARE FOUR THINGS... ESSENTIAL TO THE... EXISTENCE OF THE UNITED STATES, AS AN INDEPENDENT POWER.

1st, AN INDISSOLUBLE UNION OF THE STATES UNDER ONE FEDERAL HEAD.

2ndly. A SACRED REGARD TO PUBLIC JUSTICE;

3rdly, THE ADOPTION OF A PROPER PEACE ESTABLISHMENT, AND

4thly. ... [FOR ALL AMERICANS] TO FORGET THEIR LOCAL PREJUDICES AND POLICIES... AND IN SOME INSTANCES, TO SACRIFICE THEIR INDIVIDUAL ADVANTAGES TO THE INTEREST OF THE COMMUNITY.

MEMBERS OF WASHINGTON'S CABINET-- AND ALEXANDER HAMILTON WAS ONE OF THEM-- EXERCISED SIGNIFICANT POWERS.

WASHINGTON'S ADMINISTRATION AVERTED A NEW BREAKOUT OF WAR WITH GREAT BRITAIN. IT PLACED THE CRIPPLING DEBT ON THE ROAD TO RETIREMENT.

THE FIRST PRESIDENT EVEN PUT DOWN AN UPRISING AGAINST FEDERAL LAW: *THE WHISKEY REBELLION.*

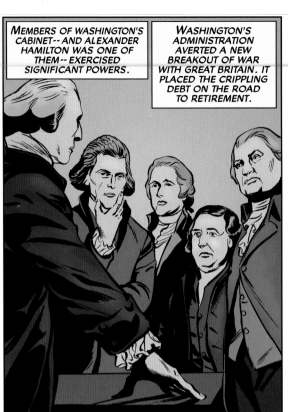

WASHINGTON HIMSELF LED TROOPS IN THE FIELD. HE REMAINS THE ONLY ACTING COMMANDER-IN-CHIEF TO EVER DO SO.

BUT WASHINGTON COULD NOT SERVE HIS COUNTRY FOREVER.

NEITHER COULD HE LIVE FOREVER.

AND AS HE BEGAN TO AGE AND FADE INTO THE BACKGROUND...

...THE OLD DISAGREEMENTS ABOUT GOVERNMENT POWER WERE EXPOSED LIKE JAGGED ROCKS IN A RECEDING TIDE.

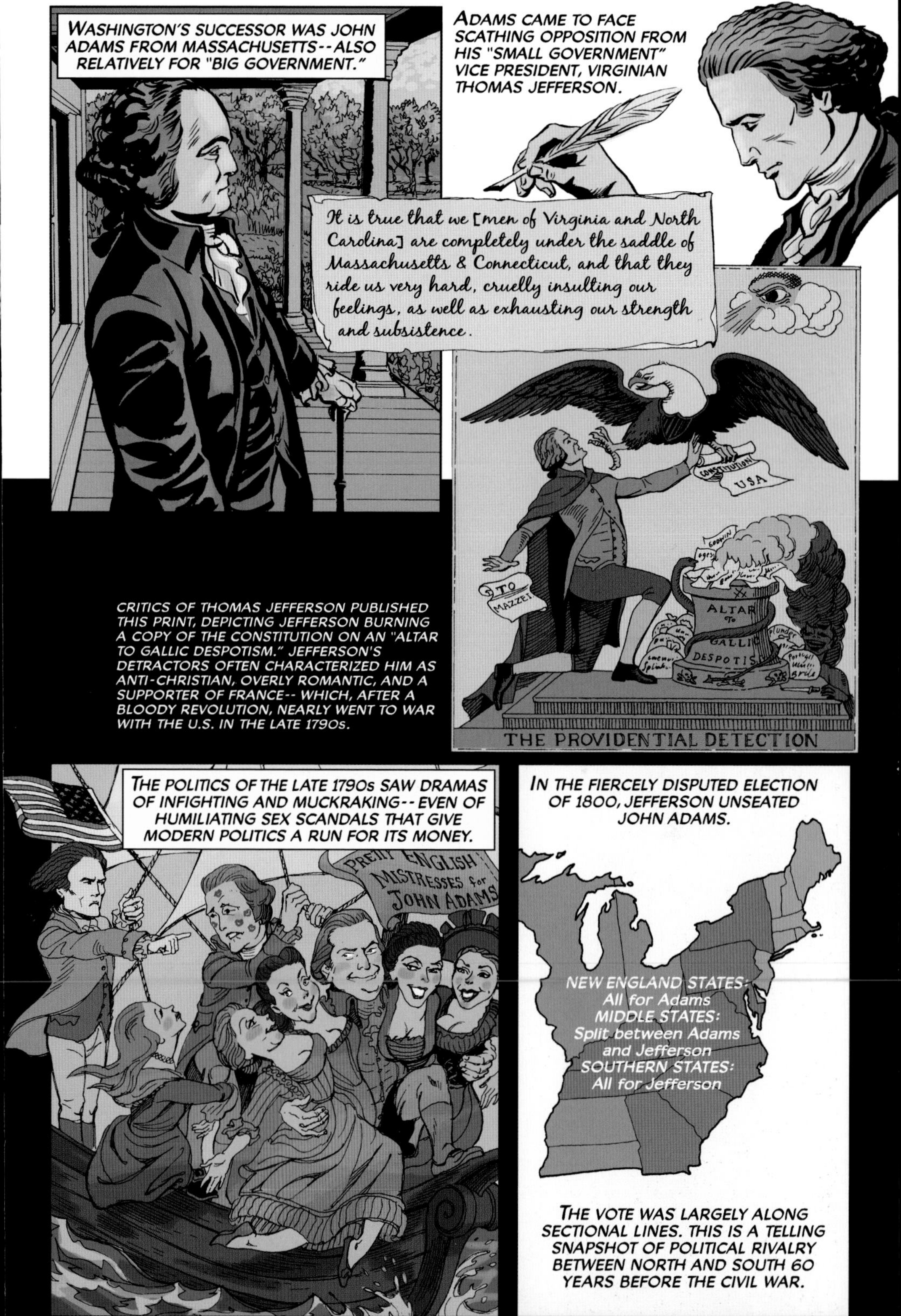
WASHINGTON'S SUCCESSOR WAS JOHN ADAMS FROM MASSACHUSETTS--ALSO RELATIVELY FOR "BIG GOVERNMENT."
ADAMS CAME TO FACE SCATHING OPPOSITION FROM HIS "SMALL GOVERNMENT" VICE PRESIDENT, VIRGINIAN THOMAS JEFFERSON.
It is true that we [men of Virginia and North Carolina] are completely under the saddle of Massachusetts & Connecticut, and that they ride us very hard, cruelly insulting our feelings, as well as exhausting our strength and subsistence.
CONSTITUTION
USA
TO MAZZEI
GODWIN
ALTAR TO GALLIC DESPOTIS
plunder
THE PROVIDENTIAL DETECTION
CRITICS OF THOMAS JEFFERSON PUBLISHED THIS PRINT, DEPICTING JEFFERSON BURNING A COPY OF THE CONSTITUTION ON AN "ALTAR TO GALLIC DESPOTISM." JEFFERSON'S DETRACTORS OFTEN CHARACTERIZED HIM AS ANTI-CHRISTIAN, OVERLY ROMANTIC, AND A SUPPORTER OF FRANCE-- WHICH, AFTER A BLOODY REVOLUTION, NEARLY WENT TO WAR WITH THE U.S. IN THE LATE 1790s.
THE POLITICS OF THE LATE 1790s SAW DRAMAS OF INFIGHTING AND MUCKRAKING-- EVEN OF HUMILIATING SEX SCANDALS THAT GIVE MODERN POLITICS A RUN FOR ITS MONEY.
ENGLISH MISTRESSES for JOHN ADAMS
IN THE FIERCELY DISPUTED ELECTION OF 1800, JEFFERSON UNSEATED JOHN ADAMS.
NEW ENGLAND STATES: All for Adams
MIDDLE STATES: Split between Adams and Jefferson
SOUTHERN STATES: All for Jefferson
THE VOTE WAS LARGELY ALONG SECTIONAL LINES. THIS IS A TELLING SNAPSHOT OF POLITICAL RIVALRY BETWEEN NORTH AND SOUTH 60 YEARS BEFORE THE CIVIL WAR.

THE TWO-PARTY SYSTEM GREW FROM THE SEEDS OF THIS CONFLICT...

...SETTING THE STAGE FOR MORE PARTISAN BICKERING OVER GOVERNMENT POWER FOR YEARS TO COME.

EXAMPLE: IN THE EARLY 1800s, WHEN IT TOOK THREE WEEKS TO GO FROM OHIO TO NEW YORK...

...THE GOVERNMENT CONSIDERED VASTLY IMPROVING TRAVEL BY BUILDING A ROAD FROM BUFFALO, NEW YORK, TO NEW ORLEANS, LOUISIANA.

MANY SOUTHERN POLITICIANS VEHEMENTLY ATTACKED THE PLAN.

SOUTHERN CONGRESS-MEN FINALLY DEFEATED THE PROJECT. ONE REJOICED THAT HIS SIDE HAD...

BUFFALO & NEW ORLEANS ROAD

"...HARPOONED THE MONSTER [OF 'BIG GOVERNMENT'], AND MADE HIS BLOOD SPOUT GLORIOUSLY."

WHAT OFTEN MOTIVATED SUCH "SMALL GOVERNMENT" ACTIVISTS?

"IF CONGRESS POSSESSES THE POWER [TO BUILD ROADS, THEN IT LOGICALLY ALSO HAS THE POWER TO] ... EMANCIPATE EVERY SLAVE IN THE UNITED STATES."

UNTIL THIS GOVERNMENT IS MADE A LIMITED GOVERNMENT... THERE IS NO LIBERTY-- NO SECURITY FOR THE SOUTH.

WORRY THAT THE FEDERAL GOVERNMENT WOULD SOMEDAY COME TO HAVE MORE POWER OVER SLAVERY.

JOHN RANDOLPH OF ROANOKE, CONGRESSMAN FROM VIRGINIA, 1824.

ROBERT BARNWELL RHETT, PROSLAVERY ACTIVIST, 1833.

BROUGHT FORTH ON THIS CONTINENT

"THIS CONTINENT" OF NORTH AMERICA-- ITS GEOGRAPHY AND CLIMATE-- PROFOUNDLY SHAPED THE CHARACTER OF THE NORTH AND SOUTH.

THE LAND ITSELF WAS LITERALLY A FACTOR THAT GAVE RISE TO THE CIVIL WAR.

IN PREHISTORIC TIMES, THE AMERICAS WERE THE LAST OF THE EARTH'S LARGE LANDMASSES TO BE DISCOVERED BY HUMANS.

THE AMERICAS WERE NOT "PRISTINE" BEFORE ITS FIRST VISITS BY EUROPEANS. NATIVE PEOPLES HAD WIDELY SETTLED THE LAND.

EVEN SO, WHEN WHITE EXPLORERS AND COLONISTS MADE THEIR EARLIEST TRIPS TO "THIS CONTINENT," THE ABUNDANCE OF NATURE THEY FOUND...

...WAS NOTHING SHORT OF STAGGERING.

AROUND A.D. 1000, VIKING LEIF ERICSON FOUND THE NORTHEAST COAST OF NORTH AMERICA SO OVERHUNG WITH WILD GRAPES HE DUBBED THE PLACE "VINLAND."

SO LARGE A QUANTITY OF SALMON ENTERS THE RIVER AT NIGHT ONE IS UNABLE TO SLEEP...

NICOLAS DENYS, FRENCH EXPLORER, MID-1600s. HIS NET CAUGHT SO MANY FISH THAT "TEN MEN COULD NOT HAUL IT TO LAND."

NOWADAYS, BISON ARE REMEMBERED AS BEASTS OF THE GREAT PLAINS. BUT IN PRE-COLONIAL TIMES THEY ROAMED AS FAR EAST AS PENNSYLVANIA.

NO SPOT ON EARTH PRODUCED AS MUCH SEAFOOD PER ACRE AS THE WATERS OF CHESAPEAKE BAY.

FROM ACROSS THE OCEAN, EUROPEANS BROUGHT **CAPITALISM** AND THE DEVELOPING IDEA OF A **MARKET ECONOMY** WITH THEM.

THEY SAW THAT THE SPECTACULAR RESOURCES OF AMERICA COULD CREATE FORTUNES.

LAND SEEMED ENDLESS. IT COULD BE ACQUIRED CHEAPLY.

BUT INVESTORS NEEDED MORE THAN LAND. THEY ALSO NEEDED MANPOWER TO WORK IT.

AND SINCE THERE WAS SUCH A SMALL POPULATION OF SETTLERS IN NORTH AMERICA, FEW PEOPLE WERE AVAILABLE TO WORK. THIS MADE LABOR HUGELY EXPENSIVE.

THESE WERE THE CONDITIONS IN THE "NEW WORLD"...

...AND THOSE CONDITIONS WERE THE POLAR OPPOSITE OF THE "OLD WORLD." THERE, PEOPLE WERE TYPICALLY EITHER PEASANTS WITH LITTLE HOPE OF OWNING THEIR OWN LAND...

...OR NOBLE ELITES WHO INHERITED LAND, STATUS, AND POWER.

AMERICA BROUGHT THE POSSIBILITY OF A VASTLY DIFFERENT WAY OF LIFE. IT INVITED *UPWARD MOBILITY*. IT PROVIDED A CHANCE FOR MEN TO BE JUDGED BY THEIR TALENTS AND CAPABILITIES -- NOT BY THE FAMILY INTO WHICH THEY WERE BORN.

THE CHEAP, ABUNDANT LAND/EXPENSIVE, SCARCE LABOR DYNAMIC ARGUABLY PUT MEN ON A MORE EQUAL "PLAYING FIELD" THAN THEY EVER HAD BEFORE.

DESPITE THIS, SOME RESPONDED BY INTRODUCING VARIOUS FORMS OF *FORCED SERVITUDE*.

...WHICH BY THE LATE 1600s EVOLVED INTO BLACK SLAVERY.

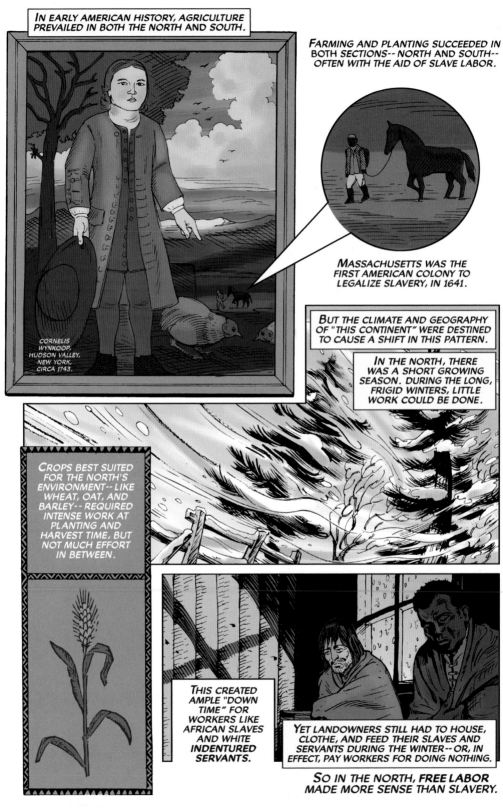

IN EARLY AMERICAN HISTORY, AGRICULTURE PREVAILED IN BOTH THE NORTH AND SOUTH.

FARMING AND PLANTING SUCCEEDED IN BOTH SECTIONS-- NORTH AND SOUTH-- OFTEN WITH THE AID OF SLAVE LABOR.

CORNELIS WYNKOOP, HUDSON VALLEY, NEW YORK, CIRCA 1743.

MASSACHUSETTS WAS THE FIRST AMERICAN COLONY TO LEGALIZE SLAVERY, IN 1641.

BUT THE CLIMATE AND GEOGRAPHY OF "THIS CONTINENT" WERE DESTINED TO CAUSE A SHIFT IN THIS PATTERN.

IN THE NORTH, THERE WAS A SHORT GROWING SEASON. DURING THE LONG, FRIGID WINTERS, LITTLE WORK COULD BE DONE.

CROPS BEST SUITED FOR THE NORTH'S ENVIRONMENT-- LIKE WHEAT, OAT, AND BARLEY-- REQUIRED INTENSE WORK AT PLANTING AND HARVEST TIME, BUT NOT MUCH EFFORT IN BETWEEN.

THIS CREATED AMPLE "DOWN TIME" FOR WORKERS LIKE AFRICAN SLAVES AND WHITE INDENTURED SERVANTS.

YET LANDOWNERS STILL HAD TO HOUSE, CLOTHE, AND FEED THEIR SLAVES AND SERVANTS DURING THE WINTER-- OR, IN EFFECT, PAY WORKERS FOR DOING NOTHING.

SO IN THE NORTH, FREE LABOR MADE MORE SENSE THAN SLAVERY.

UNDER THE FREE LABOR SYSTEM, WORKERS COULD BE HIRED ONLY WHEN NEEDED. THEY WERE LEFT TO SUPPORT THEMSELVES THE REST OF THE YEAR.

THE NORTH CAME TO CELEBRATE FREE LABOR AS EFFICIENT AND HONORABLE, WITH ITS PROMISE OF UPWARD MOBILITY IN EXCHANGE FOR WORK WELL DONE.

THE POOR SOIL OF NEW ENGLAND PARTICULARLY LIMITED FARMING.

BUT THE REGION DID OFFER AMPLE RIVERS AND STREAMS FOR WATER POWER, AND WOOD FOR BUILDINGS AND PRODUCTS LIKE SHIP MASTS.

IT BECAME CLEAR THAT, IN GENERAL, THE NORTHEAST WAS BETTER SUITED FOR INDUSTRY, SHIPBUILDING, TRANSPORTATION, AND COMMERCE.

AGRICULTURE DECLINED.

SO SLAVERY DIED OUT ACROSS THE NORTH.

ROUGHLY BETWEEN THE YEARS 1780 AND 1804, SLAVERY WAS EITHER ABOLISHED OR GRADUAL EMANCIPATION WAS ADOPTED IN THE NORTH.

AN ACT FOR THE GRADUAL ABOLITION OF SLAVERY

SEC. 1. BE it enacted by the Council and General Assembly of this State, and it is hereby enacted by the authority of the same, That every child born of a slave within this state, after the fourth day of July next, shall be free; but shall remain the servant of the owner of his or her mother, and the executors, administrators or assigns of such owner, in the same manner as if such child had been bound to service by the trustees or overseers of the poor, and shall continue in such service, if a male until the age of twenty five years; and if a female until the age of twenty one years...

STATE HOUSE, TRENTON, NEW JERSEY.

IN THE SOUTH, THERE WERE MILD WINTERS AND LONG GROWING SEASONS.

MORE TROPICAL-CLIMATE CROPS FLOURISHED THERE-- LIKE TOBACCO, RICE, AND INDIGO.

AS EXPORTS TO EUROPE, THESE PRODUCTS PROVED TO BE HIGHLY PROFITABLE.

BECAUSE THE EASIEST WAY TO EARN MONEY WAS WITH AGRICULTURE, SOUTHERNERS HAD INCENTIVE TO FARM LARGE PLANTATIONS RATHER THAN TAKE UP OTHER TRADES.

TOBACCO, RICE, AND INDIGO-- UNLIKE WHEAT-- WERE FAR MORE LABOR-INTENSIVE CROPS. THEY REQUIRED A GREAT DEAL OF WORK EVEN BETWEEN PLANTING AND HARVESTING.

SO WHAT YIELDED THE HIGHEST AND EASIEST PROFITS FOR LANDOWNERS HERE? SLAVE LABOR.

A TOBACCO PLANTATION

BECAUSE SLAVES LACKED REAL UPWARD MOBILITY, THEY TENDED TO HAVE LESS MOTIVATION TO WORK HARD. SO IN ORDER TO FUNCTION, THE SLAVERY SYSTEM REQUIRED CONSTANT OVERSIGHT. AND, OFTEN, HARSH DISCIPLINE.

MEANWHILE, SOUTHERNERS TOO POOR TO OWN SLAVES GENERALLY LOOKED DOWN ON MANUAL LABOR. THAT WAS SEEN AS "SLAVES' WORK."

LOOK CLOSELY AT THE SOUTH, HOWEVER, AND ONE SEES IT HAD DIVERSE REGIONS AND CULTURES OF ITS OWN.

IN PARTS OF SOUTH CAROLINA, THE INSTITUTION OF SLAVERY BECAME DEEPLY EMBEDDED IN THE ECONOMY AND IN DAILY LIFE...

...BECAUSE OF A LITERALLY MICROSCOPIC FACTOR.

THE MALARIA VIRUS.

THE BOGGY, MOSQUITO-INFESTED SWAMPS OR TIDEWATER OF THE SOUTH CAROLINA COAST WERE PERFECT FOR GROWING RICE AND SUPERFINE STRAINS OF COTTON.

BUT THE ENVIRONMENT WAS ALSO A PESTILENT ONE, THICK WITH INFECTION AND DISEASE. ESPECIALLY IN SUMMER.

AND ESPECIALLY FOR THOSE OF EUROPEAN EXTRACTION: THE WHITE PLANTATION OWNERS AND THEIR FAMILIES, WHO MOSTLY RULED AS ABSENTEE LANDLORDS.

SLAVES IMPORTED FROM AFRICA OR THE CARIBBEAN, HOWEVER, DEMONSTRATED A RESISTANCE TO MALARIA--AND, IT WAS BELIEVED, TO THE RIGORS OF THE STEAMY CLIMATE.

SO IT IS NO ACCIDENT THAT SOUTH CAROLINA GREW TO BECOME SLAVERY'S MOST PASSIONATE DEFENDER. BUT THE TIDEWATER'S CONDITIONS ALSO LED TO A POTENTIALLY EXPLOSIVE IMBALANCE IN THE REGION...

...WHERE THE POPULATION WAS OVER 80% BLACK AND UNDER 20% WHITE.

ENTER "KING COTTON"

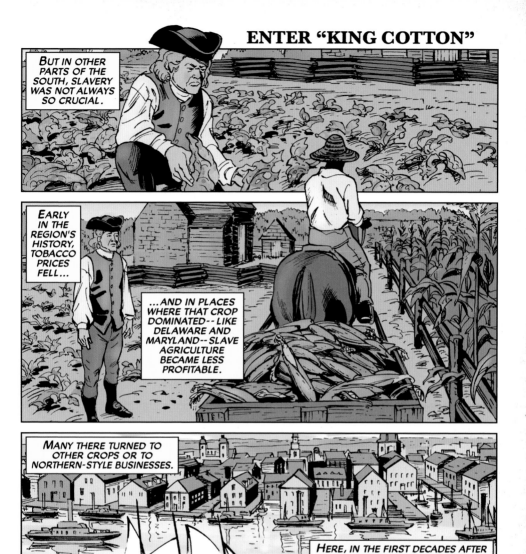

BUT IN OTHER PARTS OF THE SOUTH, SLAVERY WAS NOT ALWAYS SO CRUCIAL.

EARLY IN THE REGION'S HISTORY, TOBACCO PRICES FELL...

...AND IN PLACES WHERE THAT CROP DOMINATED-- LIKE DELAWARE AND MARYLAND-- SLAVE AGRICULTURE BECAME LESS PROFITABLE.

MANY THERE TURNED TO OTHER CROPS OR TO NORTHERN-STYLE BUSINESSES.

BALTIMORE, MARYLAND, 1830s.

HERE, IN THE FIRST DECADES AFTER THE REVOLUTION, IT SEEMED SLAVERY MIGHT BE ON THE DECLINE.

BUT IN 1793, A NEW DEVELOPMENT CHANGED EVERYTHING.

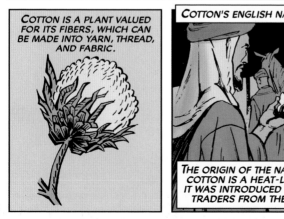

COTTON IS A PLANT VALUED FOR ITS FIBERS, WHICH CAN BE MADE INTO YARN, THREAD, AND FABRIC.

COTTON'S ENGLISH NAME COMES FROM THE ARABIC AL-QUTN.

THE ORIGIN OF THE NAME HINTS THAT COTTON IS A HEAT-LOVING PLANT. IT WAS INTRODUCED TO EUROPE BY TRADERS FROM THE NEAR EAST.

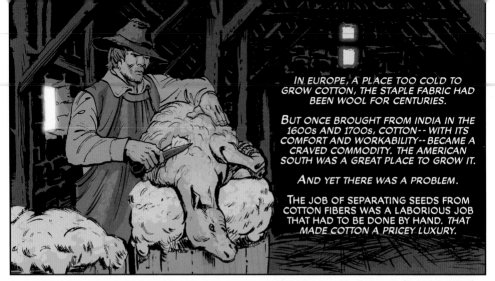

IN EUROPE, A PLACE TOO COLD TO GROW COTTON, THE STAPLE FABRIC HAD BEEN WOOL FOR CENTURIES.

BUT ONCE BROUGHT FROM INDIA IN THE 1600s AND 1700s, COTTON-- WITH ITS COMFORT AND WORKABILITY-- BECAME A CRAVED COMMODITY. THE AMERICAN SOUTH WAS A GREAT PLACE TO GROW IT.

AND YET THERE WAS A PROBLEM.

THE JOB OF SEPARATING SEEDS FROM COTTON FIBERS WAS A LABORIOUS JOB THAT HAD TO BE DONE BY HAND. *THAT MADE COTTON A PRICEY LUXURY.*

BUT IN 1793, ELI WHITNEY, A MASSACHUSETTS-BORN INVENTOR THEN LIVING IN GEORGIA, INVENTED THE COTTON GIN...

...A MACHINE WHOSE NAME IS SHORT FOR "COTTON ENGINE."

THE COTTON GIN DRAMATICALLY SPED UP THE PROCESS OF REMOVING SEEDS FROM A VARIETY OF THE PLANT KNOWN AS "SHORT-STAPLE" OR "UPLAND" COTTON.

THE AVAILABILITY OF COTTON EXPLODED.

THE WORLD'S DEMAND FOR IT RESPONDED IN KIND, CREATING AN ECONOMIC BOOM.

THIS LUCRATIVE NEW AGRICULTURE SWEPT ACROSS HUGE SWATHS OF THE "DEEP SOUTH."

AND SLAVERY, WHICH HAD BEEN STAGNATING, BECAME MORE CRUCIAL THAN EVER.

FOR COTTON WAS ANOTHER LABOR-INTENSIVE CROP. THE FORTUNES IT PROMISED WERE BEST SECURED WITH SLAVE LABOR.

AND MORE AMERICANS BEGAN TO DEFEND AND EVEN CELEBRATE SLAVERY.

"KING COTTON" DID NOT JUST TRANSFORM THE SOUTH.

NORTHERN CITIES FLOURISHED WITH INDUSTRIAL TEXTILE MILLS. NORTHERN HARBORS FILLED WITH SHIPS TRANSPORTING COTTON OVERSEAS.

THE MOST PROFITABLE WAY OF FARMING UPLAND COTTON, HOWEVER, HAD DRAWBACKS.

IT SEVERELY DEPLETED THE SOIL.

LUCKILY FOR COTTON PLANTERS, IN AMERICA LAND WAS STILL CHEAP. AND THERE WAS ONE PLACE TO WHICH SLAVE-OWNING SOUTHERN PLANTERS COULD LOOK WHEN LAND BECAME WORTHLESS FOR GROWING COTTON...

THE WEST

WESTWARD THE COURSE OF EMPIRE TAKES IT'S WAY.

TO BE CLEAR, AMERICA HAS HAD NOT ONE BUT RATHER MULTIPLE "WESTS."

EARLY ON, THOSE "WESTS" INCLUDED ALABAMA AND MISSISSIPPI IN THE SOUTH, AND OHIO AND INDIANA IN THE NORTH.

ONLY MUCH LATER WOULD THE TERM "THE WEST" PRIMARILY APPLY TO THE PLAINS, THE ROCKIES, AND THE PACIFIC.

COTTON AGRICULTURE KEPT DRAWING SLAVERY FARTHER INTO THE FRONTIER. ONE 1842 OBSERVER SAID...

...EVERY PLANTER CONSIDERS HIMSELF ONLY A TEMPORARY OCCUPANT OF THE PLANTATION ON WHICH HE IS SETTLED...

...HE THUS GOES ON FROM YEAR TO YEAR, RACKING IT OUT, AND MAKING IT YIELD AS MUCH COTTON...AS HE CAN...

...[UNTIL] HE IS READY TO GO FARTHER WEST IN QUEST OF ANOTHER LOT OF LAND...

AMERICAN CULTURE HAS LONG BEEN INFECTED WITH AN ADVENTUROUS, ROMANTIC SPIRIT TO PUSH WEST.

ANNEXATION

THAT IMPULSE IS AT LEAST PARTIALLY INSPIRED BY SLAVERY'S NEED TO CONSTANTLY EXPAND...

Clear the road. Don't you see that we are fulfilling our manifest destiny!

We are not a whit inclined to tarry there.

HEAD QUARTERS OF THE NORTHERN DEMOCRACY.

Hey! hey, there! where upon airth are you going! Come back here to your quarters!

...OR FACE ITS OWN DESTRUCTION.

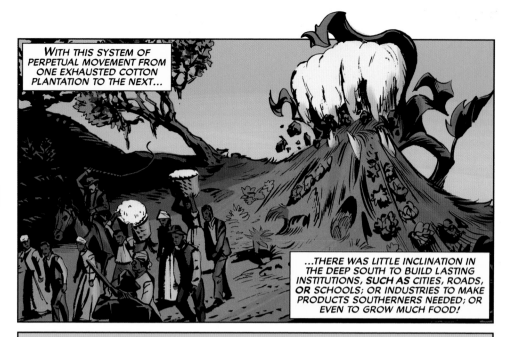

WITH THIS SYSTEM OF PERPETUAL MOVEMENT FROM ONE EXHAUSTED COTTON PLANTATION TO THE NEXT...

...THERE WAS LITTLE INCLINATION IN THE DEEP SOUTH TO BUILD LASTING INSTITUTIONS, **SUCH AS** CITIES, ROADS, **OR** SCHOOLS; OR INDUSTRIES TO MAKE PRODUCTS SOUTHERNERS NEEDED; OR EVEN TO GROW MUCH FOOD!

BUT SOUTHERNERS WERE NOT THE ONLY MEN IN THE UNITED STATES LOOKING TO THE WEST.

AMERICA HAD PROVEN ITSELF AS A "LAND OF OPPORTUNITY."

...OUR COUNTRY HAS IMPROVED AND IS FLOURISHING BEYOND ANY FORMER EXAMPLE IN THE HISTORY OF NATIONS.

FAREWELL ADDRESS OF PRESIDENT ANDREW JACKSON, 1837.

LIKE SOUTHERNERS, THOSE IN THE NORTH-- BOTH NATURAL-BORN CITIZENS AND A RISING TIDE OF IMMIGRANTS-- HAD THE SAME AMBITIONS TO PROSPER...

... AND PROSPERITY, ESPECIALLY FOR THE LOWER CLASSES, WAS GETTING TO BE HARD TO COME BY IN THE NORTHEAST.

SOME AREAS EVEN RESEMBLED THE "OLD WORLD."

TREMONT STREET, BOSTON, 1840s.

SKILLED CRAFTSMEN WERE LOSING JOBS TO INDUSTRIAL TECHNOLOGY. LAND WAS EXPENSIVE.

AND WORKERS' WAGES WERE LOW.

AS NEW TERRITORIES WERE ANNEXED BY THE U.S., OPPORTUNITIES IN THE WEST BECKONED.

ALL UNDERSTOOD THAT THESE WESTERN TERRITORIES WERE LIKELY TO BECOME STATES SOMEDAY.

BUT BEFORE THAT COULD HAPPEN, THEY WERE UNDER THE CONTROL OF THE U.S. CONGRESS.

AND OUT WEST, FORTUNE-SEEKING FREE LABORERS KNEW THERE WAS ONE THREAT THEY WOULD NEVER BE ABLE TO COMPETE WITH.

WHAT WAS THAT THREAT?

SLAVE LABOR.

FREE LABORERS FEARED THAT IF THE PLANTATION SYSTEM WITH ITS SLAVES AND HUGE ACREAGES CAME TO THE TERRITORIES, IT WOULD DRIVE UP PRICES OF LAND AND DRIVE DOWN WORKERS' WAGES.

As a noted U.S. legislator from Pennsylvania said...

I plead the cause and rights of white freemen [and] would preserve [a chance for them to] live without the disgrace which association with Negro slavery brings upon free labor.

DAVID WILMOT, SENATOR FROM PENNSYLVANIA, 1847.

The West? It was not only land.

It was the future.

The question was which system would control this future: free labor or slavery?

We are playing for a mighty stake... If we win we carry slavery to the Pacific Ocean...

If we do not exclude slavery from the territories, it will exclude us.

DAVID ATCHISON, SENATOR FROM MISSOURI, 1855.

OLIVER MORTON, GOVERNOR OF INDIANA, 1860.

Abraham Lincoln was born in Kentucky--a slave state.

His family could not afford a plantation or slaves. This, in part, provoked Lincoln's father, Thomas Lincoln, to move the family to free states: Indiana, then Illinois.

THIS PERSONALLY INVOLVED LINCOLN IN THE GREAT NARRATIVE OF AMERICA'S WESTWARD EXPANSION, MAKING HIM AN APPEALING PRESIDENTIAL CANDIDATE FOR HIS PARTY.

THE U.S. CONSTITUTION IS SET UP...

...SO THAT THE STATES EXERT CONTROL ON AND SHAPE ALL THREE BRANCHES OF THE FEDERAL GOVERNMENT.

BY ELECTING MEMBERS OF THE HOUSE AND SENATE, THE STATES INFLUENCE CONTROL IN CONGRESS.

STATES' VOTES IN THE **ELECTORAL COLLEGE** DETERMINE WHO WILL BE PRESIDENT...

...THE EXECUTIVE WITH THE AUTHORITY TO NOMINATE SUPREME COURT JUSTICES, WHO CAN THEN INFLUENCE AMERICAN LAW FOR DECADES TO COME.

THEREFORE, GROUPS OF STATES THAT POSSESS SIMILAR INTERESTS AND PRIORITIES TEND TO COMPETE WITH OTHER GROUPS OF STATES.

THE PRIZE THEY ALL SEEK IS CONTROL IN WASHINGTON-- AND THE ABILITY TO STEER THE COURSE OF THE ENTIRE NATION.

INCREASINGLY OVER THE COURSE OF THE 19th CENTURY, THE SLAVE STATES AND FREE STATES WRESTLED FOR CONTROL.

EACH FACTION FEARED THE OTHER WOULD GAIN THE UPPER HAND-- AND USE THE POWER OF THE FEDERAL GOVERNMENT AGAINST IT.

IN A WAY, IT WAS A NUMBERS GAME. EACH SIDE, SLAVE AND FREE, WANTED TO ADD MORE STATES TO ITS TOTAL.

NEW ANNEXED LAND-- PURCHASED BY CONGRESS OR CONQUERED IN WARS-- LED TO NEW TERRITORIES.

NEW TERRITORIES LED TO NEW STATES...

...AND TO MORE INFLUENCE IN THE FEDERAL GOVERNMENT.

SO EVERY TIME NEW AREAS CAME UNDER U.S. CONTROL...

...IT WOULD TOUCH OFF AN EVEN MORE RANCOROUS SCUFFLE OVER HOW SLAVERY WOULD OR WOULD NOT APPLY THERE.

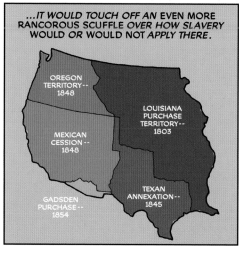

OREGON TERRITORY-- 1848

MEXICAN CESSION-- 1848

LOUISIANA PURCHASE TERRITORY-- 1803

GADSDEN PURCHASE-- 1854

TEXAN ANNEXATION-- 1845

THESE SHOWDOWNS PLAYED OUT WITH THE ADMISSION OF MISSOURI, TEXAS, AND CALIFORNIA TO THE UNION, THEN WITH THE TERRITORIES OF NEW MEXICO, KANSAS, AND NEBRASKA.

NEBRASKA TERRITORY-- ORGANIZED IN 1854

KANSAS TERRITORY-- ORGANIZED IN 1854

MISSOURI-- ADMITTED IN 1821

CALIFORNIA-- ADMITTED IN 1850

NEW MEXICO TERRITORY-- ORGANIZED IN 1850

TEXAS-- ADMITTED IN 1845

THE SLAVERY ISSUE IN KANSAS BECAME SO CONTENTIOUS THAT SETTLERS FOUGHT TO THE DEATH OVER THE ISSUE.

MARAIS des CYGNES MASSACRE, TRADING POST, KANSAS, 1858.

WHEN SUCH SECTIONAL CRISES AROSE, THEY THREATENED PEACE AND HARMONY AMONG THE STATES.

GREAT POLITICIANS OF THE DAY SCRAMBLED TO PRESERVE BALANCE AND KEEP THE UNION AFLOAT.

THE IDEAL METHOD TO KEEP PEACE WAS TO PRESERVE THE SAME NUMBER OF FREE AND SLAVE STATES. ONE SUCH MANEUVER WAS THE 1820 MISSOURI COMPROMISE...

...WHICH BALANCED THE ADMISSION OF MISSOURI, A NEW SLAVE STATE, WITH MAINE, A NEW FREE STATE.

SENATORS HENRY CLAY (KENTUCKY), JOHN C. CALHOUN (SOUTH CAROLINA), AND DANIEL WEBSTER (MASSACHUSETTS) MADE UP A "GREAT TRIUMVIRATE" THAT SECURED ORDER IN THE 1830s AND 1840s.

YET AS YEARS PASSED, EACH FACTION'S PATIENCE WITH THE OTHER WORE THIN. PARANOIA AND HOSTILITY MULTIPLIED. IN 1857, THE CLEVELAND LEADER CLAIMED:

...the people of the North and of the South have come to hate each other worse than the hatred between any two nations in the world.

TENSIONS WERE DRIVING A WEDGE INTO THE HEART OF THE UNION.

WHAT BLOW WOULD ULTIMATELY SPLIT IT IN TWO?

C-CRACK!

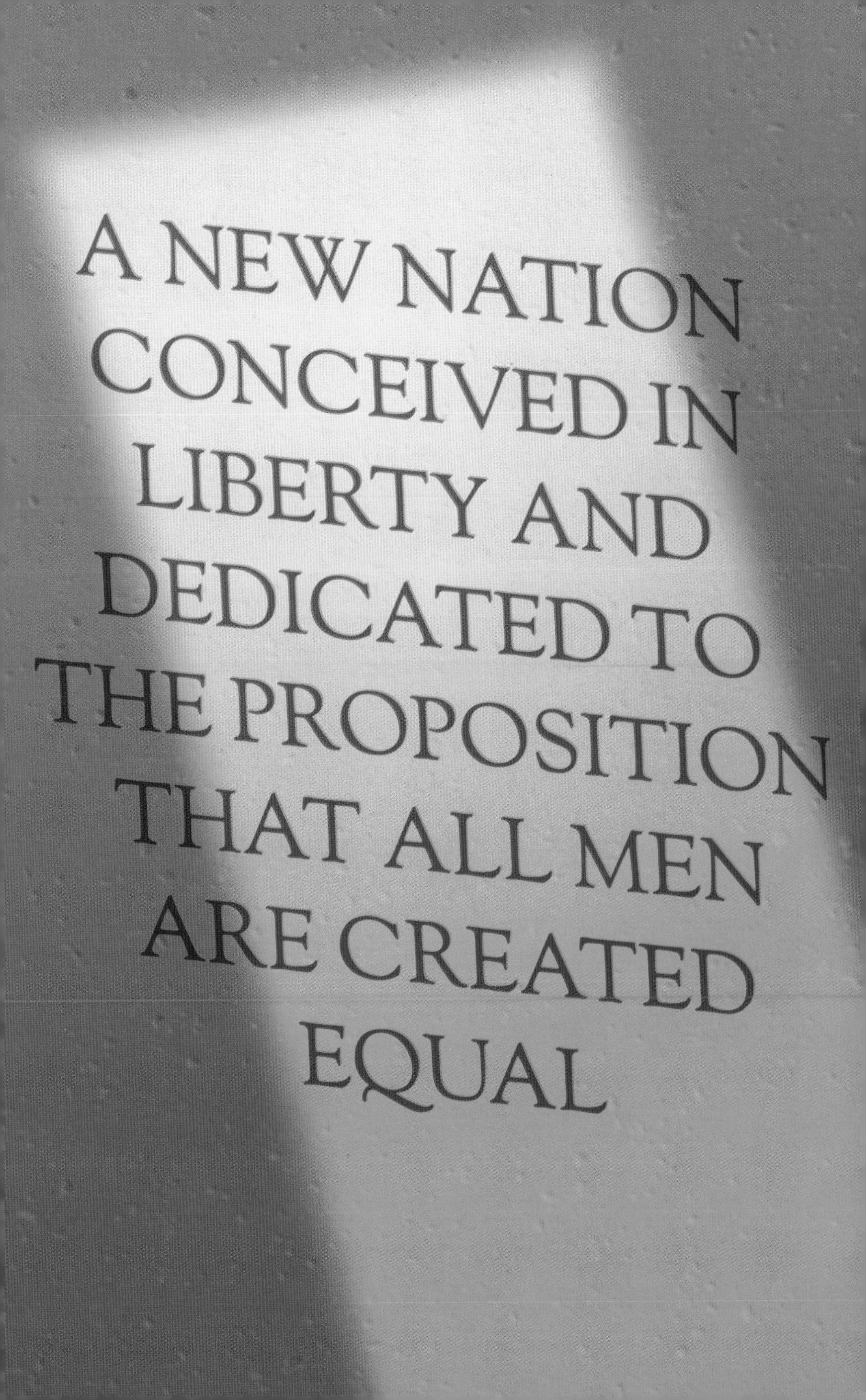
A NEW NATION
CONCEIVED IN
LIBERTY AND
DEDICATED TO
THE PROPOSITION
THAT ALL MEN
ARE CREATED
EQUAL

WE HOLD THESE TRUTHS TO BE SELF-EVIDENT: THAT ALL MEN ARE CREATED EQUAL, THAT THEY ARE ENDOWED BY THEIR CREATOR WITH CERTAIN INALIENABLE THESE ARE LIFE, LIBERTY ESS, THAT

"CREATED EQUAL" Part 1: RHETORIC

LINCOLN BELIEVED THE UNION WAS OLDER THAN--AND THUS IN MANY WAYS SUPREME OVER--THE STATES.

WE'VE SEEN HOW HE DID NOT ARRIVE AT THAT POSITION FROM THE MOST STRAIGHTFORWARD READING OF THE DECLARATION OF INDEPENDENCE.

LINCOLN'S CONCLUSION WAS INSTEAD INDIRECT, SPECULATIVE, AND PERSONAL.

WAS THE UNITED STATES GENUINELY "DEDICATED TO THE PROPOSITION THAT ALL MEN ARE CREATED EQUAL"?

ISN'T SUCH AN ASSERTION HYPOCRITICAL...

...GIVEN THAT SEVERAL MILLION PEOPLE IN AMERICA WERE FORCED INTO SLAVERY?

LINCOLN WAS CHALLENGED TIME AND AGAIN ON HIS POSITION.

I TELL YOU THAT THIS... DOCTRINE OF LINCOLN'S-- DECLARING THAT THE NEGRO AND THE WHITE MAN ARE MADE EQUAL BY THE DECLARATION OF INDEPENDENCE AND BY DIVINE PROVIDENCE--IS A *MONSTROUS HERESY.*

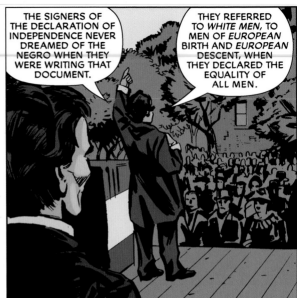

THE SIGNERS OF THE DECLARATION OF INDEPENDENCE NEVER DREAMED OF THE NEGRO WHEN THEY WERE WRITING THAT DOCUMENT.

THEY REFERRED TO *WHITE MEN,* TO MEN OF *EUROPEAN* BIRTH AND *EUROPEAN* DESCENT, WHEN THEY DECLARED THE EQUALITY OF ALL MEN.

STEPHEN A. DOUGLAS, SENATOR FROM ILLINOIS, 1858. (EMPHASIS ADDED)

YET LINCOLN STOOD BY HIS WORDS.

YES, EVEN WITH SLAVERY, HE BELIEVED THE UNITED STATES HAD MEANT ITSELF TO BECOME A SOCIETY OF EQUALITY.

THE WORDS OF KEY FOUNDING FATHERS-- AND EVEN MANY SLAVE- HOLDERS THEMSELVES-- BACKED HIM UP.

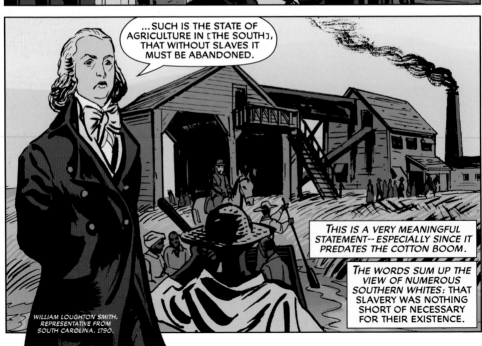

...SUCH IS THE STATE OF AGRICULTURE IN [THE SOUTH], THAT WITHOUT SLAVES IT MUST BE ABANDONED.

THIS IS A VERY MEANINGFUL STATEMENT-- ESPECIALLY SINCE IT PREDATES THE COTTON BOOM.

THE WORDS SUM UP THE VIEW OF NUMEROUS SOUTHERN WHITES: THAT SLAVERY WAS NOTHING SHORT OF NECESSARY FOR THEIR EXISTENCE.

WILLIAM LOUGHTON SMITH, REPRESENTATIVE FROM SOUTH CAROLINA, 1790.

84

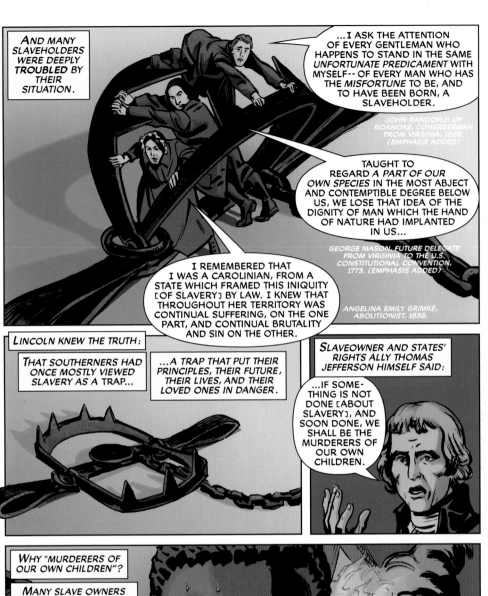

AND MANY SLAVEHOLDERS WERE DEEPLY *TROUBLED* BY THEIR SITUATION.

...I ASK THE ATTENTION OF EVERY GENTLEMAN WHO HAPPENS TO STAND IN THE SAME *UNFORTUNATE PREDICAMENT* WITH MYSELF-- OF EVERY MAN WHO HAS THE *MISFORTUNE* TO BE, AND TO HAVE BEEN BORN, A SLAVEHOLDER.

JOHN RANDOLPH OF ROANOKE, CONGRESSMAN FROM VIRGINIA, 1828. (EMPHASIS ADDED)

TAUGHT TO REGARD *A PART OF OUR OWN SPECIES* IN THE MOST ABJECT AND CONTEMPTIBLE DEGREE BELOW US, WE LOSE THAT IDEA OF THE DIGNITY OF MAN WHICH THE HAND OF NATURE HAD IMPLANTED IN US...

GEORGE MASON, FUTURE DELEGATE FROM VIRGINIA TO THE U.S. CONSTITUTIONAL CONVENTION, 1773. (EMPHASIS ADDED)

I REMEMBERED THAT I WAS A CAROLINIAN, FROM A STATE WHICH FRAMED THIS INIQUITY [OF SLAVERY] BY LAW. I KNEW THAT THROUGHOUT HER TERRITORY WAS CONTINUAL SUFFERING, ON THE ONE PART, AND CONTINUAL BRUTALITY AND SIN ON THE OTHER.

ANGELINA EMILY GRIMKÉ, ABOLITIONIST, 1838.

LINCOLN KNEW THE TRUTH:

THAT SOUTHERNERS HAD ONCE MOSTLY VIEWED SLAVERY AS A TRAP...

...A TRAP THAT PUT THEIR PRINCIPLES, THEIR FUTURE, THEIR LIVES, AND THEIR LOVED ONES IN DANGER.

SLAVEOWNER AND STATES' RIGHTS ALLY THOMAS JEFFERSON HIMSELF SAID:

...IF SOMETHING IS NOT DONE [ABOUT SLAVERY], AND SOON DONE, WE SHALL BE THE MURDERERS OF OUR OWN CHILDREN.

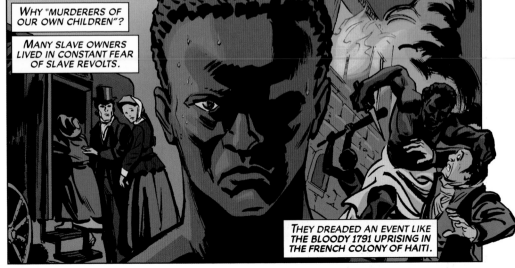

WHY "MURDERERS OF OUR OWN CHILDREN"?

MANY SLAVE OWNERS LIVED IN CONSTANT FEAR OF SLAVE REVOLTS.

THEY DREADED AN EVENT LIKE THE BLOODY 1791 UPRISING IN THE FRENCH COLONY OF HAITI.

SHORT OF ACTS OF OUTRIGHT WARFARE, SLAVES COULD--AND IN MANY CASES DID--POISON THEIR MASTERS OR BURN DOWN THEIR HOMES.

LIFE IN SLAVE STATES FREQUENTLY MEANT LIVING IN A STATE OF PARANOIA.

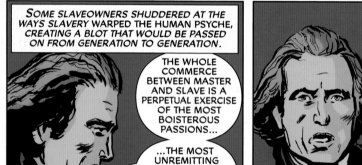

SOME SLAVEOWNERS SHUDDERED AT THE WAYS SLAVERY WARPED THE HUMAN PSYCHE, CREATING A BLOT THAT WOULD BE PASSED ON FROM GENERATION TO GENERATION.

THE WHOLE COMMERCE BETWEEN MASTER AND SLAVE IS A PERPETUAL EXERCISE OF THE MOST BOISTEROUS PASSIONS...

...THE MOST UNREMITTING DESPOTISM ON THE ONE PART, AND DEGRADING SUBMISSIONS ON THE OTHER.

OUR CHILDREN SEE THIS, AND LEARN TO IMITATE IT... THE PARENT STORMS, THE CHILD LOOKS ON... [AND IS] THUS NURSED, EDUCATED, AND DAILY EXERCISED IN TYRANNY...

JEFFERSON EVEN BLAMED GREAT BRITAIN AND KING GEORGE III FOR THE FACT THAT AMERICA HAD SLAVERY AT ALL!

THE HORSE AMERICA, throwing his Master.

waged cruel war against human nature itself, violating its most sacred rights of life and liberty in the persons of a distant people who never offended him, captivating and carrying them into slavery in another hemisphere...

THIS WAS POINTED ANTISLAVERY RHETORIC.

BUT REPRESENTATIVES FROM SOUTH CAROLINA FORCED THE DELETION OF JEFFERSON'S PASSAGE FROM THE DECLARATION.

LINCOLN ARGUED THAT JEFFERSON STILL MANAGED TO INSERT IN THE DECLARATION A SUBTLE ASSAULT ON SLAVERY.

THE DECLARATION READS:

"[ALL MEN] ARE ENDOWED BY THEIR CREATOR WITH CERTAIN UNALIENABLE RIGHTS, THAT AMONG THESE ARE LIFE, LIBERTY AND THE PURSUIT OF HAPPINESS."

THE LAST PHRASE WAS INSPIRED BY THE WORK OF ENGLISH PHILOSOPHER JOHN LOCKE-- A PROPONENT OF THE SAME "HIGHER LAW" OR NATURAL RIGHTS THAT JUSTIFIED THE AMERICAN REVOLUTION.

BUT AS LOCKE ORIGINALLY PUT IT, THE THREE UNALIENABLE RIGHTS WERE...

LIFE, LIBERTY, AND PROPERTY.

LINCOLN BELIEVED JEFFERSON HAD SUBSTITUTED "HAPPINESS" FOR "PROPERTY" TO SNUB SLAVEHOLDERS.

PROPERTY, AFTER ALL, IS PRECISELY WHAT SLAVEOWNERS HELD THEIR SLAVES TO BE.

GREAT BARGAINS SALE OF NEGROES HORSES CATTLE & OTHER PROPERTY

TO JEFFERSON, AS LONG AS SLAVERY EXISTED, THE AMERICAN REVOLUTION WAS DEGRADING AND SUBVERTING THE VERY NOTION OF LIBERTY IT WAS FIGHTING FOR.

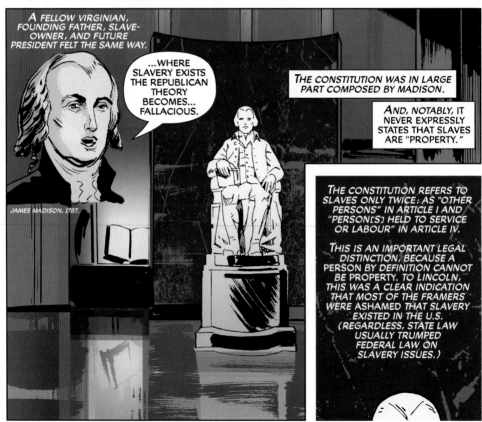

A FELLOW VIRGINIAN, FOUNDING FATHER, SLAVE-OWNER, AND FUTURE PRESIDENT FELT THE SAME WAY.

...WHERE SLAVERY EXISTS THE REPUBLICAN THEORY BECOMES... FALLACIOUS.

JAMES MADISON, 1787.

THE CONSTITUTION WAS IN LARGE PART COMPOSED BY MADISON.

AND, NOTABLY, IT NEVER EXPRESSLY STATES THAT SLAVES ARE "PROPERTY."

THE CONSTITUTION REFERS TO SLAVES ONLY TWICE: AS "OTHER PERSONS" IN ARTICLE I AND "PERSON[S] HELD TO SERVICE OR LABOUR" IN ARTICLE IV.

THIS IS AN IMPORTANT LEGAL DISTINCTION, BECAUSE A PERSON BY DEFINITION CANNOT BE PROPERTY. TO LINCOLN, THIS WAS A CLEAR INDICATION THAT MOST OF THE FRAMERS WERE ASHAMED THAT SLAVERY EXISTED IN THE U.S. (REGARDLESS, STATE LAW USUALLY TRUMPED FEDERAL LAW ON SLAVERY ISSUES.)

LINCOLN KNEW THE FOUNDING FATHERS FACED AN IMPOSSIBLE SITUATION.

HE WOULD HAVE AGREED THAT THE MEN OF THE EARLY U.S. COULD NOT SPRING THEMSELVES-- OR THOSE IN HUMAN BONDAGE-- FROM THE "TRAP" OF SLAVERY OVERNIGHT.

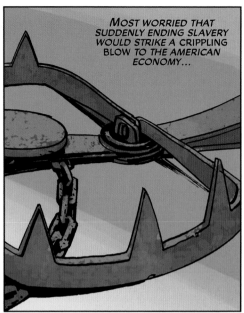

MOST WORRIED THAT SUDDENLY ENDING SLAVERY WOULD STRIKE A CRIPPLING BLOW TO THE AMERICAN ECONOMY...

...AND CREATE AN IMPOVERISHED, HOMELESS, AND UNEDUCATED BLACK POPULATION.

DURING THE FOUNDING ERA, ANY BIG PUSH TO END SLAVERY PROBABLY WOULD HAVE LED SOUTHERN STATES TO REJECT JOINING THE UNION IN THE FIRST PLACE.

THIS WOULD HAVE LEFT THE U.S. SMALL AND FRACTURED, VULNERABLE TO ENEMIES.

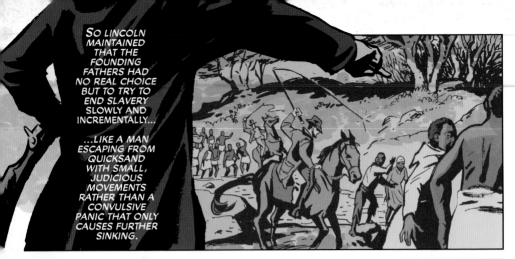

SO LINCOLN MAINTAINED THAT THE FOUNDING FATHERS HAD NO REAL CHOICE BUT TO TRY TO END SLAVERY SLOWLY AND INCREMENTALLY...

...LIKE A MAN ESCAPING FROM QUICKSAND WITH SMALL, JUDICIOUS MOVEMENTS RATHER THAN A CONVULSIVE PANIC THAT ONLY CAUSES FURTHER SINKING.

[THE FOUNDING FATHERS] MEANT SIMPLY TO DECLARE THE *RIGHT* [OF RACIAL EQUALITY], SO THAT THE *ENFORCEMENT OF IT* MIGHT FOLLOW AS FAST AS CIRCUMSTANCES SHOULD PERMIT.

AND HE OFFERED EVIDENCE TO PROVE HIS POINT.

1787

UNDER THE ARTICLES OF CONFEDERATION, THE PURPOSEFULLY WEAK CONGRESS WAS NEVERTHELESS EMPOWERED TO ABOLISH SLAVERY IN ALL U.S. TERRITORIES.

JEFFERSON HIMSELF PROPOSED THE *NORTHWEST ORDINANCE:* AN ACT THAT OUTLAWED SLAVERY IN TERRITORY THAT LATER BECAME THE STATES OF OHIO, INDIANA, ILLINOIS, MICHIGAN, WISCONSIN, AND MINNESOTA.

FURTHERMORE, CONGRESS ENDED THE IMPORTATION OF SLAVES FROM AFRICA STARTING IN 1808...

PIONEERS FROM CONNECTICUT ENTERING THE "WESTERN RESERVE" (MODERN-DAY OHIO) THAT HAD BEEN SET ASIDE FOR THEM.

...AND IN 1820 WENT SO FAR AS TO MAKE THIS PRACTICE AN ACT OF PIRACY PUNISHABLE BY DEATH.

LINCOLN KNEW THAT JEFFERSON--AND OTHER LIKE-MINDED MEN OF THAT TIME--BELIEVED IT WAS ONLY A MATTER OF TIME BEFORE AMERICANS FULLY ABOLISHED SLAVERY.

LIFE IN A CIVILIZATION BASED ON REVOLUTIONARY-ERA VALUES, JEFFERSON THOUGHT, WOULD MAKE MEN VIRTUOUS, RATIONAL, AND WISE.

AMERICANS WOULD COME TO THEIR SENSES AND REJECT SLAVERY.

JEFFERSON ALSO PREDICTED THAT THE BALMY SOUTH WOULD ATTRACT A FLOOD OF NORTHERN IMMI-GRANTS, WHO WOULD BRING THEIR FREE LABOR IDEAS WITH THEM.

CAPTAIN NATHANIEL GORDON OF THE SLAVE SHIP ERIE EXECUTED IN NEW YORK CITY, FEBRUARY 21, 1862.

IN THE ANTEBELLUM PERIOD, THIS NEVER QUITE CAME TO PASS.

BUT IT WAS BEYOND JEFFERSON'S POWERS TO FORESEE THE COTTON BOOM.

JEFFERSON DID NOT ANTICIPATE HOW MUCH MORE THE U.S. ECONOMY WOULD COME TO DEPEND ON SLAVERY.

A SLAVE POPULATION OF JUST UNDER 900,000 IN 1820 GREW TO NEARLY 4,000,000 BY 1860.

SO MANY BECAME HOOKED ON THE PROFITS OF SLAVE LABOR THAT IT NO LONGER MADE SENSE TO SINGLE OUT SOUTHERNERS.

BY THE MID-1800s MANY SPOKE OF A NATIONWIDE SLAVE-POWER ANGLING TO CONTROL THE GOVERNMENT.

THE SO-CALLED SLAVEPOWER WAS THE ENTIRE POLITICAL AND ECONOMIC STRUCTURE DESIGNED TO KEEP SLAVERY PROPPED UP. IT BENEFITED BOTH THE SLAVEOWNERS...

...AND THEIR NORTHERN PARTNERS IN INDUSTRY AND COMMERCE.

WE KNOW THE DECLARATION AND CONSTITUTION ARE IN TENSION OVER THE ISSUES OF STATES' RIGHTS AND GOVERNMENT POWER.

NOW WE SEE A THIRD TENSION. THE DECLARATION CLAIMS "ALL MEN ARE CREATED EQUAL," BUT THE CONSTITUTION ALLOWS SLAVE STATES IN THE UNION.

THESE TENSIONS ALLOWED PRO- AND ANTISLAVERY FACTIONS TO USE THE TWO FOUNDATIONS OF AMERICAN POLITICS AS WEAPONS AGAINST EACH OTHER. BOTH SIDES WOULD USE ITS OWN INTERPRETATION OF THE FOUNDING DOCUMENTS TO TRY TO PROVE IT WAS ON THE SIDE OF "TRUE" AMERICAN PATRIOTISM.

LINCOLN CONTENDED THAT THE SLAVE-POWER HAD HIJACKED THOMAS JEFFERSON, PERVERTED HIS PRINCIPLES, AND WILLFULLY IGNORED HIS TRUE STANCE ON SLAVERY.

THE SLAVEPOWER NEEDED TO PROTECT AND PERPETUATE SLAVERY. FEELING THREATENED BY LINCOLN'S ELECTION, IT DECIDED TO RAISE AN ARMY TO DEFEND ITSELF.

THIS IT ACCOMPLISHED BY UNRAVELING AND REWORKING THE DECLARATION'S IDEALS. THE SLAVEPOWER WORKED TO MAKE FIGHTING FOR SLAVERY SEEM PATRIOTIC.

THE SLAVEPOWER USED THE DECLARATION'S...

...IDEA OF WEAK, LOCAL GOVERNMENT... ...TO PAINT A PICTURE OF THE FEDERAL GOVERNMENT AS TYRANNICAL.

...IDEA OF STATES' RIGHTS... ...TO JUSTIFY COMPACT THEORY AND CREATE A LEGAL ARGUMENT FOR SECEDING FROM THE UNION.

...RIGHT OF REVOLUTION... ...TO JUSTIFY TAKING UP ARMS AGAINST FEDERAL AUTHORITY. IN HUGE NUMBERS, SOUTHERNERS TOO POOR TO OWN SLAVES WERE CONVINCED TO RISK THEIR LIVES TO FIGHT FOR THE CONFEDERACY.

AS THE CIVIL WAR RAGED, LINCOLN REALIZED THERE WAS ONLY ONE WAY TO TRULY DEFEAT THE SLAVEPOWER AND THE CONFEDERACY.

HE HAD TO EXPUNGE THEM OF THEIR KEY RHETORICAL WEAPON. LINCOLN HAD TO WIN BACK THE DECLARATION OF INDEPENDENCE.

THIS HE COULD ONLY ACHIEVE BY ENDING SLAVERY ONCE AND FOR ALL...

...BY REMAKING AMERICA AS JEFFERSON WOULD HAVE WANTED IT: TRULY A NATION WHERE "ALL MEN ARE CREATED EQUAL."

"CREATED EQUAL" Part 2: SENTIMENT

IT'S WORTH REPEATING:

LINCOLN CRAFTED A STRONG ANTISLAVERY ARGUMENT. HE CITED THE MOST INFLUENTIAL FOUNDING FATHERS TO ARGUE THAT THEY HAD ONLY TOLERATED SLAVERY AS A TEMPORARY "NECESSARY EVIL"...

...NOT SOMETHING TRUE PATRIOTS WOULD FIGHT FOR.

I wish from my soul that the legislature of this state could see the policy of a gradual abolition of slavery...

GEORGE WASHINGTON, 1797.

BUT WHAT DID BOTH JEFFERSON AND LINCOLN ACTUALLY MEAN BY UPHOLDING THE IDEA THAT ALL ARE "CREATED EQUAL"?

WERE THESE MEN BEYOND RACISM? WERE THEY MORAL GIANTS, YEARS AHEAD OF THEIR TIME?

NO.

BOTH OF THESE STATESMEN BELIEVED--AT LEAST FOR MOST OF THEIR LIVES--THAT BLACKS AND WHITES COULD NOT AND SHOULD NOT COEXIST.

AS JEFFERSON SAW IT, FREEING THE SLAVES-- BUT ALLOWING THEM TO REMAIN AS CITIZENS IN THE U.S.-- WOULD CAUSE UPHEAVAL THAT WOULD...

...PROBABLY NEVER END BUT IN THE EXTERMINATION OF THE ONE OR THE OTHER RACE.

THOMAS JEFFERSON, 1783.

NOTHING IS MORE CERTAINLY WRITTEN IN THE BOOK OF FATE THAN THAT THESE PEOPLE [BLACKS] ARE TO BE FREE.

NOR IS IT LESS CERTAIN THAT THE TWO RACES, EQUALLY FREE, CANNOT LIVE IN THE SAME GOVERNMENT.

THOMAS JEFFERSON, 1821.

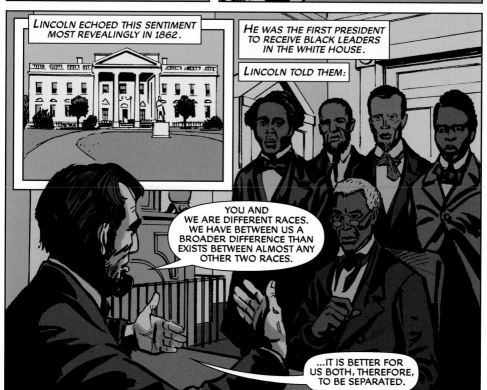

LINCOLN ECHOED THIS SENTIMENT MOST REVEALINGLY IN 1862.

HE WAS THE FIRST PRESIDENT TO RECEIVE BLACK LEADERS IN THE WHITE HOUSE.

LINCOLN TOLD THEM:

YOU AND WE ARE DIFFERENT RACES. WE HAVE BETWEEN US A BROADER DIFFERENCE THAN EXISTS BETWEEN ALMOST ANY OTHER TWO RACES.

...IT IS BETTER FOR US BOTH, THEREFORE, TO BE SEPARATED.

WHAT, THEN, WERE LINCOLN'S AND JEFFERSON'S SOLUTIONS TO THE PROBLEM OF BLACK-WHITE COEXISTENCE?

THE NEGRO PROBLEM SOLVED

BOTH PRESIDENTS--AT LEAST FOR LONG STRETCHES OF THEIR CAREERS--ADVOCATED THE SAME GENERAL PLAN.

THIS IS THE LORD'S DOING; IT IS MARVELLOUS IN OUR EYES. PSALM 118 V.

FIRST, THEY WANTED THE STATES TO GRADUALLY EMANCIPATE THE SLAVES.

SECOND, THEY ADVOCATED "COLONIZATION" FOR FREE BLACKS.

THIS MEANT SETTING UP A NEW REPUBLIC IN AFRICA OR THE CARIBBEAN, AND CONVINCING BLACKS TO VOLUNTARILY RELOCATE THERE.

A COLONIZATION ADVOCATE'S 1864 VISION OF A FUTURE AFRICA.

EXPERIMENTS ALONG THESE LINES WERE ACTUALLY CARRIED OUT.

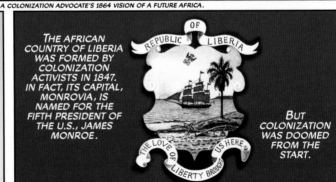

THE AFRICAN COUNTRY OF LIBERIA WAS FORMED BY COLONIZATION ACTIVISTS IN 1847. IN FACT, ITS CAPITAL, MONROVIA, IS NAMED FOR THE FIFTH PRESIDENT OF THE U.S., JAMES MONROE.

REPUBLIC OF LIBERIA

THE LOVE OF LIBERTY BROUGHT US HERE

BUT COLONIZATION WAS DOOMED FROM THE START.

FEW BLACKS OPTED TO LEAVE A COUNTRY THAT--ALTHOUGH DEEPLY RACIST--WAS THE ONLY HOME THEY HAD EVER KNOWN.

PLUS, BOTH SLAVES AND FREE BLACKS HAD INVESTED GENERATIONS' WORTH OF HARD WORK IN AMERICAN SOCIETY.

COLONIZATION PLANS WERE ALSO EXPENSIVE TO IMPLEMENT.

CONGRESS COULD NEVER AGREE ON WHO SHOULD PAY FOR IT OR HOW.

U.S. TREASURY DEPARTMENT.

SO IF FOR MUCH OF HIS LIFE LINCOLN BELIEVED THAT MILLIONS OF BLACK MEN AND WOMEN SHOULD BE SWAYED TO LEAVE THE UNITED STATES...

...WHAT DID BEING "CREATED EQUAL" ACTUALLY MEAN TO HIM?

IT MUST BE UNDERSTOOD THAT EARLIER IN AMERICAN HISTORY, THE CONCEPT OF "EQUALITY"--AND SOMETIMES EVEN "FREEDOM"--WAS MORE NUANCED THAN IT IS TODAY. LINCOLN EXPLAINED THIS:

THERE IS NO REASON IN THE WORLD WHY THE NEGRO IS NOT ENTITLED TO ALL THE NATURAL RIGHTS ENUMERATED IN THE DECLARATION OF INDEPENDENCE,-- THE RIGHT TO LIFE, LIBERTY, AND THE PURSUIT OF HAPPINESS.

I HOLD THAT HE IS AS MUCH ENTITLED TO THESE AS THE WHITE MAN.

ABRAHAM LINCOLN, 1858.

BY "LIFE, LIBERTY, AND THE PURSUIT OF HAPPINESS," LINCOLN WAS ESSENTIALLY TALKING ABOUT **CIVIL RIGHTS**.

THESE INCLUDE THE RIGHTS TO:
* OWN PROPERTY
* LEGALLY MARRY
* WORK AND RETAIN THE FRUITS OF LABOR
* SEEK JUSTICE BY BRINGING CASES TO AND TESTIFYING IN COURT
* LIVE, WORK, AND WORSHIP WHERE AND HOW ONE WISHES

...ALL OF WHICH, UNDER SLAVERY, MOST BLACKS COULD NOT DO.

POLITICAL RIGHTS

CIVIL RIGHTS

LINCOLN WAS FAR MORE GUARDED ABOUT THE IDEA OF EXTENDING **POLITICAL RIGHTS** TO BLACKS.

THESE INCLUDE THE RIGHTS TO:
* VOTE
* HOLD POLITICAL OFFICE
* SERVE ON JURIES IN STATE AND FEDERAL COURTS

SO LINCOLN'S AND JEFFERSON'S CONCEPTS OF "EQUALITY" FOR BLACKS AND WHITES ARGUABLY MEANT ONLY THAT THEY WOULD SHARE CIVIL--RATHER THAN POLITICAL--RIGHTS.

THEY THOUGHT BLACKS SHOULD ENJOY THE BENEFITS OF GOVERNMENT BUT NOT REALLY PARTICIPATE IN IT.

CLEARLY, THIS IS INCONSISTENT WITH MODERN STANDARDS.

TO BE FAIR, IT MUST BE NOTED THAT IN LINCOLN'S TIME, THE CONSTITUTION HAD NOT YET BEEN ALTERED BY THE 15 CONSTITUTIONAL AMENDMENTS THAT HAVE BEEN ADDED SINCE THE CIVIL WAR. THE "SUPREME LAW OF THE LAND" DID NOT THEN GUARANTEE POLITICAL RIGHTS, EVEN TO WHITES!

THE FEDERAL GOVERNMENT OF THE PRE-CIVIL WAR ERA-- ONE FAR LESS CENTRALIZED AND POWERFUL THAN TODAY'S-- LARGELY ALLOWED THE STATES TO DETERMINE WHO GOT TO PARTICIPATE IN GOVERNMENT. STATES COULD RESTRICT POLITICAL RIGHTS EVEN AMONG WHITE MEN-- FOR EXAMPLE, TO ONLY THOSE WHO OWNED LAND.

STATE GOVERNMENTS HAD SUCH AN UPPER HAND OVER THE FEDERAL GOVERNMENT THAT THEY WERE ALSO FREE TO ALLOW BLACKS TO VOTE IF THEY SO CHOSE. AND SEVERAL DID. BEFORE 1865, THERE WERE NO RESTRICTIONS ON BLACK MEN VOTING IN MAINE, NEW HAMPSHIRE, VERMONT, AND MASSACHUSETTS.

SO IN THE END, IT'S FAIR TO SAY THAT LINCOLN'S RECORD ON RACE IS MIXED.

BUT ONE THING HAS ALWAYS BEEN CLEAR...

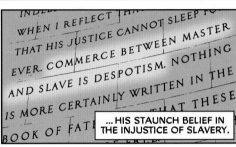

INDEE...
WHEN I REFLECT THA...
THAT HIS JUSTICE CANNOT SLEEP TO...
EVER. COMMERCE BETWEEN MASTER
AND SLAVE IS DESPOTISM. NOTHING
IS MORE CERTAINLY WRITTEN IN THE
BOOK OF FAT... THAT THESE

... HIS STAUNCH BELIEF IN THE INJUSTICE OF SLAVERY.

HISTORIANS HAVE ENDLESSLY DEBATED HOW LINCOLN REALLY FELT ABOUT RACIAL ISSUES.

ALTHOUGH AMERICANS MAY NEVER ALL AGREE ON THE FINER POINTS OF THIS SUBJECT...

...IT IS NOT HARD TO SEE WHY ABOLITIONIST FREDERICK DOUGLASS SUMMED LINCOLN UP IN THE FOLLOWING MANNER, MORE THAN 10 YEARS AFTER LINCOLN'S DEATH:

ABRAHAM LINCOLN WAS NOT, IN THE FULLEST SENSE OF THE WORD, EITHER OUR MAN OR OUR MODEL.

IN HIS INTERESTS, IN HIS ASSOCIATIONS, IN HIS HABITS OF THOUGHT, AND IN HIS PREJUDICES, HE WAS A WHITE MAN.

NOW WE ARE ENGAGED IN A GREAT CIVIL WAR

PRESSURE ON THE PEACEFUL COEXISTENCE OF NORTH AND SOUTH HAD, FOR GENERATIONS, WAXED AND WANED.

YET IN THE FIRST HALF OF THE 19th CENTURY...

[THIS MEETING] HAD NOT BEEN CALLED TO PREVENT, BUT TO PERPETUATE THE UNION.

HYMNS 141 7 PSALM 6 24

"SOUTHERN CONVENTION," NASHVILLE, TENNESSEE, JUNE 1850.

...MOST AMERICANS STILL SAW BOTH ABOLITIONISTS AND SECESSIONISTS AS EXTREMISTS...

...PEOPLE WITH RADICAL IDEAS WHO ONLY ROCKED THE BOAT.

[PROTECTOR OF SLAVERY, OUR CONSTITUTION] IS A COVENANT WITH DEATH AND AN AGREEMENT WITH HELL!

SHAME!

ABOLITION MEETING, FRAMINGHAM, MASSACHUSETTS, JULY 1854.

"A HOUSE DIVIDED AGAINST ITSELF CANNOT STAND."

I BELIEVE THIS GOVERNMENT CANNOT ENDURE, PERMANENTLY, HALF SLAVE AND HALF FREE.

WHAT DID IT TAKE FOR THE LONG WAR OF IDEAS TO TRANSFORM INTO A "SHOOTING WAR"?

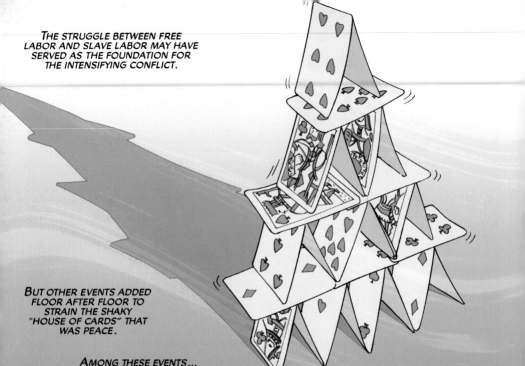

THE STRUGGLE BETWEEN FREE LABOR AND SLAVE LABOR MAY HAVE SERVED AS THE FOUNDATION FOR THE INTENSIFYING CONFLICT.

BUT OTHER EVENTS ADDED FLOOR AFTER FLOOR TO STRAIN THE SHAKY "HOUSE OF CARDS" THAT WAS PEACE.

AMONG THESE EVENTS...

THE CALIFORNIA GOLD RUSH

PROSPECTORS STRUCK IT RICH IN THE 1840s. BUT FREE LABORERS WORKING FOR THE PROSPECTORS FARED WELL TOO. IN GOLD COUNTRY, MANPOWER WAS IN SUCH HIGH DEMAND THAT MINERS COULD NEGOTIATE EXTREMELY HIGH WAGES. DETERMINED TO BLOCK COMPETITION FROM SLAVES, WORKERS IN THIS REGION (FORMERLY OF MEXICO) RUSHED TO JOIN THE UNION AS A FREE STATE.

WITH CALIFORNIA, THE NUMBER OF FREE STATES BEGAN TO OUTPACE THAT OF SLAVE STATES.

THE FIRST TRANSCONTINENTAL RAILROAD

ILLINOIS SENATOR STEPHEN A. DOUGLAS NEEDED VOTES FOR THIS PET PROJECT THAT WOULD BENEFIT HIS STATE. HE NEEDED SUPPORT FROM SOUTHERN LEGISLATORS. IN RETURN, THEY DEMANDED THAT DOUGLAS HELP ESTABLISH SLAVERY IN THE WEST.

SO DOUGLAS DELIVERED THE 1854 KANSAS-NEBRASKA ACT. IT SMASHED A LONG-HELD LEGAL PRECEDENT: THAT NO NEW SLAVE SOIL WOULD EXIST NORTH OF A LINE DRAWN ON THE MAP BY THE 1820 MISSOURI COMPROMISE. KANSAS-NEBRASKA REOPENED MANY OLD WOUNDS BETWEEN THE NORTH AND THE SOUTH.

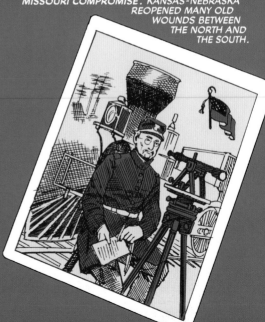

The Second Great Awakening

This Christian religious movement led many Northerners to seek to purge society of "sin"--including slavery. They began to actively oppose the South.

Their moralistic attacks on slavery infuriated many Southern slaveowners.

Massachusetts Senator Charles Sumner

In 1856, Sumner gave an antislavery speech. It insulted South Carolina Congressman Preston Brooks. In response, Brooks beat Sumner nearly to death on the Senate chamber floor.

In the free states, much of the public was shocked by this violence. Many who had once been apathetic to slavery now felt pushed to make a stand.

The novel Uncle Tom's Cabin

One of the biggest bestsellers in American history, the 1852 book (and stage productions based on it) also helped polarize the sections. In this age, most people were highly sentimental about family life--and many readers were upset by the book's depiction of slaveowners selling members of black families to different owners.

The 1857 Dred Scott Decision

This was a U.S. Supreme Court case of a slave suing for his freedom. Chief Justice Roger B. Taney made a far-reaching decision: neither slaves nor free blacks could be U.S. citizens. Government would have to protect slave property no matter where it was brought--even into free states! Abolitionists were outraged.

UNCLE TOM'S CABIN;
OR,
LIFE AMONG THE LOWLY.

BY
HARRIET BEECHER STOWE

VOL. I.
ONE HUNDRED AND FIFTH THOUSAND.

BOSTON:
JOHN P. JEWETT & COMPANY
CLEVELAND, OHIO:
JEWETT, PROCTOR & WORTHINGTON.
1852.

AMERICA'S CARD

DRED SCOTT.

LINCOLN OPPOSED SLAVERY.

BUT THE FEDERAL GOVERNMENT HAD NO POWER OVER THE INSTITUTION IN THE STATES WHERE IT ALREADY EXISTED. LINCOLN NEVER DISPUTED THIS.

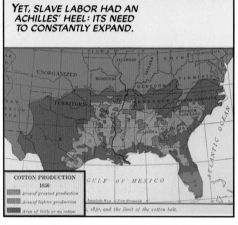

YET, SLAVE LABOR HAD AN ACHILLES' HEEL: ITS NEED TO CONSTANTLY EXPAND.

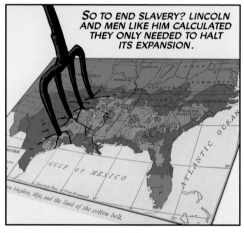

SO TO END SLAVERY? LINCOLN AND MEN LIKE HIM CALCULATED THEY ONLY NEEDED TO HALT ITS EXPANSION.

OVER TIME, THE BEST SOUTHERN SOILS FOR UPLAND COTTON WOULD WEAR OUT. THE VALUE OF SLAVES WOULD PLUMMET...

...AND THE HIGH COST OF KEEPING SLAVES WOULD FORCE MASTERS TO EMANCIPATE.

The Congress shall have Power to dispose of and make all needful Rules and Regulations respecting the Territory or other Property belonging to the United States; and nothing in this Constitution shall be so construed as to Prejudice any Claims of the United States, or of any particular State.

FREE LABOR ADOPTED THIS STRATEGY: CONTROL A MAJORITY IN CONGRESS.

FOR CONGRESS HAD THE POWER UNDER ARTICLE IV, SECTION 3 OF THE CONSTITUTION TO "MAKE ALL NEEDFUL RULES AND REGULATIONS" FOR NEW TERRITORIES.

...WHICH, EVEN IN THE TIME OF THE ARTICLES OF CONFEDERATION, INCLUDED THE POWER TO BAN SLAVERY IN THESE AREAS.

BUT THEN THE KANSAS-NEBRASKA ACT AND THE DRED SCOTT DECISION CAME ALONG.

TOGETHER, THEY EFFECTIVELY STRIPPED CONGRESS OF THIS TIME-HONORED POWER.

THIS WAS A SUCKER PUNCH TO LINCOLN AND HIS ALLIES.

...BY THIS RECKLESS MEASURE THE FREE STATES HAVE LOST ALL THE GUARANTEE FOR FREEDOM IN THE TERRITORIES...

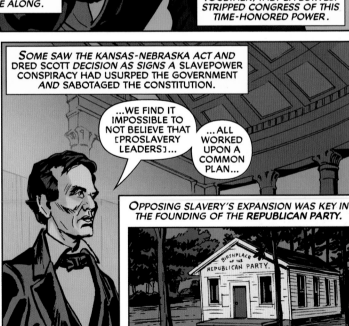

SOME SAW THE KANSAS-NEBRASKA ACT AND DRED SCOTT DECISION AS SIGNS A SLAVEPOWER CONSPIRACY HAD USURPED THE GOVERNMENT AND SABOTAGED THE CONSTITUTION.

...WE FIND IT IMPOSSIBLE TO NOT BELIEVE THAT [PROSLAVERY LEADERS]...

...ALL WORKED UPON A COMMON PLAN...

OPPOSING SLAVERY'S EXPANSION WAS KEY IN THE FOUNDING OF THE REPUBLICAN PARTY.

BIRTHPLACE OF THE REPUBLICAN PARTY.

FOR LINCOLN AND HIS ILK, THE PARTY WOULD BE THEIR INSTRUMENT TO GAIN CONTROL OF CONGRESS AND SHAPE THE FUTURE OF THE UNITED STATES.

THE REPUBLICAN PARTY DECLARED A CORNER-STONE BELIEF IN ITS 1856 PUBLIC PLATFORM:

"...it is both the right and the duty of Congress to prohibit in the Territories... [that relic] of barbarism... slavery."

THE DEMOCRATIC PARTY OPPOSED THE REPUBLICANS, BUT SOUTHERN DEMOCRATS CONSIDERED THEIR NORTHERN KIN TOO **MODERATE** WHEN IT CAME TO DEFENDING SLAVERY.

JUST BEFORE THE ELECTION OF 1860, THIS WORSENING FEUD BROKE THE PARTY INTO TWO RIVAL, SECTIONAL WINGS.

DEMOCRATS' VOTES FOR A PRESIDENTIAL CANDIDATE WOULD NOW BE SPLIT...

PROGRESSIVE DEMOCRACY—PROSPECT OF A SMASH UP.

...WHICH ALL BUT GUARANTEED *THEY WOULD LOSE THE ELECTION.*

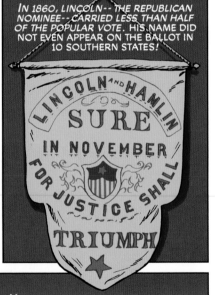

IN 1860, LINCOLN-- THE REPUBLICAN NOMINEE--CARRIED LESS THAN HALF OF THE POPULAR VOTE. HIS NAME DID NOT EVEN APPEAR ON THE BALLOT IN 10 SOUTHERN STATES!

YET BECAUSE OF THE CONSTITUTION'S COMPLEX ELECTORAL COLLEGE SYSTEM, LINCOLN WAS ABLE TO WIN BY A RAZOR-THIN MARGIN. VOTES FROM NEW ENGLAND, THE MIDWEST, CALIFORNIA, AND OREGON WERE ENOUGH TO BRING HIM TO THE WHITE HOUSE.

IN THE DEEP SOUTH, VOTERS COULD NOT ABIDE THE RESULTS OF THE ELECTION.

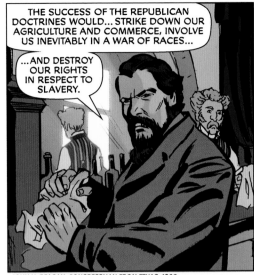

THE SUCCESS OF THE REPUBLICAN DOCTRINES WOULD... STRIKE DOWN OUR AGRICULTURE AND COMMERCE, INVOLVE US INEVITABLY IN A WAR OF RACES...

...AND DESTROY OUR RIGHTS IN RESPECT TO SLAVERY.

JOHN H. REAGAN, CONGRESSMAN FROM TEXAS, 1860.

LINCOLN WOULD NOT BE INAUGURATED-- OR ACTUALLY SERVE AS PRESIDENT-- UNTIL MARCH 4, 1861.

MONTHS BEFORE HE COULD TAKE OFFICE, AND BEFORE A REPUBLICAN-DOMINATED FEDERAL GOVERNMENT COULD ENACT ANY POLICY WHATSOEVER...

SOUTH CAROLINA DECLARED ITS SECESSION FROM THE UNION ON DECEMBER 20, 1860.

SECESSION, IN THAT REGARD, WAS A PREEMPTIVE ACT.

IN SECEDING, SOUTH CAROLINIANS DREW UP A DOCUMENT NOT UNLIKE THE DECLARATION OF INDEPENDENCE.

IN IT, THEY CITED THE CAUSES OF AND JUSTIFICATIONS FOR SECESSION.

107

THE SOUTH CAROLINA ORDINANCE OF SECESSION READ, IN PART:

"...AN INCREASING HOSTILITY ON THE PART OF THE NON-SLAVEHOLDING STATES TO THE INSTITUTION OF SLAVERY, HAS LED TO A DISREGARD OF THEIR OBLIGATIONS... AND THE CONSEQUENCE FOLLOWS THAT SOUTH CAROLINA IS RELEASED FROM HER OBLIGATION [TO REMAIN IN THE UNION]."

THE STREETS OF CHARLESTON, THE CAPITAL CITY, WERE THRONGED WITH JOY.

OPTIMISM FOR THE FUTURE ABOUNDED.

FEW THOUGHT WAR WOULD FOLLOW.

A LADY'S THIMBLE WILL HOLD ALL THE BLOOD THAT WILL BE SHED!

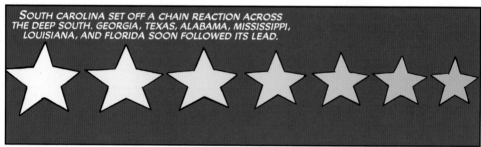

SOUTH CAROLINA SET OFF A CHAIN REACTION ACROSS THE DEEP SOUTH. GEORGIA, TEXAS, ALABAMA, MISSISSIPPI, LOUISIANA, AND FLORIDA SOON FOLLOWED ITS LEAD.

POLITICIANS LIKE THE STILL-SERVING PRESIDENT, JAMES BUCHANAN, SCRAMBLED TO APPEASE THESE STATES.

THE HOUSE AND SENATE EVEN PASSED AN UNAMENDABLE CONSTITUTIONAL AMENDMENT TO PERMANENTLY GUARANTEE CONGRESS COULD NEVER INTERFERE WITH SLAVERY IN THE SLAVE STATES.

(THE CIVIL WAR BEGAN BEFORE THE STATES COULD RATIFY THIS SO-CALLED CORWIN AMENDMENT.)

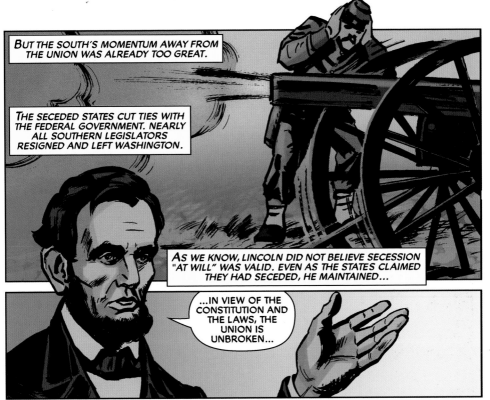

BUT THE SOUTH'S MOMENTUM AWAY FROM THE UNION WAS ALREADY TOO GREAT.

THE SECEDED STATES CUT TIES WITH THE FEDERAL GOVERNMENT. NEARLY ALL SOUTHERN LEGISLATORS RESIGNED AND LEFT WASHINGTON.

AS WE KNOW, LINCOLN DID NOT BELIEVE SECESSION "AT WILL" WAS VALID. EVEN AS THE STATES CLAIMED THEY HAD SECEDED, HE MAINTAINED...

...IN VIEW OF THE CONSTITUTION AND THE LAWS, THE UNION IS UNBROKEN...

THE FEDERAL GOVERNMENT OWNED VARIOUS FACILITIES ACROSS THE COUNTRY. IN THE SOUTH, LOCAL FORCES SEIZED THEM ONE BY ONE.

SEIZED: JAN. 1861

U.S. MINT, NEW ORLEANS, LA

SEIZED: DEC. 1860

U.S. POST OFFICE, CHARLESTON, SC

SEIZED: MAR. 1861

U.S. CUSTOMS HOUSE, GALVESTON, TX

FORT SUMTER, IN CHARLESTON HARBOR, WAS ONE OF THE LAST U.S. PROPERTIES TO REMAIN IN GOVERNMENT HANDS. LINCOLN PLEDGED TO DEFEND IT.

BUT OTHER THAN THAT, HE MADE NO OVERT THREATS TO THE SECESSIONIST STATES.

THE POWER CONFIDED TO ME, WILL BE USED TO HOLD, OCCUPY, AND POSSESS THE PROPERTY, AND PLACES BELONGING TO THE GOVERNMENT...

...BUT BEYOND [THAT], THERE WILL BE...NO USING OF FORCE AGAINST, OR AMONG THE PEOPLE ANYWHERE.

THE LINCOLN ADMINISTRATION CONTACTED THE GOVERNOR OF SOUTH CAROLINA, INFORMING HIM THAT THE U.S. SOLDIERS WHO HAD RECENTLY OCCUPIED FORT SUMTER WOULD BE SENT SUPPLY BOATS CARRYING "PROVISIONS ONLY"...

...NO "MEN, ARMS, OR AMMUNITION."

CONFEDERATE BRIGADIER GENERAL P. G. T. BEAUREGARD NEVERTHELESS DEMANDED THE SOLDIERS' SURRENDER.

WHEN THIS WAS REFUSED...

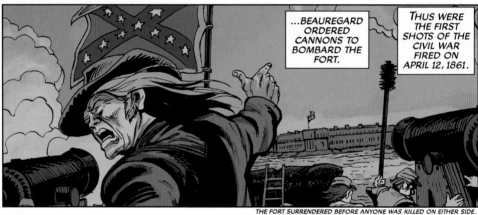

...BEAUREGARD ORDERED CANNONS TO BOMBARD THE FORT.

THUS WERE THE FIRST SHOTS OF THE CIVIL WAR FIRED ON APRIL 12, 1861.

THE FORT SURRENDERED BEFORE ANYONE WAS KILLED ON EITHER SIDE.

O'er Sumter's walls OUR FLAG again we'll wave,
And give to traitors all a bloody grave.
OUR UNION and OUR LAWS maintain we must;
And treason's banner trample in the dust.

NEWS OF THE ATTACK ON FORT SUMTER BROUGHT CELEBRATION ACROSS THE SOUTH--AND PROVOKED MANY IN THE NORTH. MEN BY THE THOUSANDS, FEELING LIKE THIS FIGHT HAD BEEN COMING FOR YEARS, RUSHED TO JOIN THE RANKS OF ONE SIDE OR THE OTHER.

...EVERY PERSON ALMOST WAS EAGER FOR THE WAR, AND WE WERE ALL AFRAID IT WOULD BE OVER AND WE NOT IN THE FIGHT.

SAM R. WATKINS, CONFEDERATE SOLDIER FROM TENNESSEE.

LINCOLN'S RESPONSE TO THE FORT SUMTER ATTACK CAME THREE DAYS LATER.

...I, ABRAHAM LINCOLN, PRESIDENT OF THE UNITED STATES...HEREBY DO CALL FORTH, THE MILITIA OF THE SEVERAL STATES OF THE UNION...IN ORDER TO SUPPRESS [THE SECESSIONISTS] ...AND TO CAUSE THE LAWS TO BE DULY EXECUTED.

THE STATES OF VIRGINIA, TENNESSEE, ARKANSAS, AND NORTH CAROLINA HAD UNTIL THAT POINT REMAINED IN THE UNION.

BUT LINCOLN'S CALL TO ARMS...

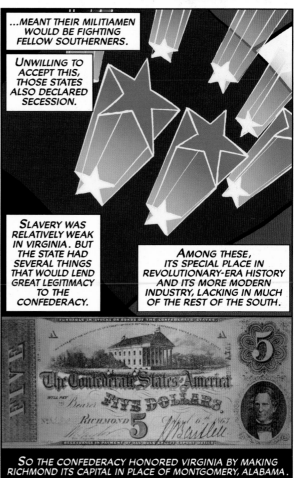

...MEANT THEIR MILITIAMEN WOULD BE FIGHTING FELLOW SOUTHERNERS.

UNWILLING TO ACCEPT THIS, THOSE STATES ALSO DECLARED SECESSION.

SLAVERY WAS RELATIVELY WEAK IN VIRGINIA. BUT THE STATE HAD SEVERAL THINGS THAT WOULD LEND GREAT LEGITIMACY TO THE CONFEDERACY.

AMONG THESE, ITS SPECIAL PLACE IN REVOLUTIONARY-ERA HISTORY AND ITS MORE MODERN INDUSTRY, LACKING IN MUCH OF THE REST OF THE SOUTH.

SO THE CONFEDERACY HONORED VIRGINIA BY MAKING RICHMOND ITS CAPITAL IN PLACE OF MONTGOMERY, ALABAMA.

IT IS WIDELY ASSUMED THAT ALL NORTHERNERS SUPPORTED THE UNION AND ALL SOUTHERNERS THE CONFEDERACY. BUT IT IS NOT SO CUT AND DRIED.

SIGNIFICANT NUMBERS OF ARDENT UNIONISTS COULD BE FOUND THROUGHOUT THE SOUTH...

MISSOURI SENT 27 REGIMENTS TO FIGHT FOR THE UNION (12 MORE THAN FOR THE CONFEDERACY); 30,000 MEN FROM TENNESSEE ALSO WORE BLUE.

TENNESSEE UNIONIST GUERRILLAS BURN A STRATEGIC, CONFEDERATE-HELD RAILROAD BRIDGE, GREENE COUNTY, TENNESSEE, NOVEMBER 1861.

LIKEWISE, SOME NORTHERN MEN FOUGHT FOR THE CONFEDERACY.

CONFEDERATE GENERALS JOHN C. PEMBERTON AND JOHNSON K. DUNCAN BOTH HAILED FROM PENNSYLVANIA.

THE FIRST FULL-SCALE BATTLE OF THE CIVIL WAR, *FIRST BULL RUN* (NORTHEASTERN VIRGINIA, JULY 1861) TOOK PLACE AT THE FRONT DOOR OF WASHINGTON, D.C.

MEMBERS OF CONGRESS -- EVEN PICNICKERS! -- FLOCKED TO HILLSIDES TO WATCH THE FIGHT. THEY EXPECTED A BRIEF, GLORIOUS ENCOUNTER AND A DECISIVE UNION VICTORY.

INSTEAD, WHEN CONFEDERATE REINFORCEMENTS ARRIVED BY TRAIN, FEDERAL TROOPS WERE ROUTED.

SOLDIERS AND SPECTATORS ALIKE DESPERATELY FLED BEHIND THE DEFENSES OF THE NATION'S CAPITAL.

IT WAS A HUMILIATING DEFEAT FOR WASHINGTON.

IT WAS ALSO ONE OF MANY SOBERING MOMENTS FOR LINCOLN.

THOUGH SERVING AS COMMANDER IN CHIEF, HIS ONLY MILITARY EXPERIENCE HAD BEEN A BRIEF STINT WITH THE ILLINOIS MILITIA IN THE 1832 *BLACK HAWK WAR* AGAINST SAUK INDIANS.

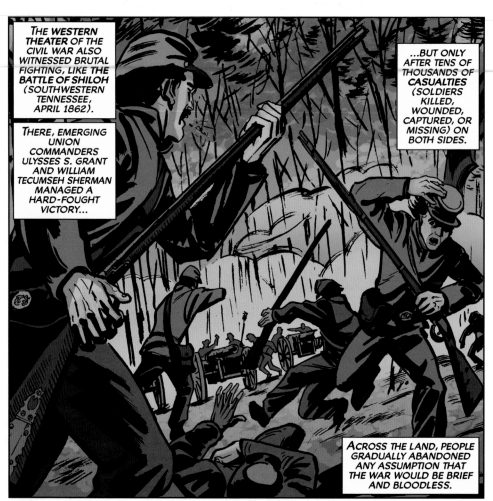

THE WESTERN THEATER OF THE CIVIL WAR ALSO WITNESSED BRUTAL FIGHTING, LIKE THE BATTLE OF SHILOH (SOUTHWESTERN TENNESSEE, APRIL 1862).

THERE, EMERGING UNION COMMANDERS ULYSSES S. GRANT AND WILLIAM TECUMSEH SHERMAN MANAGED A HARD-FOUGHT VICTORY...

...BUT ONLY AFTER TENS OF THOUSANDS OF CASUALTIES (SOLDIERS KILLED, WOUNDED, CAPTURED, OR MISSING) ON BOTH SIDES.

ACROSS THE LAND, PEOPLE GRADUALLY ABANDONED ANY ASSUMPTION THAT THE WAR WOULD BE BRIEF AND BLOODLESS.

SOLDIERS, DIPLOMATS, AND SPIES WERE NOT THE ONLY ONES WORKING TO AFFECT THE WAR'S OUTCOME...

...SLAVES DID AS WELL.

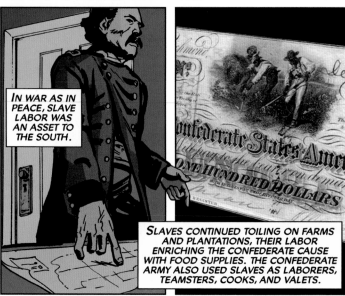

IN WAR AS IN PEACE, SLAVE LABOR WAS AN ASSET TO THE SOUTH.

SLAVES CONTINUED TOILING ON FARMS AND PLANTATIONS, THEIR LABOR ENRICHING THE CONFEDERATE CAUSE WITH FOOD SUPPLIES. THE CONFEDERATE ARMY ALSO USED SLAVES AS LABORERS, TEAMSTERS, COOKS, AND VALETS.

IN GETTYSBURG, ROBERT E. LEE'S ARMY OF NORTHERN VIRGINIA IS ESTIMATED TO HAVE BEEN ACCOMPANIED BY 6,000-10,000 SLAVES.

BUT A GREAT MANY SLAVES RISKED THEIR LIVES TO UNDERMINE THE CONFEDERATE ARMY. SOME ABANDONED OR SABOTAGED THEIR MASTERS.

OFTEN SLAVES BROUGHT VALUABLE MILITARY INFORMATION TO UNION FORCES.

THE CHIEF SOURCE OF INFORMATION TO THE ENEMY IS THROUGH OUR NEGROES.

ROBERT E. LEE, 1863.

BEFORE THE WAR, NUMEROUS NORTHERN WHITES HAD NEVER SEEN AN AFRICAN AMERICAN IN THE FLESH!

BY THE THOUSANDS, ESCAPED SLAVES FOLLOWED THE UNION ARMIES. THIS PERSONAL CONTACT CHALLENGED INEXPERIENCED SOLDIERS' PRESUMPTIONS ABOUT SLAVERY, ABOUT RACE. MEN IN UNIFORM SOON CAME TO SUPPORT ANTISLAVERY POLICIES EVEN MORE THAN NORTHERN CIVILIANS DID.

LINCOLN RECOGNIZED THAT THE CONFEDERATE WAR EFFORT RELIED ON SLAVERY.

BUT EARLY IN THE WAR, HE DID VERY LITTLE TO TARGET THE INSTITUTION.

...ALL WHO DESIRE THE UNQUALIFIED SUPPRESSION OF THE REBELLION...

...ARE SORELY DISAPPOINTED AND DEEPLY PAINED BY THE POLICY YOU SEEM TO BE PURSUING WITH REGARD TO THE SLAVES OF REBELS.

HORACE GREELEY, REPUBLICAN NEWSPAPER EDITOR, 1862.

WITH MUCH HAND-WRINGING, LINCOLN BEGAN TO PONDER...

...WAS THERE ANY CONSTITUTIONAL METHOD HE COULD USE TO EMANCIPATE THE CONFEDERACY'S SLAVES?

EVEN IN WARTIME, A PRESIDENT HAS NO UNILATERAL POWER TO MAKE LAW BY DECREE. YET IN HIS ROLE AS COMMANDER IN CHIEF, THE PRESIDENT IS ABLE TO CALL ON HIS CONSTITUTIONAL **WAR POWERS.** UNDER THIS UMBRELLA, A PRESIDENT CAN MAKE WIDE-RANGING DECISIONS THAT AFFECT MILITARY, IF NOT CIVILIAN, AFFAIRS. IN THIS WAR POWER "MODE," LINCOLN SAW AN OPPORTUNITY. HE HAD NO AUTHORITY TO EMANCIPATE ALL SLAVES. BUT HE COULD EMANCIPATE A FRACTION OF THEM IN SOME PLACES, IF NOT OTHERS.

IN ARMED CONFLICT, ENEMIES ALWAYS ATTACK EACH OTHER'S ABILITY TO MAKE WAR. FOR INSTANCE, DURING THE REVOLUTION, CONGRESS LICENSED AMERICAN **PRIVATEERS** TO SEIZE BRITISH WARSHIPS--AND ANY PROVISIONS, AMMUNITION, MONEY, OR WEAPONS ON BOARD.

SUCH SEIZURE OF **MATERIEL** (ARMS, EQUIPMENT, AND THE LIKE) WAS-- AND REMAINS-- A COMMON METHOD OF COMBATING AN ENEMY. LINCOLN INCREASINGLY FELT THAT SLAVES COULD BE REGARDED AS THE SAME TYPE OF PROPERTY: ASSETS THAT COULD BE TAKEN FROM THE CONFEDERACY AND USED AGAINST IT. SO LINCOLN ASSERTED IT WAS WITHIN HIS POWERS TO EMANCIPATE SLAVES-- BUT ONLY IN "REBEL" AREAS! NOT, FOR INSTANCE, IN THE SLAVE STATES OF DELAWARE, MARYLAND, MISSOURI, AND KENTUCKY, WHICH HAD NOT SECEDED.

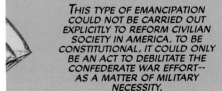

THIS TYPE OF EMANCIPATION COULD NOT BE CARRIED OUT EXPLICITLY TO REFORM CIVILIAN SOCIETY IN AMERICA. TO BE CONSTITUTIONAL, IT COULD ONLY BE AN ACT TO DEBILITATE THE CONFEDERATE WAR EFFORT-- AS A MATTER OF MILITARY NECESSITY.

EVEN SO, LINCOLN FULLY REALIZED THAT ISSUING ANY KIND OF EMANCIPATION ORDER WOULD BE A GRAVE POLITICAL RISK.

FREEING ANY SLAVES, UNDER ANY CIRCUMSTANCES, MIGHT COMPEL THE BORDER STATES TO SECEDE.

...TO WAGE [THIS WAR] FOR THE... ABOLITION OF SLAVERY, WOULD BE A FRAUD SO INFAMOUS THAT IT WOULD CALL DOWN UPON ITS AUTHORS THE ANATHEMAS OF ALL GOOD AND HONEST MEN!

HOWEVER, WITHOUT DIRECT ACTION TO END SLAVERY, SOME NORTHERN STATES REFUSED TO SEND NEW UNION ARMY VOLUNTEERS.

TO FIGHT AGAINST SLAVEHOLDERS, WITHOUT FIGHTING AGAINST SLAVERY, IS BUT A HALF-HEARTED BUSINESS...

CHARLES A. WICKLIFFE, CONGRESSMAN FROM KENTUCKY, 1862.

FREDERICK DOUGLASS, 1861.

LINCOLN AGONIZED. SHOULD HE EMANCIPATE? HE YEARNED FOR A SIGN THAT IT WAS THE RIGHT THING TO DO.

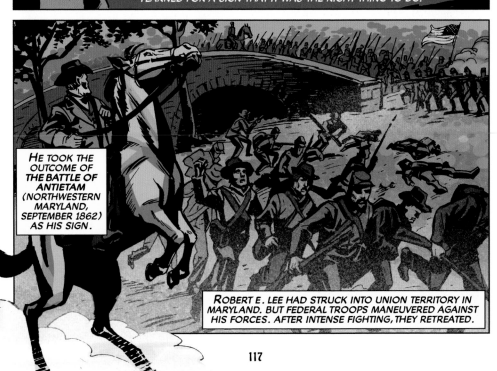

HE TOOK THE OUTCOME OF THE BATTLE OF ANTIETAM (NORTHWESTERN MARYLAND, SEPTEMBER 1862) AS HIS SIGN.

ROBERT E. LEE HAD STRUCK INTO UNION TERRITORY IN MARYLAND. BUT FEDERAL TROOPS MANEUVERED AGAINST HIS FORCES. AFTER INTENSE FIGHTING, THEY RETREATED.

ANTIETAM WAS A SUCCESS FOR LINCOLN, THOUGH A PRECARIOUS ONE. OUTNUMBERED NEARLY TWO TO ONE, CONFEDERATE TROOPS STILL INFLICTED HEAVY CASUALTIES ON THEIR OPPONENTS.

LINCOLN ANNOUNCED HIS *EMANCIPATION PROCLAMATION* ON SEPTEMBER 22, 1862.

IT WAS NOT A POETIC EULOGY LIKE THE GETTYSBURG ADDRESS. IT WAS A PLAINLY PHRASED MILITARY ORDER.

EMANCIPATION WOULD NOT GO INTO EFFECT UNTIL JANUARY 1, 1863. A TIMELINE OF SEVERAL MONTHS WAS IMPOSED. WASHINGTON HOPED A "TICKING CLOCK" WOULD TEMPT THE CONFEDERACY TO CUT ITS LOSSES AND SURRENDER.

BUT IT DID NOT.

...THE DETERMINATION OF [THE SOUTH'S] PEOPLE HAS, WITH EACH SUCCEEDING MONTH, BECOME MORE UNALTERABLY FIXED TO ENDURE ANY SUFFERING...

...UNTIL THEIR RIGHT TO SELF-GOVERNMENT, AND THE SOVEREIGNTY AND INDEPENDENCE OF THESE STATES, SHALL HAVE BEEN TRIUMPHANTLY VINDICATED...

JEFFERSON DAVIS, JANUARY 1863.

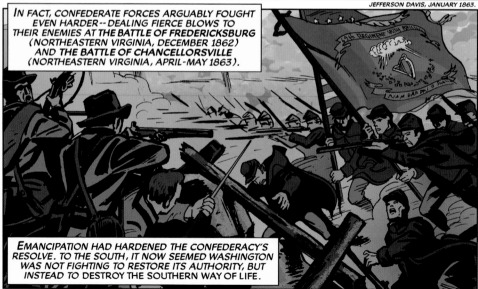

IN FACT, CONFEDERATE FORCES ARGUABLY FOUGHT EVEN HARDER -- DEALING FIERCE BLOWS TO THEIR ENEMIES AT *THE BATTLE OF FREDERICKSBURG* (NORTHEASTERN VIRGINIA, DECEMBER 1862) AND *THE BATTLE OF CHANCELLORSVILLE* (NORTHEASTERN VIRGINIA, APRIL-MAY 1863).

EMANCIPATION HAD HARDENED THE CONFEDERACY'S RESOLVE. TO THE SOUTH, IT NOW SEEMED WASHINGTON WAS NOT FIGHTING TO RESTORE ITS AUTHORITY, BUT INSTEAD TO DESTROY THE SOUTHERN WAY OF LIFE.

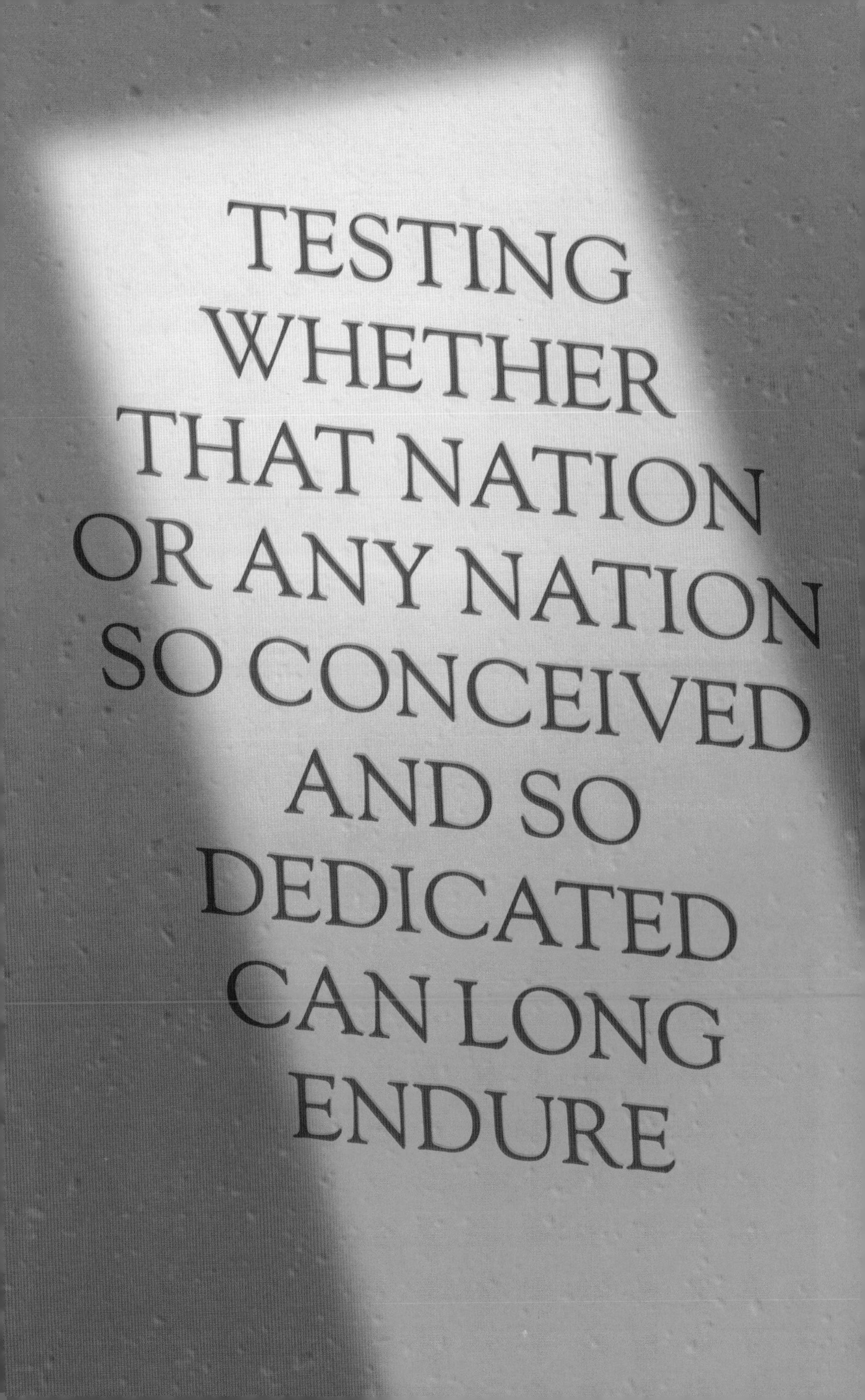
TESTING
WHETHER
THAT NATION
OR ANY NATION
SO CONCEIVED
AND SO
DEDICATED
CAN LONG
ENDURE

THE CIVIL WAR WAS A "TEST" OF THE CONSTITUTION.

THE DILEMMA OF CONDUCTING WAR ON THE COUNTRY'S HOME SOIL-- AGAINST PART OF ITS OWN PEOPLE-- THREATENED TO CRACK THE BEDROCK OF AMERICAN POLITICAL PHILOSOPHY.

AGAIN, LINCOLN BELIEVED THE UNITED STATES WAS "CONCEIVED IN LIBERTY" AND "DEDICATED TO THE PROPOSITION THAT ALL MEN ARE CREATED EQUAL."

BUT HE KNEW THAT FREEDOM AND EQUALITY COME AT A GREAT PRICE.

THE SAME FREEDOM THAT IS A STRENGTH IN PEACE CAN BE A STINGING HANDICAP IN CRISIS AND DANGER...

...WHEN THE RIGHTS OF POTENTIAL ENEMIES MUST BE AS RESPECTED AS THOSE OF AFFIRMED FRIENDS.

IN OTHER WORDS, A FREE SOCIETY CAN UNDERMINE ITS OWN SECURITY, ITS OWN ABILITY TO "LONG ENDURE."

LINCOLN FELT THE UNITED STATES WAS CARRYING OUT A DARING AND UNIQUE EXPERIMENT WITH FREEDOM, POPULAR SOVEREIGNTY, AND RULE OF LAW.

TO HIM, THE VALUES OF THE UNION-- NOT THE CONFEDERACY-- WERE THE TRUE EMBODIMENT OF THAT EXPERIMENT.

IF THE UNION WAS LOST, THE GREAT AMERICAN EXPERIMENT WOULD FAIL...

...AND THIS WOULD BE A CRIPPLING BLOW TO THE PEOPLE OF THE WHOLE WORLD.

IN THE MID-1800s, MUCH OF THE GLOBE STILL LIVED UNDER A **FEUDAL SYSTEM** OF PEASANTS AND NOBILITY.

EVEN IN EUROPE, THE MIDDLE AND WORKING CLASSES HAD SUFFERED HARSH REPRESSION AFTER THE FAILED REVOLUTIONS OF 1848, WHEN PEOPLE HAD DEMANDED MORE RIGHTS AND POLITICAL POWER.

IT SEEMED THAT NOWHERE COULD DEMOCRATIC IDEALS "LONG ENDURE" WITHOUT BEING SHATTERED BY THE IRON GRIP OF TYRANNY.

FOREIGN COUNTRIES WERE WATCHING THE CIVIL WAR AND JUDGING THE U.S. FROM AFAR.

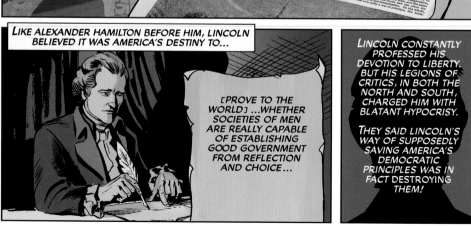

LIKE ALEXANDER HAMILTON BEFORE HIM, LINCOLN BELIEVED IT WAS AMERICA'S DESTINY TO...

[PROVE TO THE WORLD] ...WHETHER SOCIETIES OF MEN ARE REALLY CAPABLE OF ESTABLISHING GOOD GOVERNMENT FROM REFLECTION AND CHOICE...

LINCOLN CONSTANTLY PROFESSED HIS DEVOTION TO LIBERTY. BUT HIS LEGIONS OF CRITICS, IN BOTH THE NORTH AND SOUTH, CHARGED HIM WITH BLATANT HYPOCRISY.

THEY SAID LINCOLN'S WAY OF SUPPOSEDLY SAVING AMERICA'S DEMOCRATIC PRINCIPLES WAS IN FACT DESTROYING THEM!

GOVERNMENT VS. FREEDOM IN THE NORTH

ROGER B. TANEY, CHIEF JUSTICE OF THE SUPREME COURT, 1861.

ABRAHAM LINCOLN, 1861.

...IN THE CONSTITUTION... I CAN SEE NO GROUND WHATEVER FOR SUPPOSING THAT THE PRESIDENT, IN ANY EMERGENCY, OR IN ANY STATE OF THINGS, CAN AUTHORIZE THE SUSPENSION OF THE PRIVILEGE OF THE WRIT OF *HABEAS CORPUS*...

...ARE ALL THE LAWS BUT ONE TO GO UNEXECUTED, AND THE GOVERNMENT ITSELF GO TO PIECES LEST THAT ONE BE VIOLATED?

DURING THE WAR, THE FEDERAL GOVERNMENT DID INDEED VIOLATE MANY PEOPLE'S FREEDOMS. LINCOLN STRETCHED THE CONSTITUTION TO THE LIMIT AND, IN SOME CASES, FLAUNTED IT ALTOGETHER.

PERHAPS MOST FAMOUSLY, LINCOLN SUSPENDED HABEAS CORPUS: THE LEGAL PRINCIPLE THAT PROTECTS PEOPLE FROM BEING ARBITRARILY JAILED.

THE UNION STATE OF MARYLAND WAS HOME TO MANY CONFEDERATE SYMPATHIZERS. IN 1861, AN ANGRY MOB ATTACKED UNION TROOPS MARCHING THROUGH BALTIMORE. LINCOLN HAD GRAVE CONCERNS THAT MARYLAND WOULD SECEDE AND LEAVE WASHINGTON, D.C., SURROUNDED BY ENEMY TERRITORY. SO LINCOLN SUSPENDED HABEAS CORPUS, EMPOWERING HIS MILITARY TO ARREST AND DETAIN ANYONE WHOSE ACTIVITIES WERE DEEMED HOSTILE TO THE UNION. THEY ALSO APPREHENDED DULY ELECTED MEMBERS OF MARYLAND'S LEGISLATURE WHO LINCOLN FEARED WOULD PUSH THE STATE TOWARD SECESSION.

THE CONSTITUTION DOES GRANT THE FEDERAL GOVERNMENT THE POWER TO SUSPEND HABEAS CORPUS "IN CASES OF REBELLION OR INVASION." BUT MANY HAD ASSUMED THIS POWER BELONGED TO CONGRESS, NOT THE PRESIDENT.

ABOUT 13,000 CIVILIANS WERE HELD UNDER MILITARY ARREST BY THE UNION DURING THE COURSE OF THE WAR.

EVEN NEWSPAPERS IN NORTHERN STATES WERE SHUT DOWN DURING LINCOLN'S PRESIDENCY, LIKE THE *CHICAGO TIMES* AND THE *NEW YORK WORLD*.

LIBERTY

GOVERNMENT VS. FREEDOM IN THE SOUTH

BUT THE ANTEBELLUM AND CIVIL WAR-ERA SOUTH ALSO INFRINGED ON CONSTITUTIONAL LIBERTIES.

OF COURSE, SOUTHERN SLAVES HAD FEW LEGAL RIGHTS TO SPEAK OF

BUT SLAVERY ALSO LIMITED THE RIGHTS OF WHITES.

SERVITUDO ESTO PERPETUA

Old Rye

Cotton. Tobacco. Sugar.

G.H.Heap Inv.   H.H.Tilley Del. 1860.

ARMS of ye CONFEDERACIE.

IN THE SOUTH, SLAVERY BECAME SUCH AN ENTRENCHED INSTITUTION THAT GOVERNMENT AT BOTH THE STATE AND FEDERAL LEVEL HAD TO BE RIGGED TO DEFEND IT--AT THE EXPENSE OF DEMOCRATIC IDEALS.

AMERICANS NOW TAKE "ONE PERSON, ONE VOTE" FOR GRANTED. BUT THIS PRINCIPLE DID NOT ALWAYS APPLY IN THE SOUTH. STATES OFTEN INCLUDED PROPERTY AND WEALTH IN DETERMINING POLITICAL REPRESENTATION. SO AREAS WITH WHITE MEN WHO OWNED MANY SLAVES (LIKE THE ALABAMA "BLACK BELT") HAD MORE VOTING POWER IN THE STATE HOUSE THAN AREAS WITH WHITES WHO OWNED FEW OR NO SLAVES (LIKE WINSTON COUNTY, ALABAMA, NOTED FOR ITS OPPOSITION TO SECESSION).

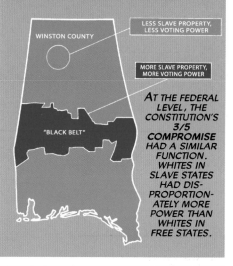

WINSTON COUNTY

LESS SLAVE PROPERTY, LESS VOTING POWER

MORE SLAVE PROPERTY, MORE VOTING POWER

"BLACK BELT"

AT THE FEDERAL LEVEL, THE CONSTITUTION'S 3/5 COMPROMISE HAD A SIMILAR FUNCTION. WHITES IN SLAVE STATES HAD DIS-PROPORTION-ATELY MORE POWER THAN WHITES IN FREE STATES.

JURY TRIALS AND FREEDOM OF SPEECH AND OF THE PRESS HAVE SUPPOSEDLY ALWAYS BEEN SACRED IN AMERICA. BUT IN THE ANTEBELLUM SOUTH, THE NEED TO PROTECT SLAVERY CAME FIRST. ANTISLAVERY PUBLICATIONS WERE COLLECTED AND DESTROYED BY THE U.S. POST OFFICE BEFORE THEY COULD BE DELIVERED. WHITES ACCUSED OF PREACHING ABOLITION WERE SOMETIMES CONVICTED BY KANGAROO COURTS AND LYNCHED, SUCH AS IN MADISON COUNTY, MISSISSIPPI, IN 1835.

NEITHER SIDE IN THE CIVIL WAR CAN CLAIM A PERFECT RECORD OF UPHOLDING LIBERTY AND EQUALITY.

AND BY 1863, THE QUESTION OF WHETHER THE UNITED STATES COULD "LONG ENDURE" ITS "TEST" BEGAN TO DEPEND LESS ON THE RULE OF LAW AND MORE ON THE STRENGTH OF ARMIES...

...IN FIELDS THAT WERE GROWING STEADILY BLOODIER.

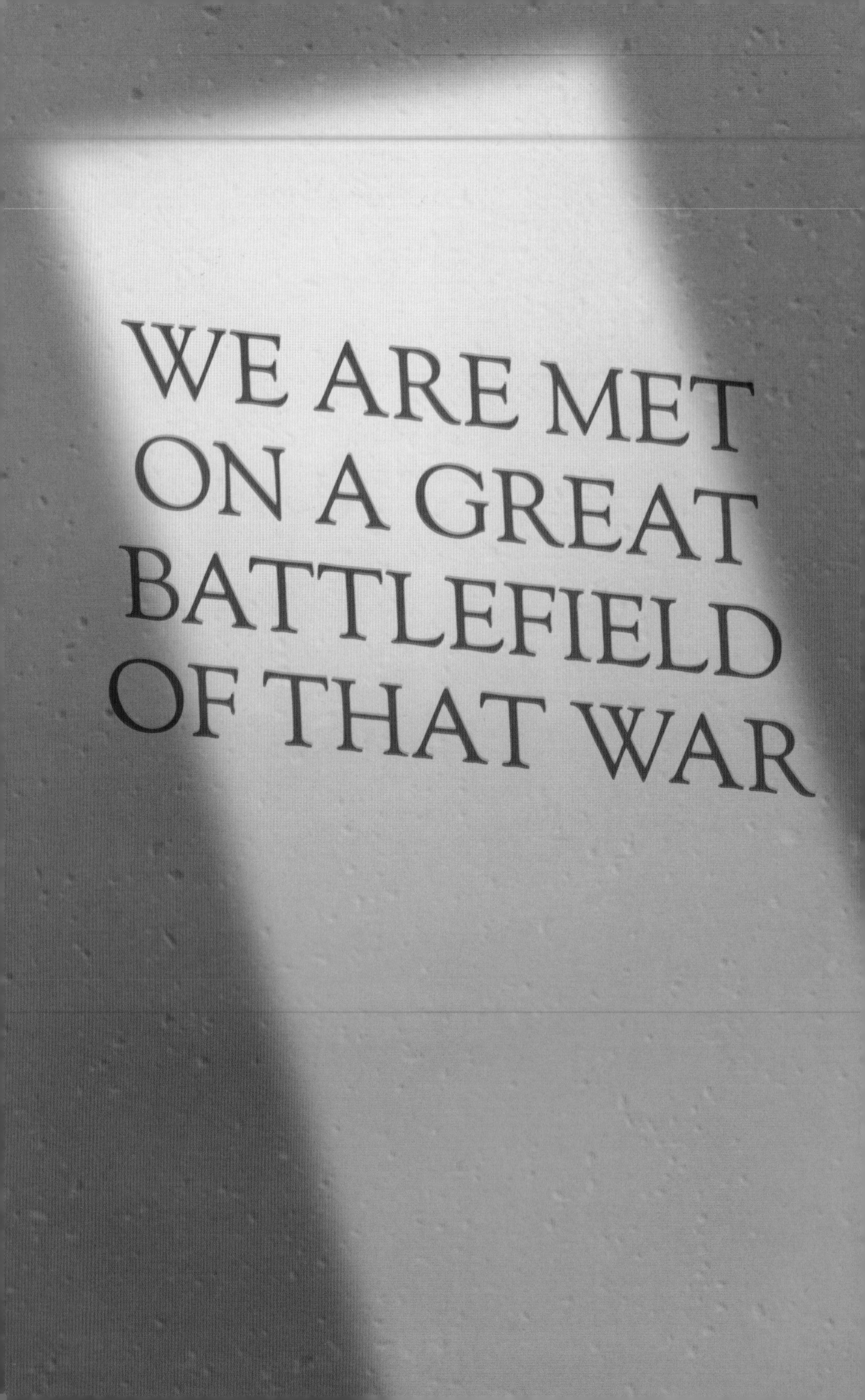
WE ARE MET
ON A GREAT
BATTLEFIELD
OF THAT WAR

IN THE SUMMER OF 1863, THE CONFEDERATES INVADED THE NORTH.

LINCOLN AND HIS ARMIES HAD TO DRIVE THEM OUT OF PENNSYLVANIA...

...OR FACE THE POSSIBILITY OF A RUINOUS DEFEAT THAT WOULD FOREVER ALTER AMERICA'S FUTURE.

IT WAS INEVITABLE A MAJOR CLASH WAS GOING TO HAPPEN SOMEWHERE IN PENNSYLVANIA.

BUT WHERE?

ANDREW CURTIN, GOVERNOR OF PENNSYLVANIA

GETTYSBURG WAS DESTINED TO BE THIS "GREAT BATTLEFIELD."

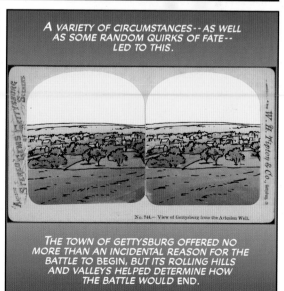

A VARIETY OF CIRCUMSTANCES-- AS WELL AS SOME RANDOM QUIRKS OF FATE-- LED TO THIS.

THE TOWN OF GETTYSBURG OFFERED NO MORE THAN AN INCIDENTAL REASON FOR THE BATTLE TO BEGIN, BUT ITS ROLLING HILLS AND VALLEYS HELPED DETERMINE HOW THE BATTLE WOULD END.

WHY HAD ROBERT E. LEE TAKEN HIS CONFEDERATES TO PENNSYLVANIA IN THE FIRST PLACE?

IT'S IMPOSSIBLE TO SAY FOR SURE. BUT THERE ARE SEVERAL KEY THEORIES.

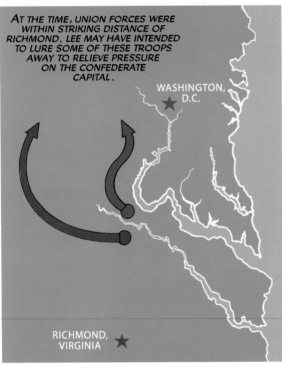

AT THE TIME, UNION FORCES WERE WITHIN STRIKING DISTANCE OF RICHMOND. LEE MAY HAVE INTENDED TO LURE SOME OF THESE TROOPS AWAY TO RELIEVE PRESSURE ON THE CONFEDERATE CAPITAL.

WASHINGTON, D.C.

RICHMOND, VIRGINIA

YEARS OF FIGHTING HAD LAID VIRGINIA'S COUNTRYSIDE BARREN. LEE MAY HAVE RAIDED THE FRUITFUL CUMBERLAND VALLEY (ON THE MARYLAND-PENNSYLVANIA BORDER) SIMPLY IN SEARCH OF FOOD AND SUPPLIES. INDEED, CONFEDERATES SEIZED MASSES OF TOOLS, CLOTHING, AND PROVISIONS--TENS OF THOUSANDS OF CATTLE, SHEEP, HORSES, AND HOGS--WHILE THERE.

ANOTHER POSSIBILITY IS THAT LEE WANTED TO CAPTURE HARRISBURG, PENNSYLVANIA'S CAPITAL. SUCH A MOVE WOULD MAKE THE CONFEDERACY LOOK STRONG AND UNDEFEATABLE. FOREIGN COUNTRIES MIGHT OFFER IT MORE AID. DIPLOMATIC AND POLITICAL PRESSURE MIGHT FORCE WASHINGTON TO END THE WAR AND LET THE SOUTH SECEDE.

HARRISBURG

HARRISBURG--HELD HOSTAGE-- COULD ALSO BE USED AS A BARGAINING CHIP. LEE MAY HAVE BEEN ANGLING TO FORCE WASHINGTON TO ABANDON ITS NAVAL BLOCKADE OF SOUTHERN PORTS. THE BLOCKADE HAD NEARLY CUT THE CONFEDERACY OFF FROM OVERSEAS MERCHANTS WITH SUPPLIES OF WEAPONS AND AMMUNITION, WHICH THE SOUTH DEARLY NEEDED TO CONTINUE ITS WAR EFFORT.

WARFARE IS A DAUNTINGLY COMPLEX INTERPLAY OF STRATEGY, TACTICS, POLITICS, AND LOGISTICS.

AND IT MUST BE CONDUCTED IN THE "REAL WORLD" OF VARIABLE TERRAIN, WEATHER EXTREMES, AND THE COMPLEXITIES OF COMMUNICATION AND SUPPLY LINES.

THE 1860s WERE A TIME BEFORE THE INVENTION OF FLIGHT, AND WHEN TECHNOLOGY LIKE SATELLITE CAMERAS WAS ALL BUT UNIMAGINABLE.

TO TRACK THE MOVEMENT EVEN OF VAST ARMIES, ONE NEEDED EYEWITNESSES, SCOUTS, AND SPIES.

TO CONCEAL HIS MEN FROM ENEMY EYES AND MAKE THEIR PRECISE MISSION HARD TO GUESS, ROBERT E. LEE EMPLOYED TERRAIN.

HE MARCHED HIS ARMY THROUGH HIDDEN MOUNTAIN PASSES AS THEY HEADED FROM VIRGINIA INTO PENNSYLVANIA.

LIKE THEIR UNION COUNTERPARTS, LEE'S MEN TRAVELED ON VARIOUS ROADS. THEY WERE NOT ALL TOGETHER, BUT IN SEGMENTS OFTEN MILES APART-- LIKE THE CLOUDS OF A STORM SYSTEM SWEEPING ACROSS THE LAND.

LEE HAD ORDERED GENERAL "JEB" STUART'S **CAVALRY** (SOLDIERS ON HORSEBACK) ON THEIR OWN SEPARATE COURSE.

STUART'S MEN WERE TO CONDUCT RAIDS, CUT TELEGRAPH AND RAIL LINES, AND GUARD MOUNTAIN PASSES.

THIS WOULD DISTRACT THE UNION MILITARY AND KEEP IT FROM TRACKING THE CONFEDERATE **INFANTRY** (SOLDIERS MARCHING ON FOOT).

CAVALRY WERE THE "EYES AND EARS" OF THE ARMY. FAST-MOVING RIDERS COULD GATHER INTELLIGENCE ON THE ENEMY AND RUSH IT TO HEAD-QUARTERS.

BUT FOR REASONS THAT HISTORIANS STILL DEBATE, STUART'S CAVALRY LOST CONTACT WITH LEE FOR SEVERAL DAYS.

WITHOUT BULLETINS FROM STUART, LEE HAD ONLY AN INCOMPLETE PICTURE OF THE UNION ARMY AND ITS WHEREABOUTS.

BOTH ARMIES CRITICALLY NEEDED INFORMATION ON THE OTHER AS JULY 1863 NEARED. SMALL UNITS OF CONFEDERATES AND UNIONISTS WERE ENCOUNTERING EACH OTHER NEAR THE PENNSYLVANIA BORDER. SOMETIMES THEY CLASHED, SOMETIMES THEY CAUTIOUSLY WITHDREW ON SIGHT. WHY?

ARMIES DON'T EXIST SIMPLY TO ATTACK.

THEY ALSO SEEK TO MOVE AND MANIPULATE *THE ENEMY.* LIKE IN A GAME OF CHESS, THEY MAY ANGLE FOR AN ADVANTAGE SEVERAL "MOVES" IN THE FUTURE.

ALL THE MINOR SKIRMISHES FAILED TO TOUCH OFF A LARGE BATTLE BECAUSE NEITHER SIDE YET KNEW THE FULL STATUS OF THE OTHER.

ONLY TWO CONDITIONS COULD MAKE ONE SIDE COMMIT TO A FULL-SCALE CONFRONTATION.

1. BEING ABLE TO SOMEHOW DRAW ALL ITS SCATTERED TROOPS TOGETHER *BEFORE* A FIGHT.

2. FINDING AN ACTUAL PLACE ON A BATTLEFIELD THAT WOULD BE ADVANTAGEOUS AND EASIER TO DEFEND.

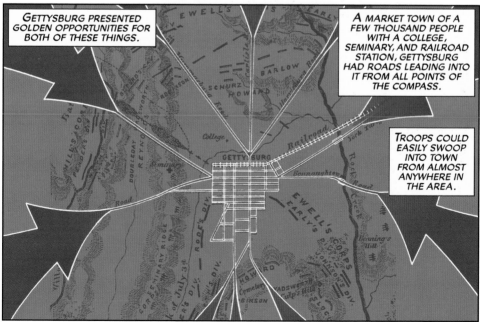

GETTYSBURG PRESENTED GOLDEN OPPORTUNITIES FOR BOTH OF THESE THINGS.

A MARKET TOWN OF A FEW THOUSAND PEOPLE WITH A COLLEGE, SEMINARY, AND RAILROAD STATION, GETTYSBURG HAD ROADS LEADING INTO IT FROM ALL POINTS OF THE COMPASS.

TROOPS COULD EASILY SWOOP INTO TOWN FROM ALMOST ANYWHERE IN THE AREA.

GETTYSBURG ALSO HAD HIGH GROUND-- POTENTIAL BATTLEFIELD POSITIONS WORTH SCRAMBLING FOR.

CULP'S HILL.

THAT REGION OF PENNSYLVANIA IS LARGELY MADE UP OF LONG, UNDULATING RIDGES AND VALLEYS-- LIKE A RIPPLED POTATO CHIP.

ALL OTHER THINGS BEING EQUAL, AN ARMY CONTROLLING ONE OF THESE RIDGES CAN FIGHT FAR BETTER THAN THE OTHER.

WHY? THE **FRONT LINES** OR **FRONT** OF MANY CIVIL WAR BATTLES STRETCHED AS MUCH AS 5 MILES ACROSS. BEFORE RADIO COMMUNICATIONS, THE VISIBILITY OF ELEVATED SPOTS HELPED AN ARMY'S **SIGNAL CORPS** PASS ALONG COMMUNICATIONS-- CRITICAL FOR FAR-FLUNG UNITS TO FUNCTION AS A WHOLE.

HIGH GROUND ALSO GIVES AN ARMY A BETTER VANTAGE POINT TO OBSERVE ITS OPPONENT.

WHEN SOLDIERS ATTEMPT TO ATTACK UPHILL, GRAVITY SLOWS AND TIRES THEM, MAKING THEM TARGETS THAT ARE EASIER TO HIT.

PLUS, THOSE DEFENDING HIGH GROUND EXPOSE ONLY THEIR FORWARD RANKS-- WHILE TARGETING ATTACKERS IN FRONT AND BACK.

UNION GENERAL JOHN BUFORD HAD BEEN SENT INTO GETTYSBURG ON JUNE 30, 1863, TO SCOUT THE AREA.

HE SAW VALUABLE HIGH GROUND JUST SOUTH OF TOWN: **CULP'S HILL** AND **CEMETERY HILL** (PLUS THE LONG **CEMETERY RIDGE** PROCEEDING SOUTHWARD).

BUFORD REASONED THAT IF THERE WAS GOING TO BE A FIGHT IN GETTYSBURG, THERE WOULD BE A RACE TO OCCUPY THOSE HEIGHTS ABOVE TOWN.

SO HE TOOK ACTION. BUFORD DISPATCHED COURIERS TO SUMMON THE MAIN UNION ARMY--

AND HOPEFULLY LET IT TAKE THE HIGH GROUND.

BUFORD HAD APPROXIMATELY 2,750 MEN UNDER HIS COMMAND. THEY COULD NOT STOP THE CONFEDERATES...

...BUT THEY COULD SLOW THEM DOWN.

AT 7 A.M. ON JULY 1, 1863...

...UNION LIEUTENANT MARCELLUS E. JONES WAS AMONG THE FIRST TO SPOT A UNIT OF CONFEDERATES HEADED TOWARD GETTYSBURG.

JONES TOOK AIM AND FIRED WHAT MOST CREDIT AS THE FIRST ROUND OF THE BATTLE.

THE CONFEDERATES HALTED AND ORGANIZED A COUNTER-ATTACK.

THE BATTLE: DAY 1

A NEARBY FARMER SAW CONFEDERATES READYING A CANNON ON HIS LAND.

MY GOD...

YOU ARE NOT GOING TO FIRE HERE, ARE YOU?

OUTNUMBERED THREE TO ONE, BUFORD'S MEN FELL BACK TOWARD TOWN.

NEWS OF THE SKIRMISH RAN LIKE WILDFIRE IN ALL DIRECTIONS. SOON, THE ENTIRETIES OF BOTH ARMIES WERE CONVERGING ON GETTYSBURG.

THE ERA OF THE CIVIL WAR WAS ONE OF EVOLVING WEAPONS TECHNOLOGY.

FIREARMS HAD ONCE BEEN SMOOTHBORE, MEANING THEIR BARRELS WERE LIKE DRINKING STRAWS, WITH SLICK CYLINDER WALLS.

.58 Caliber 1861 Springfield Musket

IN SUCH BARRELS, AMMUNITION WOULD LITERALLY BOUNCE AROUND. (IMAGINE A PINBALL MACHINE'S BALL RICOCHETING THROUGH BUMPERS ON ITS WAY DOWN THE PLAYING FIELD.)

THE DIRECTION IN WHICH A PROJECTILE WOULD FINALLY FIRE WAS DETERMINED BY ITS LAST "BOUNCE."

SMOOTHBORE WEAPONS, THEREFORE, WERE NOT VERY ACCURATE.

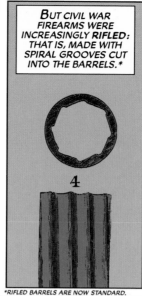

BUT CIVIL WAR FIREARMS WERE INCREASINGLY **RIFLED**: THAT IS, MADE WITH SPIRAL GROOVES CUT INTO THE BARRELS.*

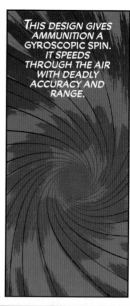

THIS DESIGN GIVES AMMUNITION A GYROSCOPIC SPIN. IT SPEEDS THROUGH THE AIR WITH DEADLY ACCURACY AND RANGE.

*RIFLED BARRELS ARE NOW STANDARD.

FORWARD MEN, FORWARD, FOR GOD'S SAKE, AND DRIVE THOSE FELLOWS OUT OF THE WOODS!

UNLIKE TODAY, 19TH-CENTURY OFFICERS OF HIGH RANK WERE OFTEN EXPECTED TO LEAD MEN INTO COMBAT.

SO DURING THE CIVIL WAR, OFFICERS WERE MORE LIKELY TO BE KILLED IN ACTION THAN LOWER-RANKING ENLISTED MEN.

THIS WAS THE FATE OF UNION MAJOR GENERAL JOHN F. REYNOLDS. AFTER RUSHING HIS MEN TO GETTYSBURG, HE WAS SHOT DEAD OFF HIS HORSE-- LIKELY BY THE RIFLES OF THE 14TH TENNESSEE INFANTRY.

IN THE ESCALATING BATTLE, MISSISSIPPI MEN UNDER BRIGADIER GENERAL JOSEPH DAVIS-- THE CONFEDERATE PRESIDENT'S NEPHEW-- TOOK COVER IN A "RAILROAD CUT"...

...A HOLLOWED-OUT CONSTRUCTION AREA FOR A PLANNED TRAIN BRIDGE.

AN ATTACK BY SOLDIERS OF THE 6th WISCONSIN FORCED THEM TO SURRENDER.

ROBERT E. LEE ARRIVED ON THE SCENE ABOUT 2:30 P.M. HE SOON ESTABLISHED A HEADQUARTERS ON *SEMINARY RIDGE*.

IT WAS ALSO HIGH GROUND, ALTHOUGH THE AREA'S SECOND BEST.

THE CONFEDERATES ADVANCED WITH SHATTERING FORCE.

UNION MEN ABANDONED THEIR POSTS. TROOPS FROM STATES LIKE MAINE, OHIO, AND NEW YORK-- ALL UNFAMILIAR WITH GETTYSBURG-- GOT LOST AND WERE TAKEN CAPTIVE BY THE SCORE.

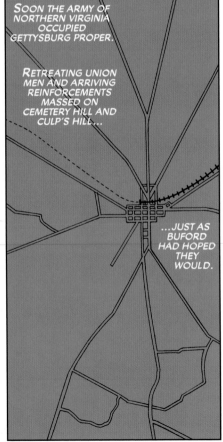

SOON THE ARMY OF NORTHERN VIRGINIA OCCUPIED GETTYSBURG PROPER.

RETREATING UNION MEN AND ARRIVING REINFORCEMENTS MASSED ON CEMETERY HILL AND CULP'S HILL...

...JUST AS BUFORD HAD HOPED THEY WOULD.

136

THE UNION MEN DUG INTO THEIR HILL POSITIONS AND ERECTED WOODEN FORTIFICATIONS CALLED BREASTWORKS.

NIGHT-FIGHTING WAS NOT TYPICAL DURING THE CIVIL WAR. MOST SOLDIERS MADE CAMP, ATE, AND RESTED FOR THE NEXT DAY.

UNION MAJOR GENERAL GEORGE MEADE HAD JUST BEEN APPOINTED COMMANDER OF THE ARMY OF THE POTOMAC.

...A BATTLE AT GETTYSBURG IS NOW FORCED ON US, AND... IF WE CAN GET UP OUR PEOPLE AND ATTACK WITH OUR WHOLE FORCE, TO-MORROW, WE OUGHT TO DEFEAT THE FORCE THE ENEMY HAS.

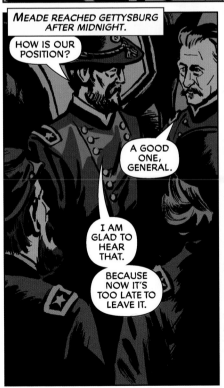

MEADE REACHED GETTYSBURG AFTER MIDNIGHT.

HOW IS OUR POSITION?

A GOOD ONE, GENERAL.

I AM GLAD TO HEAR THAT.

BECAUSE NOW IT'S TOO LATE TO LEAVE IT.

THE ARMY OF THE POTOMAC HAD SUFFERED ABOUT 9,000 CASUALTIES ON THE FIRST DAY OF BATTLE—THOUSANDS MORE THAN ITS OPPONENT.

MEADE WOULD HAVE PREFERRED TO FACE LEE SOMEWHERE IN MARYLAND. BUT NOW A MAJOR ENGAGEMENT WAS IMPOSSIBLE TO AVOID.

GENERALLY, THE "LOSER" OF A FIGHT WAS THE ARMY THAT LEFT THE FIELD FIRST.

THE BATTLE: DAY 2

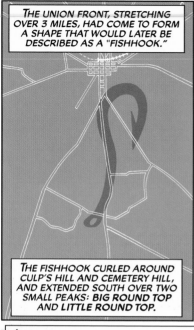

THE UNION FRONT, STRETCHING OVER 3 MILES, HAD COME TO FORM A SHAPE THAT WOULD LATER BE DESCRIBED AS A "FISHHOOK."

THE FISHHOOK CURLED AROUND CULP'S HILL AND CEMETERY HILL, AND EXTENDED SOUTH OVER TWO SMALL PEAKS: BIG ROUND TOP AND LITTLE ROUND TOP.

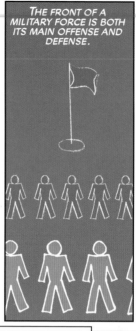

THE FRONT OF A MILITARY FORCE IS BOTH ITS MAIN OFFENSE AND DEFENSE.

ONE WAY TO DEFEAT A FORCE IS TO PENETRATE OR BYPASS ITS FRONT AND ATTACK THE REAR...

...TYPICALLY THE LOCATION OF ITS COMMAND AND CONTROL, SUPPORT, SUPPLIES, AND LINES OF COMMUNICATION.

LEE'S CHALLENGE WAS TO DETERMINE WHERE THE UNION FRONT WAS WEAKEST-- OR COULD BE MADE THE WEAKEST.

I'VE LEARNED MUCH ABOUT THE TOPOGRAPHY OF THIS COUNTRY ON MY MARCH FROM YORK.

AND THE RIGHT SIDE IS WHERE MEADE IS STRETCHED THIN.

THE ARMY OF NORTHERN VIRGINIA WOULD THEN MOUNT AN ATTACK ON THAT VULNERABLE POINT.

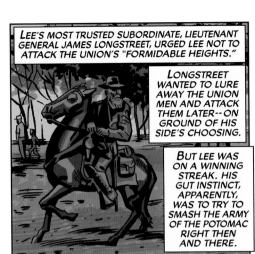

LEE'S MOST TRUSTED SUBORDINATE, LIEUTENANT GENERAL JAMES LONGSTREET, URGED LEE NOT TO ATTACK THE UNION'S "FORMIDABLE HEIGHTS."

LONGSTREET WANTED TO LURE AWAY THE UNION MEN AND ATTACK THEM LATER-- ON GROUND OF HIS SIDE'S CHOOSING.

BUT LEE WAS ON A WINNING STREAK. HIS GUT INSTINCT, APPARENTLY, WAS TO TRY TO SMASH THE ARMY OF THE POTOMAC RIGHT THEN AND THERE.

LEE HAD A TOP COMMANDER, GENERAL RICHARD S. EWELL, ASSAULT THE NORTH SIDE OF THE FISH-HOOK-- THE UNION'S RIGHT FLANK.

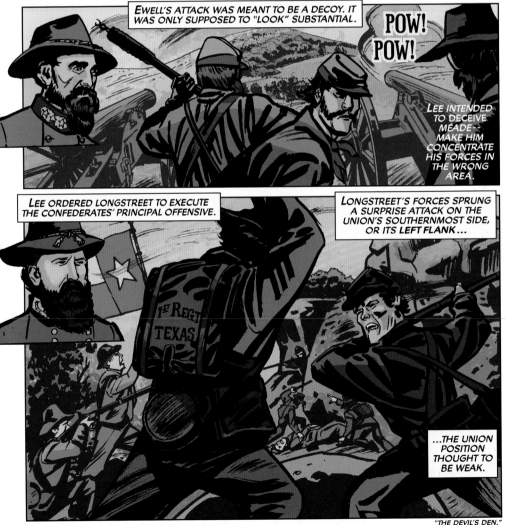

EWELL'S ATTACK WAS MEANT TO BE A DECOY. IT WAS ONLY SUPPOSED TO "LOOK" SUBSTANTIAL.

POW! POW!

LEE INTENDED TO DECEIVE MEADE-- MAKE HIM CONCENTRATE HIS FORCES IN THE WRONG AREA.

LEE ORDERED LONGSTREET TO EXECUTE THE CONFEDERATES' PRINCIPAL OFFENSIVE.

LONGSTREET'S FORCES SPRUNG A SURPRISE ATTACK ON THE UNION'S SOUTHERNMOST SIDE, OR ITS LEFT FLANK...

1ST REGT TEXAS

...THE UNION POSITION THOUGHT TO BE WEAK.

"THE DEVIL'S DEN."

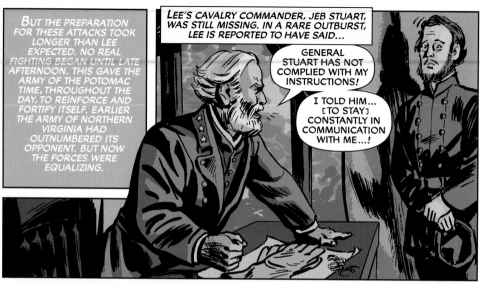

BUT THE PREPARATION FOR THESE ATTACKS TOOK LONGER THAN LEE EXPECTED. NO REAL FIGHTING BEGAN UNTIL LATE AFTERNOON. THIS GAVE THE ARMY OF THE POTOMAC TIME, THROUGHOUT THE DAY, TO REINFORCE AND FORTIFY ITSELF. EARLIER THE ARMY OF NORTHERN VIRGINIA HAD OUTNUMBERED ITS OPPONENT. BUT NOW THE FORCES WERE EQUALIZING.

LEE'S CAVALRY COMMANDER, JEB STUART, WAS STILL MISSING. IN A RARE OUTBURST, LEE IS REPORTED TO HAVE SAID...

GENERAL STUART HAS NOT COMPLIED WITH MY INSTRUCTIONS!

I TOLD HIM... [TO STAY] CONSTANTLY IN COMMUNICATION WITH ME...!

THAT CHANGED ON THE AFTERNOON OF JULY 2, WHEN STUART WAS FOUND AND FINALLY REJOINED THE MAIN FORCE.

I-I ⇍PANT⇍ FOUND THE MAIN ARMY 30 MILES SOUTH, AT ⇍PANT⇍ GETTYSBURG.

GENERAL LEE'S ORDERS ARE FOR YOU TO COME AT ONCE--!

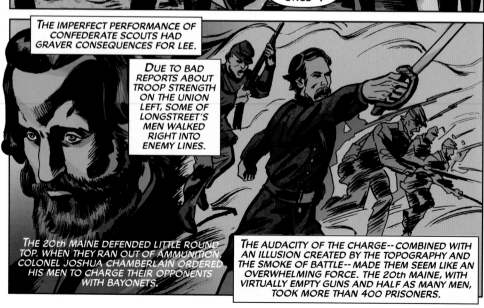

THE IMPERFECT PERFORMANCE OF CONFEDERATE SCOUTS HAD GRAVER CONSEQUENCES FOR LEE.

DUE TO BAD REPORTS ABOUT TROOP STRENGTH ON THE UNION LEFT, SOME OF LONGSTREET'S MEN WALKED RIGHT INTO ENEMY LINES.

THE 20th MAINE DEFENDED LITTLE ROUND TOP. WHEN THEY RAN OUT OF AMMUNITION, COLONEL JOSHUA CHAMBERLAIN ORDERED HIS MEN TO CHARGE THEIR OPPONENTS WITH BAYONETS.

THE AUDACITY OF THE CHARGE-- COMBINED WITH AN ILLUSION CREATED BY THE TOPOGRAPHY AND THE SMOKE OF BATTLE-- MADE THEM SEEM LIKE AN OVERWHELMING FORCE. THE 20th MAINE, WITH VIRTUALLY EMPTY GUNS AND HALF AS MANY MEN, TOOK MORE THAN 400 PRISONERS.

By the end of the day, Meade's side had sustained approximately 10,000 casualties.

But the union line had held.

THE BATTLE: DAY 3

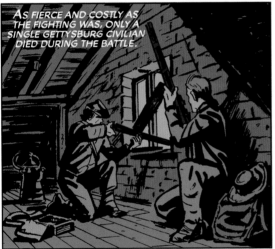

As fierce and costly as the fighting was, only a single Gettysburg civilian died during the battle.

Around 8 A.M. on July 3, a sharpshooter's stray bullet struck and killed 20-year-old Ginnie Wade.

CORRECT PHOTO · GINNIE WADE

She had been baking bread to help feed union soldiers.

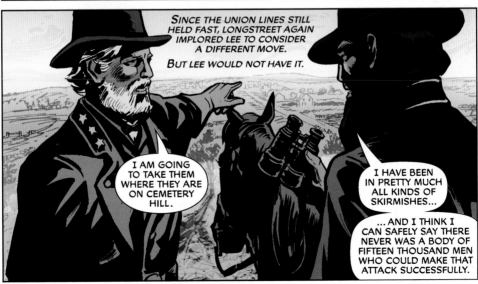

Since the union lines still held fast, Longstreet again implored Lee to consider a different move.

But Lee would not have it.

I am going to take them where they are on Cemetery Hill.

I have been in pretty much all kinds of skirmishes...

...and I think I can safely say there never was a body of fifteen thousand men who could make that attack successfully.

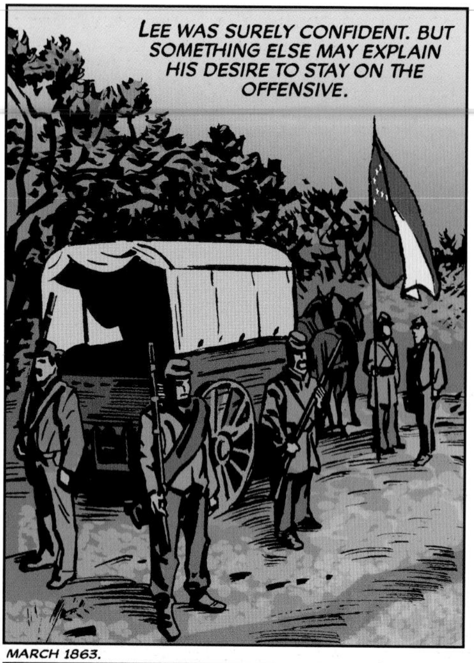
LEE WAS SURELY CONFIDENT. BUT SOMETHING ELSE MAY EXPLAIN HIS DESIRE TO STAY ON THE OFFENSIVE.

MARCH 1863.

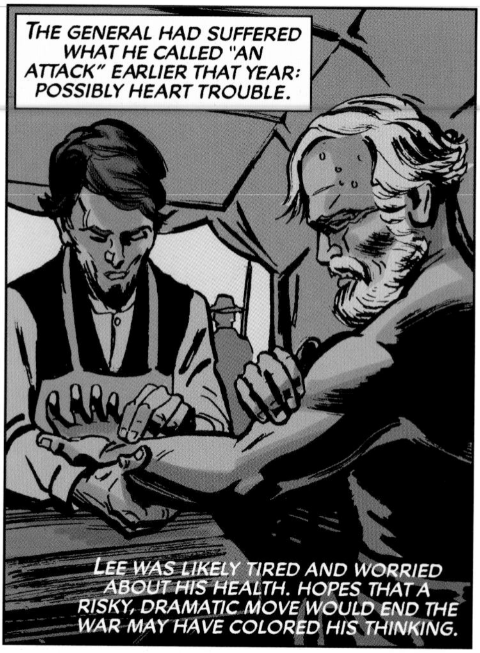
THE GENERAL HAD SUFFERED WHAT HE CALLED "AN ATTACK" EARLIER THAT YEAR: POSSIBLY HEART TROUBLE.
LEE WAS LIKELY TIRED AND WORRIED ABOUT HIS HEALTH. HOPES THAT A RISKY, DRAMATIC MOVE WOULD END THE WAR MAY HAVE COLORED HIS THINKING.

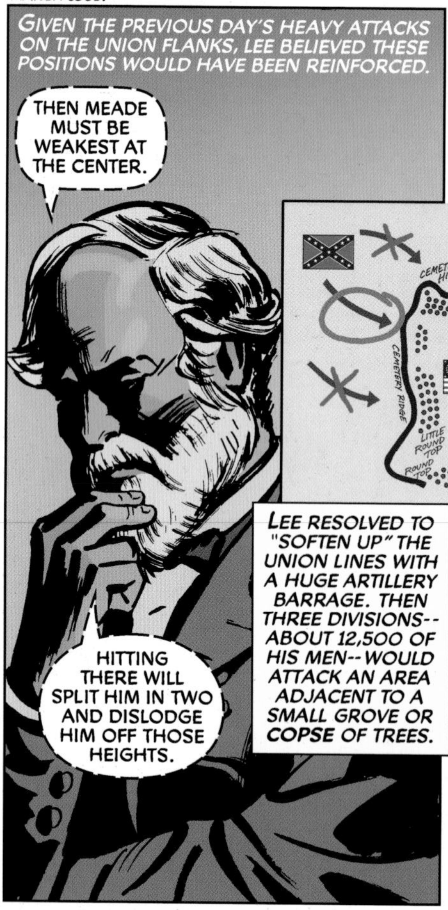
GIVEN THE PREVIOUS DAY'S HEAVY ATTACKS ON THE UNION FLANKS, LEE BELIEVED THESE POSITIONS WOULD HAVE BEEN REINFORCED.
THEN MEADE MUST BE WEAKEST AT THE CENTER.
CEMETERY HILL
CULP'S HILL
CEMETERY RIDGE
LITTLE ROUND TOP
ROUND TOP
LEE RESOLVED TO "SOFTEN UP" THE UNION LINES WITH A HUGE ARTILLERY BARRAGE. THEN THREE DIVISIONS--ABOUT 12,500 OF HIS MEN--WOULD ATTACK AN AREA ADJACENT TO A SMALL GROVE OR COPSE OF TREES.
HITTING THERE WILL SPLIT HIM IN TWO AND DISLODGE HIM OFF THOSE HEIGHTS.

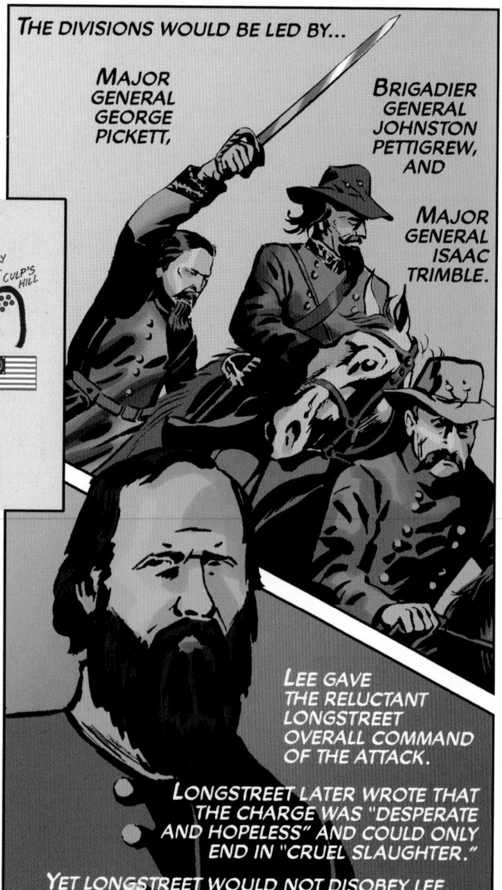
THE DIVISIONS WOULD BE LED BY...
MAJOR GENERAL GEORGE PICKETT,
BRIGADIER GENERAL JOHNSTON PETTIGREW, AND
MAJOR GENERAL ISAAC TRIMBLE.
LEE GAVE THE RELUCTANT LONGSTREET OVERALL COMMAND OF THE ATTACK.
LONGSTREET LATER WROTE THAT THE CHARGE WAS "DESPERATE AND HOPELESS" AND COULD ONLY END IN "CRUEL SLAUGHTER."
YET LONGSTREET WOULD NOT DISOBEY LEE.

K-THOOM!

K-THOOM!

THE CONFEDERATE ARTILLERY OPENED UP ABOUT 1 P.M. WITH 164 CANNONS.

FIRING CONTINUED FOR TWO HOURS. THE BARRAGE HAS GONE DOWN IN HISTORY AS THE LARGEST IN THE CIVIL WAR.

BUT CANNON FIRE BEGAN TO OVERSHOOT THE UNION FRONT.

BECAUSE OF THE DIFFICULTY OF SEEING THROUGH SO MUCH SMOKE...

...THE CONFEDERATE COMMAND FAR OVERESTIMATED THE DAMAGE THEIR ARTILLERY WOULD DO.

UP MEN, AND TO YOUR POSTS!

DON'T FORGET TODAY THAT YOU ARE FROM OLD VIRGINIA!

"PICKETT'S CHARGE" BEGAN AT 3 P.M.

IT WAS NOT AN ALL-OUT, GO-FOR-BROKE DASH. SUCH A THING WOULD EXHAUST THE SOLDIERS BEFORE THEY EVEN REACHED THEIR DESTINATION.

IT WAS INSTEAD AN ORGANIZED PROGRESSION ACROSS NEARLY A MILE OF FARM FIELDS, TAKING ABOUT 25 MINUTES.

STEADY, MEN. NOT TOO FAST.

DRESS TO THE RIGHT. KEEP WELL IN LINE...

THE 69th PENNSYLVANIA'S COLONEL DENNIS O'KANE REALIZED THE ENEMY WAS FUNNELING RIGHT TOWARD HIS POSITION.

THE JOB OF HOLDING THE LINE WOULD FALL HEAVILY ON HIS MEN.

SHOULD ANY MAN AMONG US FLINCH IN OUR DUTY, KILL HIM ON THE SPOT.

ONCE THE CONFEDERATES WERE WITHIN RANGE, THE UNION ARTILLERY FIRED ON THEM WITH BRUTAL FORCE.

DOUBLE CANNISTER!

FIRE!

K-FOOM!

LEE'S CANNONS COULD NOT EFFECTIVELY RETURN FIRE. THEY WERE CLOSE TO EMPTY, AND THEIR SUPPLY WAGONS, SENT MILES AWAY FOR PROTECTION, COULD NOT BE QUICKLY SUMMONED BACK.

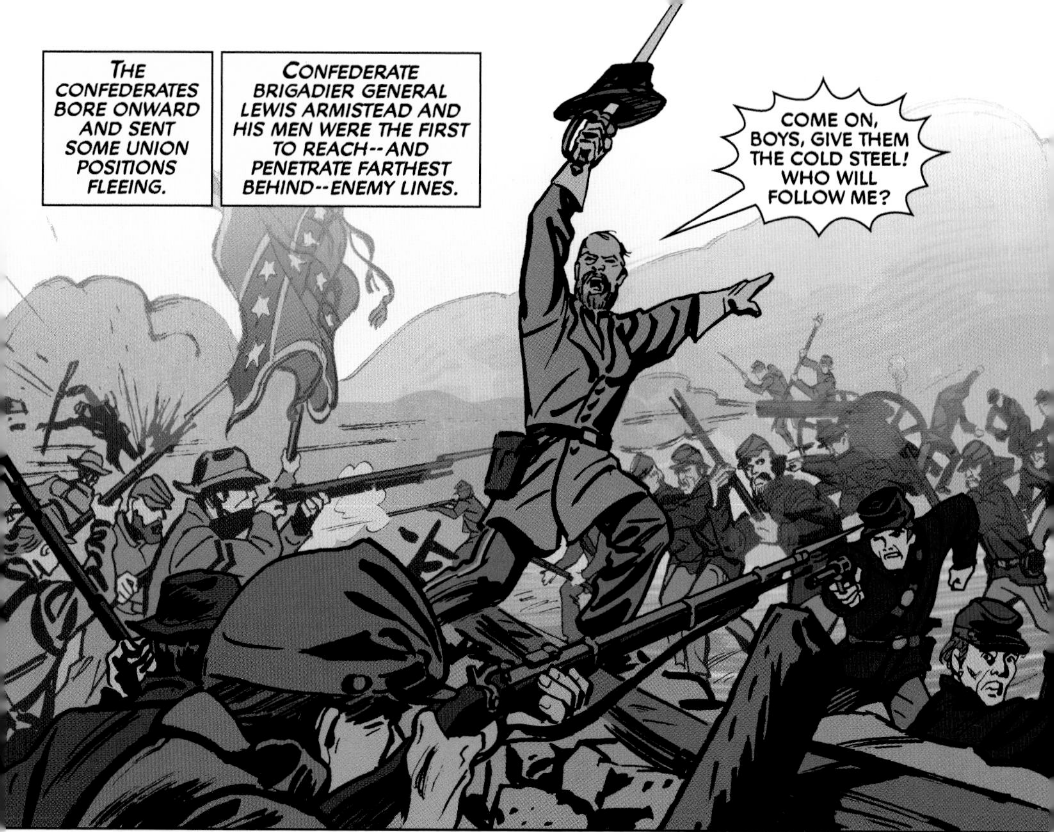
THE CONFEDERATES BORE ONWARD AND SENT SOME UNION POSITIONS FLEEING.
CONFEDERATE BRIGADIER GENERAL LEWIS ARMISTEAD AND HIS MEN WERE THE FIRST TO REACH--AND PENETRATE FARTHEST BEHIND--ENEMY LINES.
COME ON, BOYS, GIVE THEM THE COLD STEEL! WHO WILL FOLLOW ME?

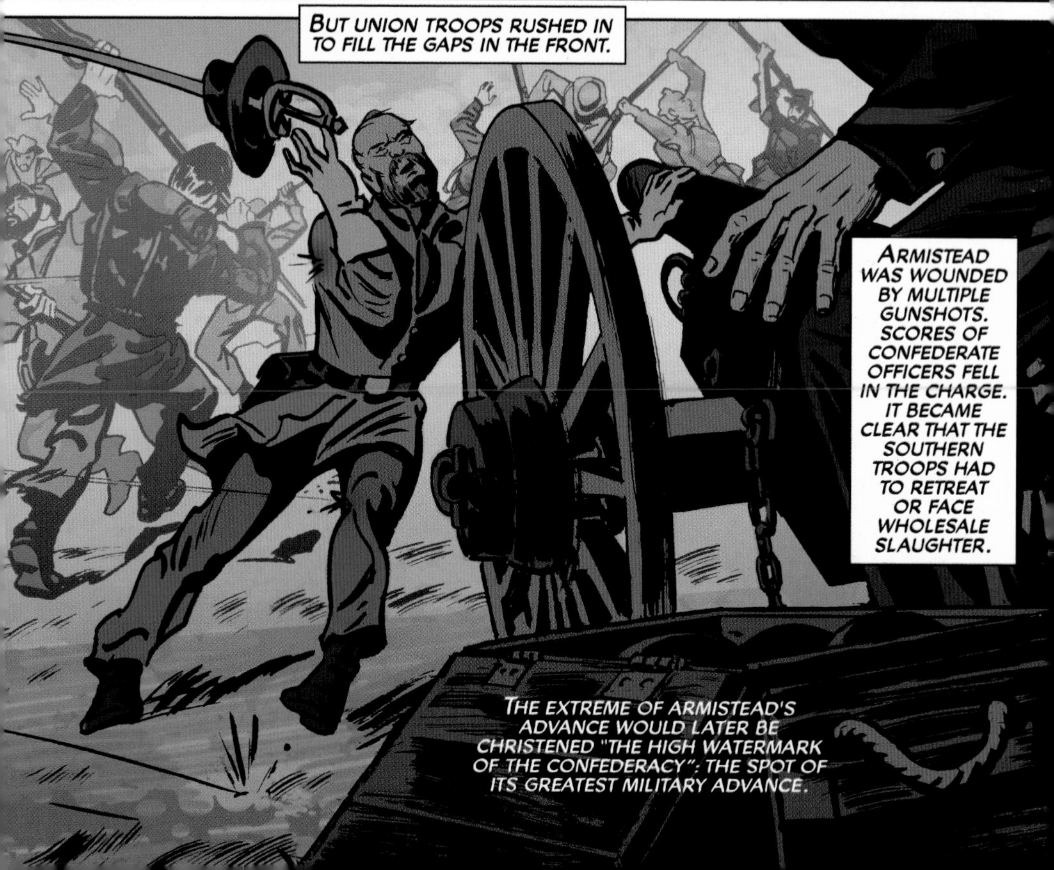
BUT UNION TROOPS RUSHED IN TO FILL THE GAPS IN THE FRONT.
ARMISTEAD WAS WOUNDED BY MULTIPLE GUNSHOTS. SCORES OF CONFEDERATE OFFICERS FELL IN THE CHARGE. IT BECAME CLEAR THAT THE SOUTHERN TROOPS HAD TO RETREAT OR FACE WHOLESALE SLAUGHTER.
THE EXTREME OF ARMISTEAD'S ADVANCE WOULD LATER BE CHRISTENED "THE HIGH WATERMARK OF THE CONFEDERACY": THE SPOT OF ITS GREATEST MILITARY ADVANCE.

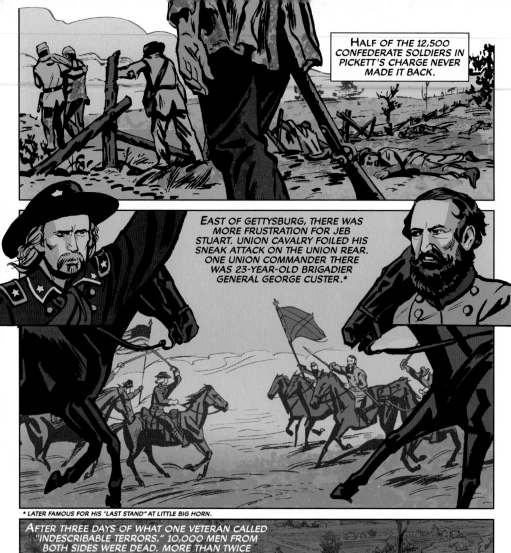

HALF OF THE 12,500 CONFEDERATE SOLDIERS IN PICKETT'S CHARGE NEVER MADE IT BACK.

EAST OF GETTYSBURG, THERE WAS MORE FRUSTRATION FOR JEB STUART. UNION CAVALRY FOILED HIS SNEAK ATTACK ON THE UNION REAR. ONE UNION COMMANDER THERE WAS 23-YEAR-OLD BRIGADIER GENERAL GEORGE CUSTER.*

* LATER FAMOUS FOR HIS "LAST STAND" AT LITTLE BIG HORN.

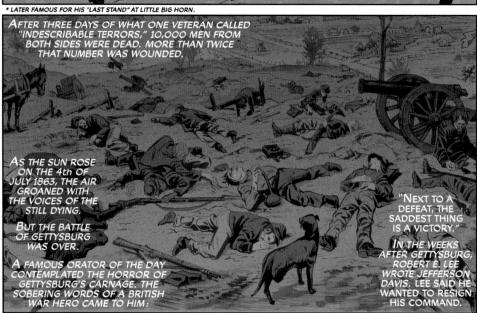

AFTER THREE DAYS OF WHAT ONE VETERAN CALLED "INDESCRIBABLE TERRORS," 10,000 MEN FROM BOTH SIDES WERE DEAD. MORE THAN TWICE THAT NUMBER WAS WOUNDED.

AS THE SUN ROSE ON THE 4th OF JULY 1863, THE AIR GROANED WITH THE VOICES OF THE STILL DYING.

BUT THE BATTLE OF GETTYSBURG WAS OVER.

A FAMOUS ORATOR OF THE DAY CONTEMPLATED THE HORROR OF GETTYSBURG'S CARNAGE. THE SOBERING WORDS OF A BRITISH WAR HERO CAME TO HIM:

"NEXT TO A DEFEAT, THE SADDEST THING IS A VICTORY."

IN THE WEEKS AFTER GETTYSBURG, ROBERT E. LEE WROTE JEFFERSON DAVIS. LEE SAID HE WANTED TO RESIGN HIS COMMAND.

IMMEDIATELY AFTER THE BATTLE, THE ARMY OF NORTHERN VIRGINIA FACED A 45-MILE RETREAT...

...MADE ARDUOUS BY 700-FOOT PEAKS, DRIVING RAIN, WASHED-OUT ROADS, ENEMY PURSUERS, AND THE LOOMING THREAT THAT THE POTOMAC RIVER WOULD FLOOD AND LEAVE THEM SITTING DUCKS.

THE CONFEDERATES ALSO HAD TO TRANSPORT PRISONERS, LIVESTOCK, AND A VAST NUMBER OF THEIR OWN WOUNDED AND SICK.

MORE THAN 6,000 OF LEE'S MEN TOO ILL OR INJURED TO MOVE WERE LEFT BEHIND.

LEE PLANNED TO ESCAPE BACK TO VIRGINIA BY THE SAME BRIDGE HIS ENGINEERS HAD BUILT TO LAUNCH THE INVASION.

BUT A SMALL FORCE OF UNION SOLDIERS HAD AMBUSHED THE BRIDGE ON JULY 4. IT WAS CUT TO PIECES AND BURNED.

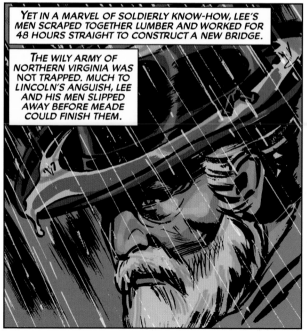

YET IN A MARVEL OF SOLDIERLY KNOW-HOW, LEE'S MEN SCRAPED TOGETHER LUMBER AND WORKED FOR 48 HOURS STRAIGHT TO CONSTRUCT A NEW BRIDGE.

THE WILY ARMY OF NORTHERN VIRGINIA WAS NOT TRAPPED. MUCH TO LINCOLN'S ANGUISH, LEE AND HIS MEN SLIPPED AWAY BEFORE MEADE COULD FINISH THEM.

WHEN LEE TRIED TO RESIGN, JEFFERSON DAVIS RESPONDED...

TO ASK ME TO SUBSTITUTE YOU BY SOME ONE IN MY JUDGMENT MORE FIT TO COMMAND, OR WHO WOULD POSSESS MORE OF THE CONFIDENCE OF THE ARMY... IS TO DEMAND AN IMPOSSIBILITY.

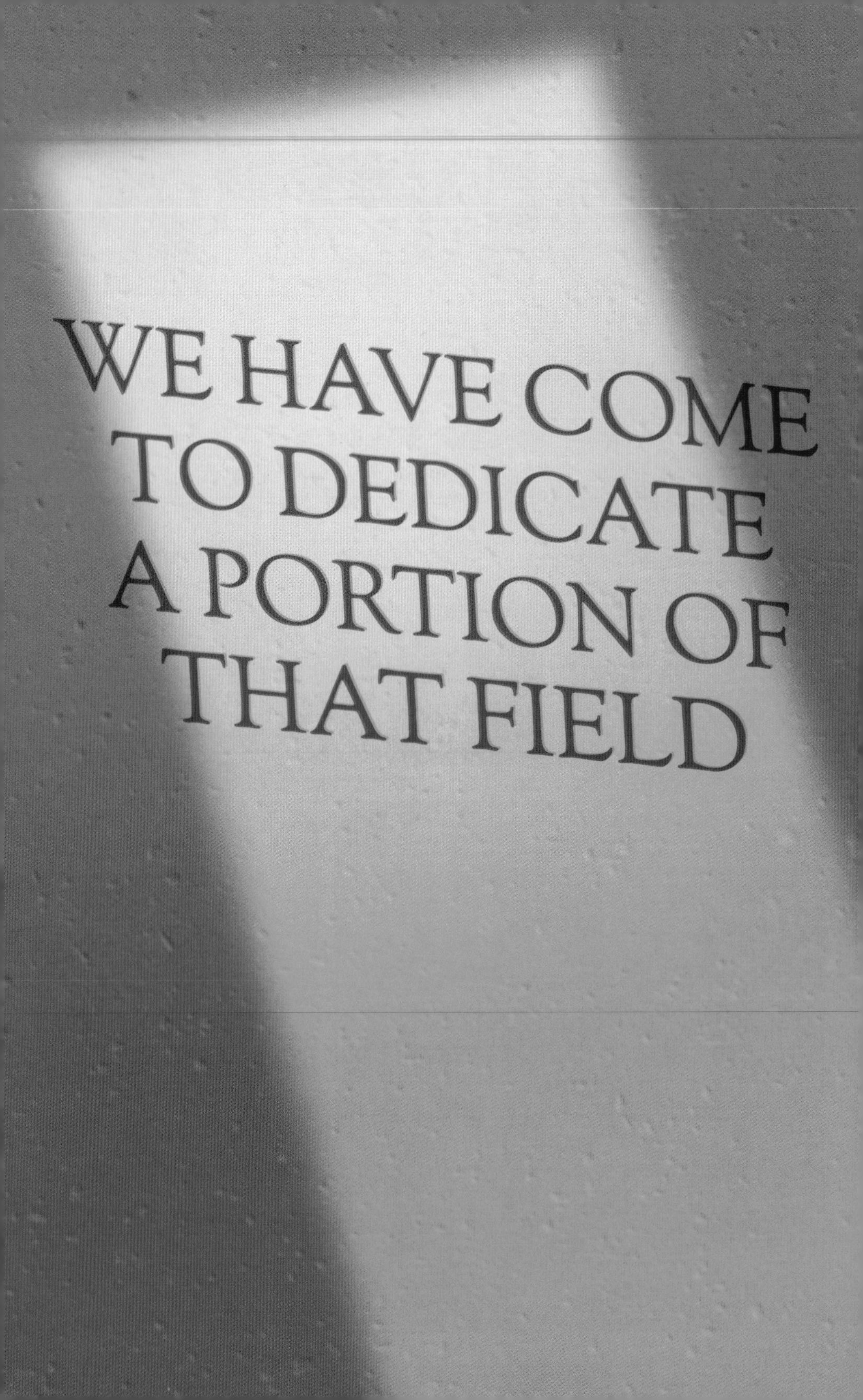
WE HAVE COME
TO DEDICATE
A PORTION OF
THAT FIELD

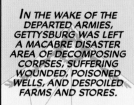

IN THE WAKE OF THE DEPARTED ARMIES, GETTYSBURG WAS LEFT A MACABRE DISASTER AREA OF DECOMPOSING CORPSES, SUFFERING WOUNDED, POISONED WELLS, AND DESPOILED FARMS AND STORES.

RELIEF WORKERS AND THOSE SEARCHING FOR LOVED ONES FLOODED IN.

RIGHT. WHAT I HEARD WAS THAT THOSE MEN FROM THE ANDREWS SHARPSHOOTERS WERE BURIED OVER HERE BY...

PARDON ME. ARE YOU THE GENTLE-MEN SENT BY THE BOSTON CITY COUNCIL?

AT YOUR SERVICE.

THIS IS JANE CLARK, OF HARRISBURG. SHE IS THE WIFE OF A SOLDIER FROM YOUR STATE'S 13TH REGIMENT...

...A MISSING SOLDIER.

I'VE HAD NO NEWS OF HIM SINCE THE 1st OF JULY.

THEY SAY YOU'VE BEEN SENT TO FIND AND BURY DEAD MASSACHUSETTS MEN. CAN YOU HELP ME?

YEP. THE 13th HAD A HARD TIME OF IT RIGHT ABOUT HERE ON JULY 1.

HERE, EVERYONE. I JUST FOUND A MARKER.

CHLORIDE OF LIME

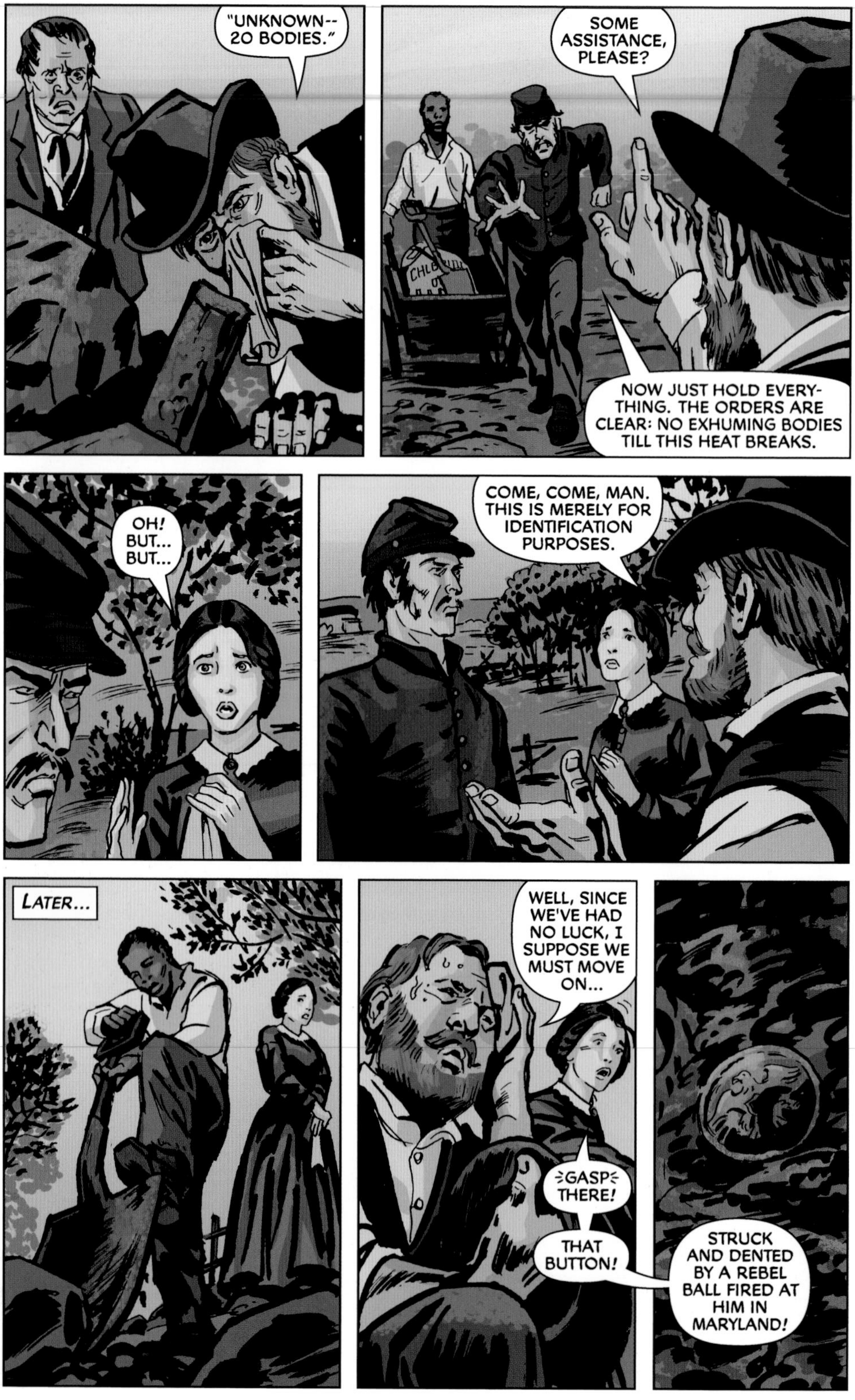
"UNKNOWN--
20 BODIES."
SOME ASSISTANCE, PLEASE?
NOW JUST HOLD EVERY-THING. THE ORDERS ARE CLEAR: NO EXHUMING BODIES TILL THIS HEAT BREAKS.
OH! BUT... BUT...
COME, COME, MAN. THIS IS MERELY FOR IDENTIFICATION PURPOSES.
LATER...
WELL, SINCE WE'VE HAD NO LUCK, I SUPPOSE WE MUST MOVE ON...
GASP THERE!
THAT BUTTON!
STRUCK AND DENTED BY A REBEL BALL FIRED AT HIM IN MARYLAND!

HE SAID HE WAS GOING TO SEND IT TO ME AS A MEMENTO.

≈SOB≈ IT'S HIM!

SOME DEAD WERE TAKEN HOME TO BE BURIED. BUT THOUSANDS MORE WERE NEVER CLAIMED OR EVEN IDENTIFIED.

AN IDEA WAS HATCHED FOR PENNSYLVANIA AND OTHER UNION STATES TO CREATE A "SOLDIERS' NATIONAL CEMETERY" FOR THE BODIES STILL AT GETTYSBURG.

(CONFEDERATE DEAD WERE EXEMPTED. INSTEAD, THEY WERE MOSTLY BURIED, BY THE SCORE, IN TRENCHES. AFTER THE WAR, SOUTHERN AID SOCIETIES EXHUMED ALL CONFEDERATE SOLDIERS THEY COULD FIND AND REBURIED THEM IN THEIR HOMEPLACES.)

FOR REASONS BOTH PERSONAL AND POLITICAL, LINCOLN AGREED TO HELP DEDICATE THE NEW CEMETERY AT A NOVEMBER 19, 1863, CEREMONY.

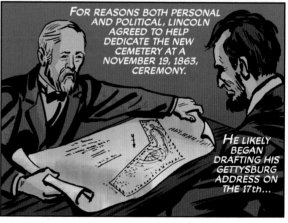

HE LIKELY BEGAN DRAFTING HIS GETTYSBURG ADDRESS ON THE 17th...

...JUST OVER A WEEK AFTER LINCOLN ATTENDED A PLAY AT WASHINGTON'S FORD'S THEATRE: THE MARBLE HEART, STARRING POPULAR ACTOR JOHN WILKES BOOTH.

Monday Evening, November 9, 1863,

MARBLE HEART!

Or, The Sculptor's Dream:

SUPERIOR CAST:

ACT I THE DREAM.

PHIDIAS, the Sculptor · · · · JOHN WILKES BOOTH

ONE FOLK LEGEND HAS LONG SURROUNDED THE GETTYSBURG ADDRESS...

...NAMELY THAT LINCOLN, IN A FLASH OF INSPIRATION, SCRAWLED THE SPEECH ON A NAPKIN OR PAPER SCRAP DURING THE RAIL TRIP TO GETTYSBURG.

WHILE NO ONE KNOWS EXACTLY WHEN LINCOLN BEGAN THE ADDRESS, THIS COMMON MYTH IS ALMOST CERTAINLY FALSE.

LINCOLN WAS A METICULOUS WORDSMITH. IT WAS NOT HIS NATURE TO COMPOSE ANYTHING SO HASTILY.

THE "NAPKIN" FABLE-- ONE THAT GENERATIONS HAVE TAKEN FOR GRANTED AS TRUE-- CAN ACTUALLY BE TRACED TO A WORK OF FICTION:

THE PERFECT TRIBUTE

A SHORT STORY WRITTEN AROUND 1906 BY THE NOW-OBSCURE AUTHOR MARY RAYMOND SHIPMAN ANDREWS.

THE PERFECT TRIBUTE

"Mr. Seward, may I have this to do a little writing?"

"NICKELODEONS" AND SILENT, SHORT-SUBJECT MOVIES LIKE THIS WERE BECOMING POPULAR AROUND THE TIME ANDREWS'S STORY WAS FIRST PUBLISHED.

DROVES OF VISITORS CRAMMED INTO GETTYSBURG ON THE EVE OF THE CEMETERY DEDICATION. REVELERS LENT THE TOWN A PARTY ATMOSPHERE.

I THANK MY GOD FOR THE HOPE THAT THIS IS THE LAST FRATRICIDAL WAR WHICH WILL FALL UPON THE COUNTRY...

...THE MOST BEAUTIFUL, MOST MAGNIFICENT... THAT HAS EVER BEEN GIVEN TO ANY PART OF THE HUMAN RACE!

HEAR!

HEAR!

CLAP CLAP

CLAP CLAP

CLAP

CLAP

WILLIAM H. SEWARD, SECRETARY OF STATE, 1863.

LINCOLN PROBABLY SPENT PART OF THE NIGHT WORKING ON HIS SPEECH.

THE MORNING OF NOVEMBER 19, THE PRESIDENT-- DRESSED IN BLACK-- TOURED THE BATTLEFIELD. LATER, ON HORSEBACK, HE JOINED A SOMBER PARADE TOWARD THE CEMETERY.

MOST EARLY AMERICAN PRESIDENTS WOULD HAVE HAD A VERY DIFFERENT SORT OF BURIAL GROUND WAITING FOR THEM ON SUCH AN OCCASSION.

THE SOLDIERS' NATIONAL CEMETERY AT GETTYSBURG WAS PART OF SOMETHING NEW...

...FOR LIKE MANY ASPECTS OF LIFE IN THE 1800s, THE MANNER OF BURYING THE DEAD HAD DRAMATICALLY CHANGED.

LINCOLN WANTED THE GETTYSBURG ADDRESS TO BE PROFOUND. WHAT HE MAY NOT HAVE REALIZED WAS THAT THE CEMETERY ITSELF WAS ITS OWN STIRRING MEDITATION ON THE SOUL OF AMERICA.

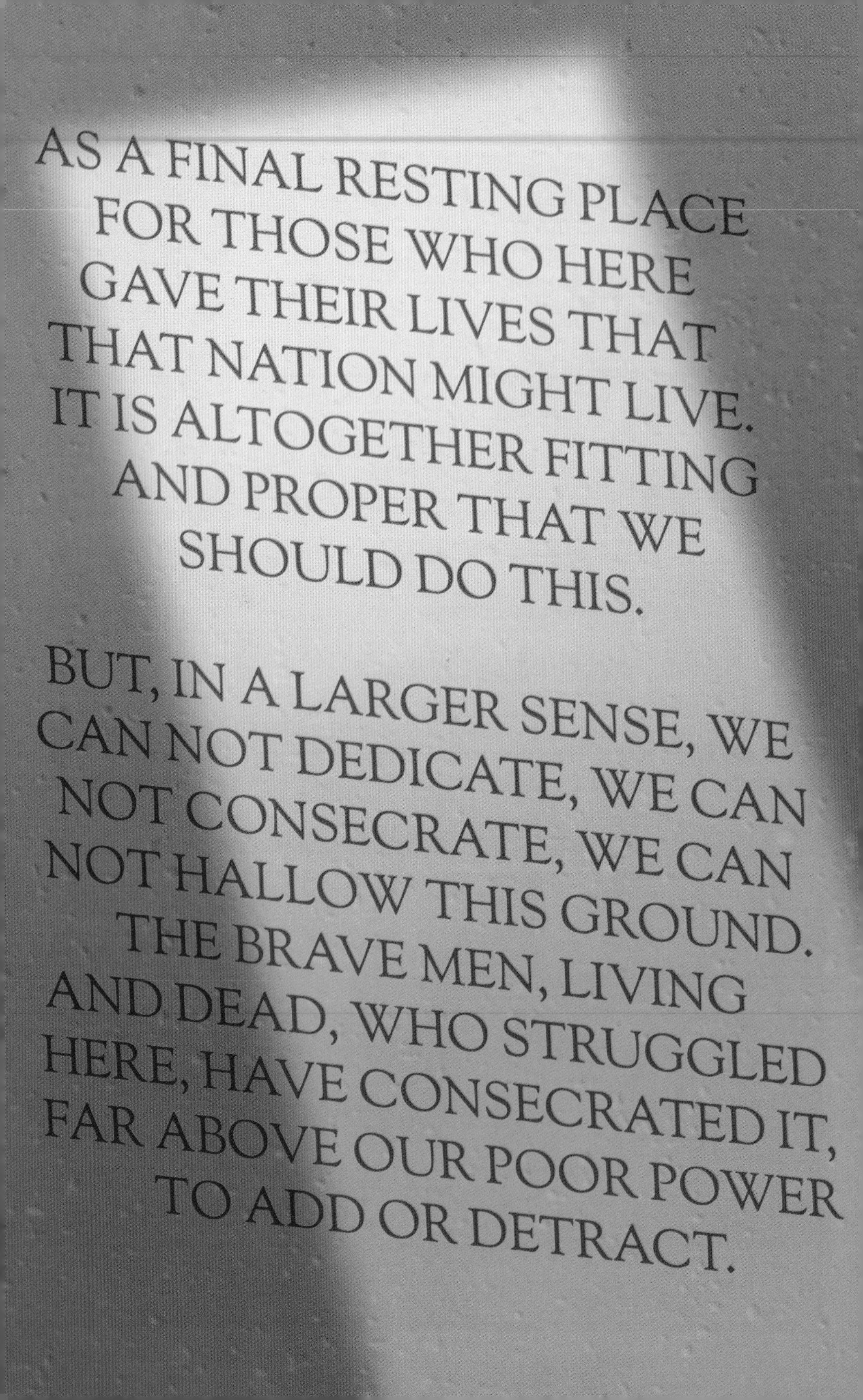
AS A FINAL RESTING PLACE
FOR THOSE WHO HERE
GAVE THEIR LIVES THAT
THAT NATION MIGHT LIVE.
IT IS ALTOGETHER FITTING
AND PROPER THAT WE
SHOULD DO THIS.
BUT, IN A LARGER SENSE, WE
CAN NOT DEDICATE, WE CAN
NOT CONSECRATE, WE CAN
NOT HALLOW THIS GROUND.
THE BRAVE MEN, LIVING
AND DEAD, WHO STRUGGLED
HERE, HAVE CONSECRATED IT,
FAR ABOVE OUR POOR POWER
TO ADD OR DETRACT.

FOR CENTURIES, MOST AMERICANS' "FINAL RESTING PLACES" WERE BLEAK GRAVEYARDS DESIGNED TO PROVOKE DISGUST AND FEAR.

IN TOWNS AND CITIES, THE DECEASED WERE CROWDED INTO CHURCHYARDS AND VACANT LOTS-- WHERE "MOURNERS SINK ANKLE DEEP IN A RANK AND OFFENSIVE MOULD, MIXED WITH BROKEN BONES AND FRAGMENTS OF COFFINS."

AS CITIES EXPANDED, CORPSES WERE CALLOUSLY PITCHED AWAY.

OFTEN, THE WORDS ENGRAVED INTO HEADSTONES FORCED THE READER TO PONDER THE GRIMNESS AND FINALITY OF DEATH.

"ALL YOU THAT DOTH MY GRAVE PASS BY,
AS YOU ARE NOW SO ONCE WAS I
AS I AM NOW SO YOU MUST BE,
PREPARE FOR DEATH & FOLLOW ME"

THIS APPROACH WAS INTENDED TO FRIGHTEN SINNERS TO REPENT TO A PURITANICAL GOD.

BUT IN THE TIME OF THE CIVIL WAR, A NEW PHILOSOPHY ABOUT LIFE AND NATURE WAS TAKING HOLD. AND IT CHANGED HOW AMERICA THOUGHT ABOUT-- AND BURIED-- THE DEAD.

IN THE ERA OF THE FOUNDING FATHERS, MEN WERE LARGELY SEEN AS IGNORANT, SELF-SERVING CREATURES.

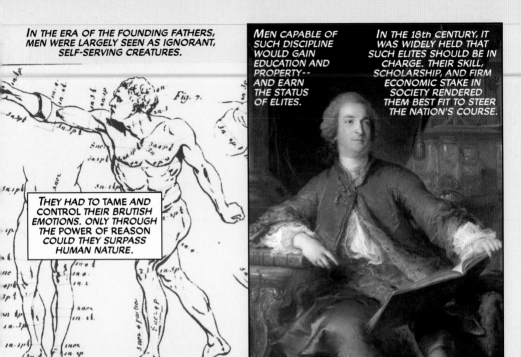

THEY HAD TO TAME AND CONTROL *THEIR BRUTISH EMOTIONS.* ONLY THROUGH THE POWER OF REASON COULD THEY SURPASS HUMAN NATURE.

MEN CAPABLE OF SUCH DISCIPLINE WOULD GAIN EDUCATION AND PROPERTY-- AND EARN THE STATUS OF ELITES.

IN THE 18th CENTURY, IT WAS WIDELY HELD THAT SUCH ELITES SHOULD BE IN CHARGE. THEIR SKILL, SCHOLARSHIP, AND FIRM ECONOMIC STAKE IN SOCIETY RENDERED THEM BEST FIT TO STEER THE NATION'S COURSE.

THIS NOTION WAS PARTICULARLY LONG-LIVED IN THE SOUTH, WHERE THE LANDED GENTRY DOMINATED LOCAL POLITICS: "MASTERS" OF SLAVES, PLANTATIONS, FAMILIES, AND THEIR OWN SELVES.

BUT OVER THE COURSE OF THE 19th CENTURY, THIS ATTITUDE SHIFTED. A REVERENCE FOR PASSION OVER REASON WAS BORN. ELITISM GAVE WAY TO EGALITARIANISM.

Concord River.

The actual experience of even the most ordinary life is full of events that never explain themselves, either as regards their origin or their tendency.

The Marble Faun.

A NEW ROMANTICISM CHAMPIONED THE IDEA THAT PEOPLE ARE INHERENTLY GOOD.

STRONG AND COMPLICATED EMOTIONS WERE NOT REJECTED, BUT EMBRACED.

TO ROMANTICS, NEITHER NATURE NOR HUMAN EMOTION WAS SEEN AS A DANGEROUS ADVERSARY TO BE CONQUERED.

THEY WERE THE HANDIWORK OF A LOVING GOD. THEY WERE TO BE COMMUNED WITH...

...IN WAYS THAT ELEVATED THE DEAD AND EDIFIED THE LIVING.

...WHY SHOULD WE THUS SEEK TO CLOTHE DEATH WITH UNNECESSARY TERRORS, AND TO SPREAD HORRORS ROUND THE TOMB OF THOSE WE LOVE?

THE GRAVE SHOULD BE SURROUNDED BY EVERY THING THAT MIGHT INSPIRE TENDERNESS AND VENERATION FOR THE DEAD; OR THAT MIGHT WIN THE LIVING TO VIRTUE.

WASHINGTON IRVING, 1820.

SO GRAVEYARDS BECAME OBSOLETE. THE REVOLTING LOTS OF FORSAKEN CORPSES WERE REPLACED BY FINE CEMETERIES.

"CEMETERY" IS FROM THE GREEK WORD KOIMETERION (A SLEEPING PLACE OR DORMITORY). IT IMPLIES PEACEFUL "REST" RATHER THAN DEATH.

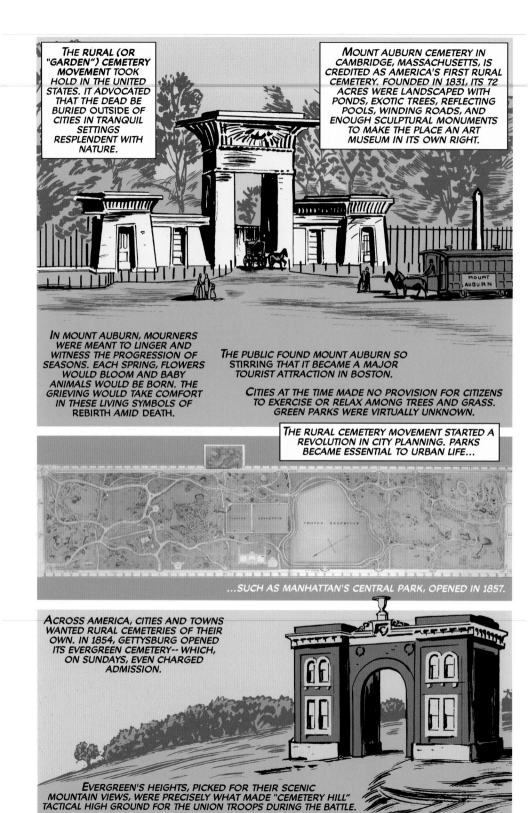

THE RURAL (OR "GARDEN") CEMETERY MOVEMENT TOOK HOLD IN THE UNITED STATES. IT ADVOCATED THAT THE DEAD BE BURIED OUTSIDE OF CITIES IN TRANQUIL SETTINGS RESPLENDENT WITH NATURE.

MOUNT AUBURN CEMETERY IN CAMBRIDGE, MASSACHUSETTS, IS CREDITED AS AMERICA'S FIRST RURAL CEMETERY. FOUNDED IN 1831, ITS 72 ACRES WERE LANDSCAPED WITH PONDS, EXOTIC TREES, REFLECTING POOLS, WINDING ROADS, AND ENOUGH SCULPTURAL MONUMENTS TO MAKE THE PLACE AN ART MUSEUM IN ITS OWN RIGHT.

IN MOUNT AUBURN, MOURNERS WERE MEANT TO LINGER AND WITNESS THE PROGRESSION OF SEASONS. EACH SPRING, FLOWERS WOULD BLOOM AND BABY ANIMALS WOULD BE BORN. THE GRIEVING WOULD TAKE COMFORT IN THESE LIVING SYMBOLS OF REBIRTH AMID DEATH.

THE PUBLIC FOUND MOUNT AUBURN SO STIRRING THAT IT BECAME A MAJOR TOURIST ATTRACTION IN BOSTON.

CITIES AT THE TIME MADE NO PROVISION FOR CITIZENS TO EXERCISE OR RELAX AMONG TREES AND GRASS. GREEN PARKS WERE VIRTUALLY UNKNOWN.

THE RURAL CEMETERY MOVEMENT STARTED A REVOLUTION IN CITY PLANNING. PARKS BECAME ESSENTIAL TO URBAN LIFE...

...SUCH AS MANHATTAN'S CENTRAL PARK, OPENED IN 1857.

ACROSS AMERICA, CITIES AND TOWNS WANTED RURAL CEMETERIES OF THEIR OWN. IN 1854, GETTYSBURG OPENED ITS EVERGREEN CEMETERY-- WHICH, ON SUNDAYS, EVEN CHARGED ADMISSION.

EVERGREEN'S HEIGHTS, PICKED FOR THEIR SCENIC MOUNTAIN VIEWS, WERE PRECISELY WHAT MADE "CEMETERY HILL" TACTICAL HIGH GROUND FOR THE UNION TROOPS DURING THE BATTLE.

IN 1863, IT WAS A GIVEN THAT THE UNION'S SOLDIERS WHO DIED AT GETTYSBURG WOULD HAVE THEIR OWN RURAL-STYLE BURIAL SITE.

IN THE SOLDIERS' NATIONAL CEMETERY, ONLY SMALL, UNIFORM HEADSTONES WERE USED.

THIS REFLECTED THE ERA'S REJECTION OF ELITISM AND EMBRACE OF EGALITARIAN THINKING. ROMANTICS PLACED A HIGH VALUE ON HUMAN LIFE.

SOLDIERS OF BOTH HIGH AND LOW RANK-- AND THOSE FROM EVERY UNION STATE-- WERE ALL TO BE TREATED THE SAME...

...SOMETHING THAT ALSO STRUCK A CHORD WITH LINCOLN'S CONTENTION THAT "ALL MEN ARE CREATED EQUAL."

(THOUGH CONFEDERATE SOLDIERS WERE EXCLUDED FROM THE CEMETERY, LINCOLN'S GETTYSBURG ADDRESS STILL PAYS THEM HOMAGE. THE SPEECH JUDICIOUSLY USES ONLY ALL-INCLUSIVE TERMS LIKE "BRAVE MEN"-- NOT "BRAVE UNION MEN.")

THE HEADSTONES ALSO KEPT THE CEMETERY FROM ECLIPSING ITS NATURAL SETTING.

ROMANTICS BELIEVED IN THE SUPERIORITY OF NATURE. ITS CONSTANT CYCLE OF DEATH AND REBIRTH WOULD "HALLOW" AND "CONSECRATE" THE DEAD.

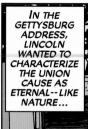

IN THE GETTYSBURG ADDRESS, LINCOLN WANTED TO CHARACTERIZE THE UNION CAUSE AS ETERNAL--LIKE NATURE...

...AND THE BATTLE DEAD NOT AS VANISHED FROM THE EARTH BUT HAVING ATTAINED IMMORTALITY THROUGH THEIR SACRIFICE.

THE RURAL CEMETERIES (AND URBAN PARKS) RESPONDED TO PEOPLE'S YEARNING FOR NATURE AND A SIMPLER PAST. THEY DID SO AT A TIME OF GROWING ANXIETY ABOUT THE AMERICAN DREAM.

THUS THE SPEECH IS FULL OF WORDS AND SYMBOLS SUGGESTING BIRTH AND REBIRTH.

OUR **FATHERS BROUGHT FORTH** A NEW NATION

CONCEIVED IN LIBERTY

NEW BIRTH OF FREEDOM

AS WE KNOW, BEFORE THE CIVIL WAR, MANY FELT THAT LAND AND OPPORTUNITY WERE RAPIDLY DISAPPEARING. THE PEOPLE OF THE SOUTH AND THE NORTH WERE, IN A WAY, MOURNING THE LOSS OF THE UNSPOILED EARLY REPUBLIC.

TO SURVIVE, FREE LABOR AND SLAVE LABOR BOTH LOOKED TO WHERE NATURE WAS STILL MOST ABUNDANT: THE WESTERN TERRITORIES.

UNCLE SAM HAS LAND ENOUGH TO GIVE US EACH A FARM

WIDE AWAKE

THE RESULTING LAND GRAB, OF COURSE, HELPED JUMP-START THE WAR.

BUT WHEN THE FIGHTING WAS OVER, THE WEST WOULD ALSO HELP RECONCILE AMERICA IN A NEWFOUND PEACE.

REPUBLICAN PARTY RALLY, NEW YORK CITY, 1860.

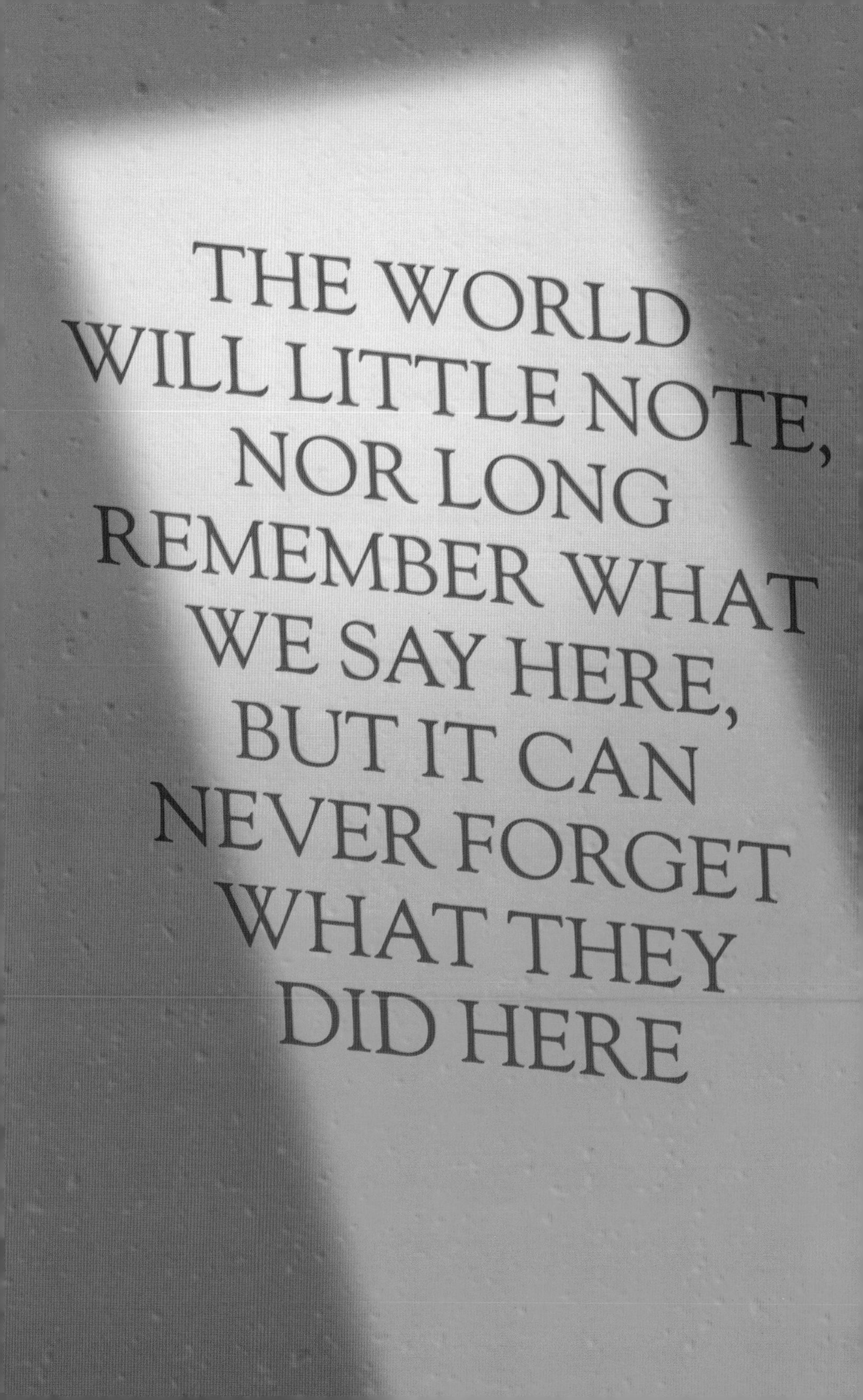
THE WORLD
WILL LITTLE NOTE,
NOR LONG
REMEMBER WHAT
WE SAY HERE,
BUT IT CAN
NEVER FORGET
WHAT THEY
DID HERE

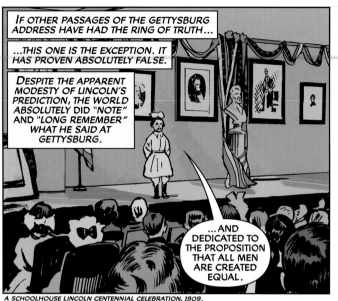

IF OTHER PASSAGES OF THE GETTYSBURG ADDRESS HAVE HAD THE RING OF TRUTH...

...THIS ONE IS THE EXCEPTION. IT HAS PROVEN ABSOLUTELY FALSE.

DESPITE THE APPARENT MODESTY OF LINCOLN'S PREDICTION, THE WORLD ABSOLUTELY DID "NOTE" AND "LONG REMEMBER" WHAT HE SAID AT GETTYSBURG.

...AND DEDICATED TO THE PROPOSITION THAT ALL MEN ARE CREATED EQUAL.

A SCHOOLHOUSE LINCOLN CENTENNIAL CELEBRATION, 1909.

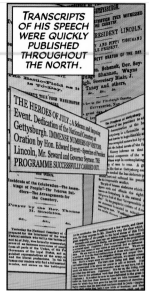

TRANSCRIPTS OF HIS SPEECH WERE QUICKLY PUBLISHED THROUGHOUT THE NORTH.

REPUBLICAN NEWSPAPER EDITORS PRAISED IT. BUT DEMOCRATIC PARTY PUBLICATIONS TENDED TO DENOUNCE THE ADDRESS. FOR EXAMPLE, THE CHICAGO TIMES CALLED LINCOLN'S PRONOUNCEMENT THAT THE UNITED STATES WAS FOUNDED ON THE EQUALITY OF ALL MEN A "FLAGRANT" "PERVERSION OF HISTORY."

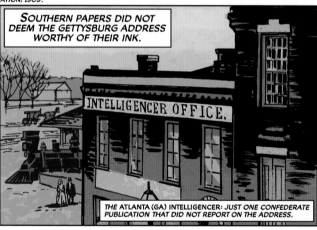

SOUTHERN PAPERS DID NOT DEEM THE GETTYSBURG ADDRESS WORTHY OF THEIR INK.

INTELLIGENCER OFFICE.

THE ATLANTA (GA) INTELLIGENCER: JUST ONE CONFEDERATE PUBLICATION THAT DID NOT REPORT ON THE ADDRESS.

SINCE 1863, THE GETTYSBURG ADDRESS HAS BEEN ENDLESSLY REPRODUCED, MEMORIZED, ANALYZED, TRANSLATED, AND CELEBRATED AROUND THE WORLD.

IN 1913, THE BRITISH CHANCELLOR OF OXFORD UNIVERSITY PRAISED IT AS "THE MASTERPIECE OF MODERN ENGLISH ELOQUENCE."

THE MORE CLOSELY THE ADDRESS IS ANALYZED THE MORE ONE MUST CONFESS ASTONISHMENT AT ITS CHOICE OF WORDS, THE PRECISION OF ITS THOUGHT, ITS SIMPLICITY, DIRECTNESS, AND EFFECTIVENESS.

IN 1978, ISRAELI PRIME MINISTER MENACHEM BEGIN-- BORN IN RUSSIA AND EDUCATED IN POLAND-- SURPRISED FIRST LADY ROSALYNN CARTER BY RECITING THE SPEECH FROM MEMORY.

WE ARE MET ON A GREAT BATTLEFIELD OF THAT WAR...

THE GLORIFICATION OF THE GETTYSBURG ADDRESS IS EVEN MORE NOTEWORTHY GIVEN THE FACT THAT LINCOLN WAS NOT THE "HEADLINER" AT THE CEMETERY DEDICATION.

GIVEN THE BURDEN OF WAR AND THE DEMANDS OF HIS OFFICE, HE WOULD LIKELY HAVE BEEN CRITICIZED FOR MAKING A LONG, ELABORATE SPEECH.

BUT IN THIS ERA BEFORE RECORDED MUSIC, MOVIES, AND RADIO, LONG AND ELABORATE SPEECHES WERE MAINSTREAM ENTERTAINMENT. ORATORS BASKED IN CELEBRITY STATUS-- LIKE POP STARS.

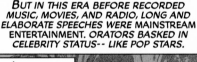

AND THEIR LECTURES WOULD SEEM OUTLANDISHLY LONG TO OUR 21st-CENTURY ATTENTION SPANS.

AT THE NATIONAL CEMETERY DEDICATION, THE "STAR" ORATOR WAS EDWARD EVERETT...

...FORMER PRESIDENT OF HARVARD UNIVERSITY, SECRETARY OF STATE, AND MASSACHUSETTS GOVERNOR, SENATOR, AND CONGRESSMAN.

EVERETT

EVERETT'S SPEECH HAS BEEN CALLED "THE FORGOTTEN GETTYSBURG ADDRESS." SO LINCOLN'S PREDICTION THAT THE SPEAKERS' WORDS WOULD NOT BE "LONG REMEMBERED" WAS AT LEAST PARTIALLY CORRECT.

EVERETT LECTURED FOR MORE THAN 2 HOURS AND ENTIRELY FROM MEMORY.

HIS SPEECH WAS FAR MORE PARTISAN THAN LINCOLN'S. EVERETT'S LABELED CONFEDERATES "DISLOYAL SLAVEHOLDERS" AND EVEN CALLED THEM "TRAITORS."

HE ALSO SOUGHT TO REFUTE A CENTRAL CONFEDERATE BELIEF: THAT SECESSION WAS AS MORALLY JUSTIFIABLE AS THE AMERICAN REVOLUTION.

WHAT WOULD HAVE BEEN THOUGHT BY AN IMPARTIAL POSTERITY OF THE AMERICAN REBELLION AGAINST GEORGE III, IF THE COLONISTS HAD AT ALL TIMES BEEN MORE THAN EQUALLY REPRESENTED IN PARLIAMENT...?

EVERETT POINTED OUT THAT, UNLIKE THE DISENFRANCHISED FOUNDERS...

...SOUTHERNERS HAD HELD GREAT SWAY IN THE FEDERAL GOVERNMENT SINCE ITS FOUNDING.

BEFORE LINCOLN, THERE HAD BEEN MORE SOUTHERN PRESIDENTS THAN NORTHERN ONES...

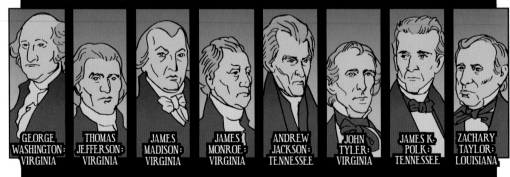

GEORGE WASHINGTON: VIRGINIA

THOMAS JEFFERSON: VIRGINIA

JAMES MADISON: VIRGINIA

JAMES MONROE: VIRGINIA

ANDREW JACKSON: TENNESSEE

JOHN TYLER: VIRGINIA

JAMES K. POLK: TENNESSEE

ZACHARY TAYLOR: LOUISIANA

SOUTHERNERS HAD ALSO MORE OFTEN THAN NOT CONTROLLED BOTH HOUSES OF CONGRESS. THEY HAD ALWAYS HAD A MAJORITY ON THE SUPREME COURT OF THE UNITED STATES.

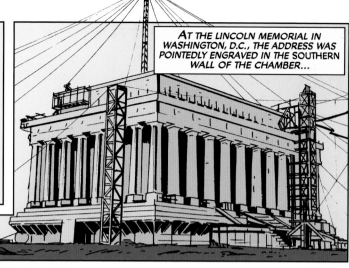

LINCOLN, WHO HOPED TO REUNITE NORTH AND SOUTH, DID NOT DWELL ON SUCH ISSUES. THE GETTYSBURG ADDRESS NEVER MENTIONS SLAVERY OR SECESSION. IT NEVER CRITICIZES THE CONFEDERATE GOVERNMENT OR ITS PEOPLE. IN FACT, NO SPEECH OF LINCOLN'S EVER CALLED SOUTHERNERS "TRAITORS."

AT THE LINCOLN MEMORIAL IN WASHINGTON, D.C., THE ADDRESS WAS POINTEDLY ENGRAVED IN THE SOUTHERN WALL OF THE CHAMBER...

...FOR MANY HAVE SEEN IT AS ACKNOWLEDGING THE SACRIFICE OF BOTH SIDES.

THE WORLD CAN NEVER FORGET WHAT THEY DID HERE.

EDWARD EVERETT BELIEVED THE SECTIONS WOULD PUT BLOODSHED BEHIND THEM.

THE BONDS THAT UNITE US AS A PEOPLE...

...ARE OF PERENNIAL FORCE AND ENERGY, WHILE THE CAUSES OF ALIENATION ARE IMAGINARY, FACTITIOUS AND TRANSIENT.

TODAY, SUCH OPTIMISM SEEMS VALID. BUT IN 1863, IT MIGHT HAVE LOOKED LIKE WISHFUL THINKING.

FOR THE CIVIL WAR HAD NO END IN SIGHT.

ARGUABLY, THE UNION RESOLVED THAT IT MUST BRING THE FULL BRUNT OF ITS GREATER NUMBERS AND RESOURCES. IT WOULD BLUDGEON AND STARVE THE CONFEDERACY INTO SUBMISSION.

IN RESPONSE, SOUTHERNERS FOUGHT MORE AND MORE LIKE MEN WITH NOTHING TO LOSE.

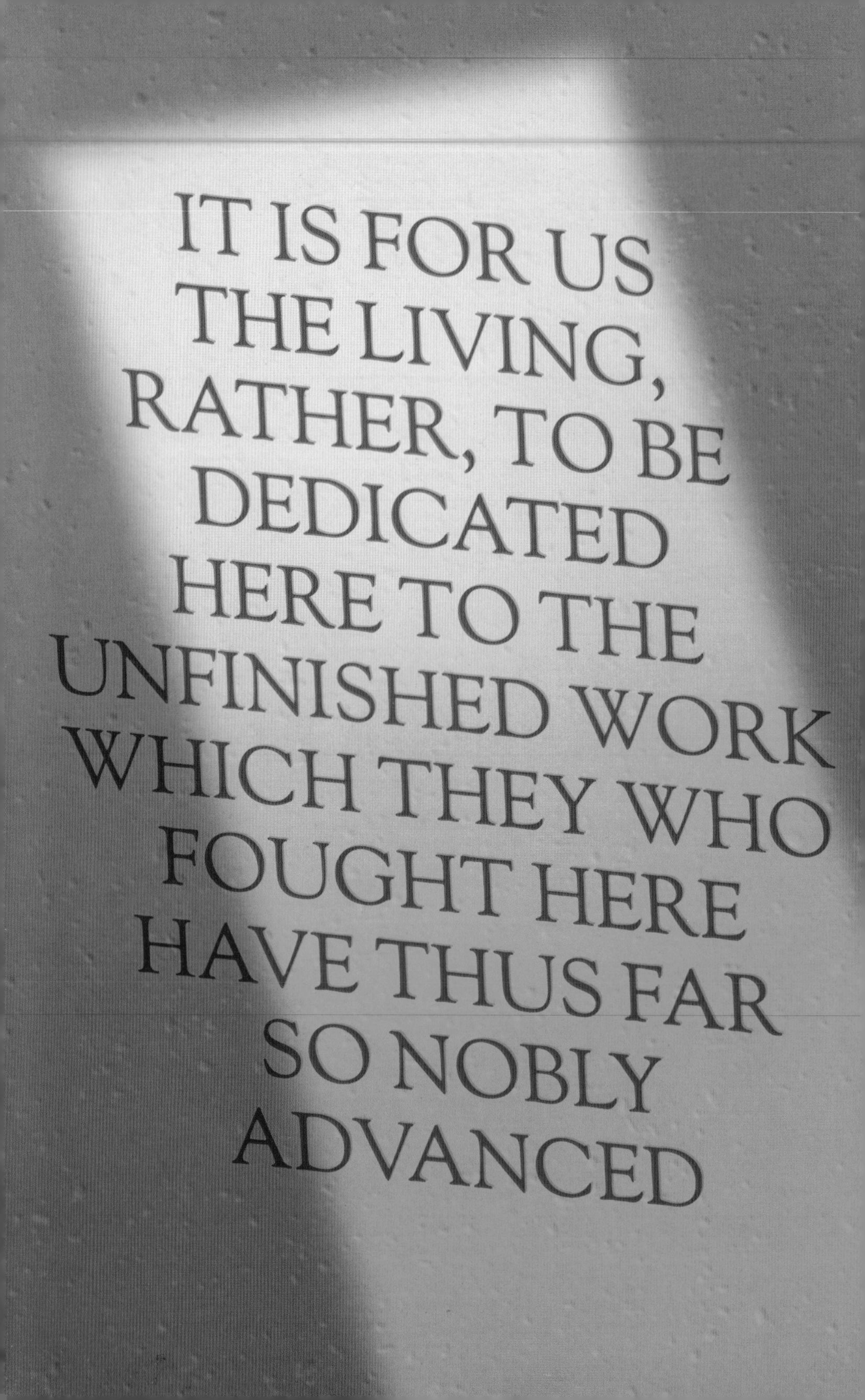
IT IS FOR US
THE LIVING,
RATHER, TO BE
DEDICATED
HERE TO THE
UNFINISHED WORK
WHICH THEY WHO
FOUGHT HERE
HAVE THUS FAR
SO NOBLY
ADVANCED

"UNFINISHED WORK": WAR

IN THE WEEKS AFTER THE BATTLE OF GETTYSBURG, UNIONISTS INDEED FACED A HARROWING AMOUNT OF "UNFINISHED WORK"...

DEFEAT OF UNION FORCES AT THE BATTLE OF CHICKAMAUGA (NORTHWESTERN GEORGIA, SEPTEMBER 1863).

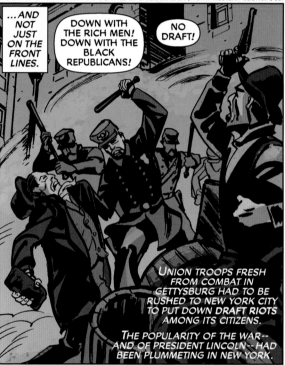

...AND NOT JUST ON THE FRONT LINES.

DOWN WITH THE RICH MEN! DOWN WITH THE BLACK REPUBLICANS!

NO DRAFT!

UNION TROOPS FRESH FROM COMBAT IN GETTYSBURG HAD TO BE RUSHED TO NEW YORK CITY TO PUT DOWN DRAFT RIOTS AMONG ITS CITIZENS.

THE POPULARITY OF THE WAR-- AND OF PRESIDENT LINCOLN-- HAD BEEN PLUMMETING IN NEW YORK.

SHOWING THE DEEP-SEATED RACISM OF MUCH OF THE NORTH, RIOTERS ATTACKED AFRICAN AMERICANS...

...WHOM THEY BLAMED FOR THE COUNTRY'S CRISIS.

THAT SAME RACISM HAD MADE LINCOLN HESITANT TO ALLOW BLACKS TO SERVE AS UNION SOLDIERS.

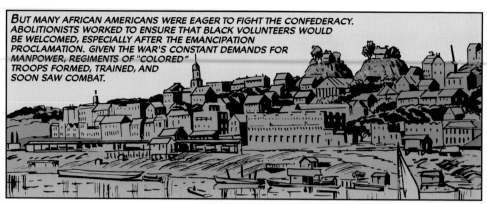

BUT MANY AFRICAN AMERICANS WERE EAGER TO FIGHT THE CONFEDERACY. ABOLITIONISTS WORKED TO ENSURE THAT BLACK VOLUNTEERS WOULD BE WELCOMED, ESPECIALLY AFTER THE EMANCIPATION PROCLAMATION. GIVEN THE WAR'S CONSTANT DEMANDS FOR MANPOWER, REGIMENTS OF "COLORED" TROOPS FORMED, TRAINED, AND SOON SAW COMBAT.

THOUSANDS OF FREED SLAVES CAME TO AID THE SIEGE OF THE KEY CONFEDERATE RIVER PORT OF VICKSBURG, MISSISSIPPI.

THESE NEW TROOPS PROVED THEMSELVES TO ONCE-DOUBTFUL WHITE SOLDIERS.

THE BRAVERY OF THE BLACKS AT MILLIKEN'S BEND COMPLETELY REVOLUTIONIZED THE SENTIMENT OF THE ARMY WITH REGARD TO EMPLOYMENT OF NEGRO TROOPS.

CHARLES A. DANA, U.S. ASSISTANT SECRETARY OF WAR, 1863.

WITH AFRICAN AMERICANS SERVING IN UNIFORM, HOPES THAT THE COUNTRY MIGHT REUNITE AND RETURN TO THE ANTEBELLUM STATUS QUO WERE DEAD ON ARRIVAL.

RATHER DIE FREEMAN THAN LIVE TO BE SLAVES

IF IT WERE TO RETURN EVEN A SINGLE UNION SOLDIER TO SLAVERY, UNION VICTORY WOULD BE A MOCKERY.

UNITED STATES COLORED TROOPS

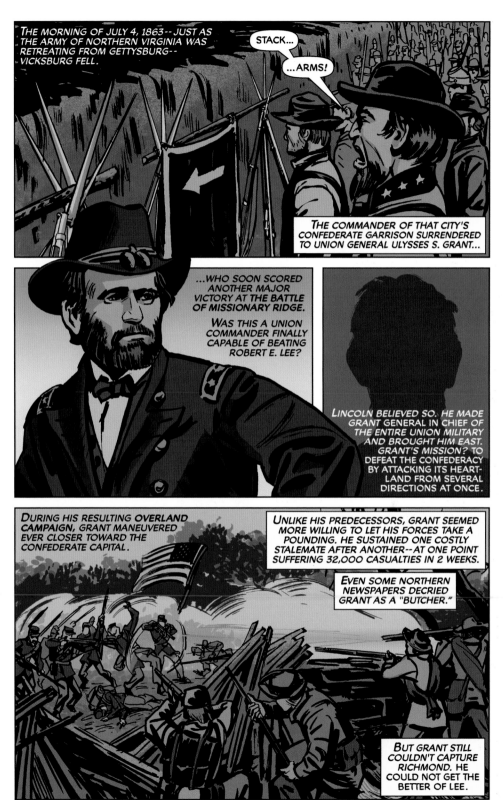

THE MORNING OF JULY 4, 1863-- JUST AS THE ARMY OF NORTHERN VIRGINIA WAS RETREATING FROM GETTYSBURG-- VICKSBURG FELL.

STACK...

...ARMS!

THE COMMANDER OF THAT CITY'S CONFEDERATE GARRISON SURRENDERED TO UNION GENERAL ULYSSES S. GRANT...

...WHO SOON SCORED ANOTHER MAJOR VICTORY AT THE BATTLE OF MISSIONARY RIDGE.

WAS THIS A UNION COMMANDER FINALLY CAPABLE OF BEATING ROBERT E. LEE?

LINCOLN BELIEVED SO. HE MADE GRANT GENERAL IN CHIEF OF THE ENTIRE UNION MILITARY AND BROUGHT HIM EAST. GRANT'S MISSION? TO DEFEAT THE CONFEDERACY BY ATTACKING ITS HEART-LAND FROM SEVERAL DIRECTIONS AT ONCE.

DURING HIS RESULTING OVERLAND CAMPAIGN, GRANT MANEUVERED EVER CLOSER TOWARD THE CONFEDERATE CAPITAL.

UNLIKE HIS PREDECESSORS, GRANT SEEMED MORE WILLING TO LET HIS FORCES TAKE A POUNDING. HE SUSTAINED ONE COSTLY STALEMATE AFTER ANOTHER-- AT ONE POINT SUFFERING 32,000 CASUALTIES IN 2 WEEKS.

EVEN SOME NORTHERN NEWSPAPERS DECRIED GRANT AS A "BUTCHER."

BUT GRANT STILL COULDN'T CAPTURE RICHMOND. HE COULD NOT GET THE BETTER OF LEE.

THE BATTLE OF COLD HARBOR (TEN MILES NORTHEAST OF RICHMOND, VIRGINIA), MAY-JUNE, 1864.

"UNFINISHED WORK": POLITICS

THE WAR'S DIM OUTLOOK...

There is very great discouragement [in] the North... strong disposition for peace, and even among republicans of long standing [an] inclination for a change of rulers.

UNION GENERAL JOHN H. MARTINDALE, 1864.

...CAST A GLOOM OVER THE QUESTION OF WHETHER LINCOLN WOULD BE REELECTED IN NOVEMBER 1864.

FRANKLY, MR. PRESIDENT, IT IS THE JUDGMENT OF ALL THE BEST POLITICIANS THAT YOU WON'T EVEN CARRY THREE STATES.

LEONARD SWETT, ADVISER TO PRESIDENT LINCOLN, 1864.

BUT THEN...

...THE TABLES TURNED.

THOOM!!

ON SEPTEMBER 1, 1864, CONFEDERATE FORCES UNDER GENERAL JOHN BELL HOOD WERE FORCED TO EVACUATE THE BESIEGED CITY OF ATLANTA, GEORGIA.

RETREATING CONFEDERATES BURNED THEIR OWN AMMUNITION STORES TO KEEP THEM OUT OF ENEMY HANDS.

ATLANTA FELL AS A RESULT OF SUCCESSFUL MANEUVERS BY MAJOR GENERAL WILLIAM TECUMSEH SHERMAN.

...THERE SHALL BE FIRED A SALUTE OF ONE HUNDRED GUNS...

...FOR THE BRILLIANT ACHIEVEMENTS OF THE ARMY UNDER COMMAND OF MAJOR-GENERAL SHERMAN... AND THE CAPTURE OF ATLANTA.

THIS AND SEVERAL OTHER MILITARY VICTORIES BROUGHT A SWELL OF SUPPORT FOR LINCOLN.

IN A GESTURE OF GOODWILL TO THE SOUTH, LINCOLN TOOK ON TENNESSEE DEMOCRAT ANDREW JOHNSON AS HIS VICE PRESIDENTIAL RUNNING MATE.

THE LINCOLN-JOHNSON TICKET TOOK ALL BUT THREE STATES, WITH OVERWHELMING VOTING SUPPORT COMING FROM THOSE ACTUALLY SERVING IN THE UNION ARMY.

(CONFEDERATE STATES, OF COURSE, DID NOT VOTE IN U.S. ELECTIONS.)

LINCOLN'S REELECTION WAS DEVASTATING FOR THE CONFEDERACY. THE SOUTH HAD HOPED THAT A NEW PRESIDENT--LIKE LINCOLN'S OPPONENT AND FORMER COMMANDER, GEORGE B. McCLELLAN-- WOULD NOT CONTINUE THE WAR BUT INSTEAD NEGOTIATE FOR PEACEFUL SOUTHERN INDEPENDENCE.

"UNFINISHED WORK": SLAVERY

COASTING ON THE MOMENTUM OF HIS ELECTORAL VICTORY...

...I GIVE THANKS TO THE ALMIGHTY FOR THIS EVIDENCE OF THE PEOPLE'S RESOLUTION TO STAND BY FREE GOVERNMENT AND THE RIGHTS OF HUMANITY.

...LINCOLN PUSHED CONGRESS TO PASS A 13th AMENDMENT TO THE U.S. CONSTITUTION TO FOREVER ABOLISH SLAVERY.

THE AMENDMENT HAD ALREADY BEEN APPROVED BY THE SENATE. BUT BY JUNE 1864, IT HAD STALLED OUT IN THE HOUSE OF REPRESENTATIVES.

GIVE UP OUR RIGHT TO HAVE SLAVERY... AND IN WHAT RIGHT ARE WE SECURE?

ONE AFTER ANOTHER WILL BE USURPED BY THE PRESIDENT AND CONGRESS... AND A GRAND IMPERIAL DESPOTISM ERECTED ON THE RUINS OF OUR RIGHTS AND LIBERTIES!

ROBERT MALLORY, CONGRESSMAN FROM KENTUCKY, 1864.

BUT WITH INTENSE POLITICAL PRESSURE, LINCOLN AND HIS ALLIES FINALLY PUSHED THE AMENDMENT THROUGH ON JANUARY 31, 1865.

THE OFFICIAL REPORT OF THE PROCEEDINGS DESCRIBED THE SCENE AFTER THE YEAS AND NAYS WERE TALLIED.

THE VOTE WAS 119-56 IN FAVOR.

The members of the Republican side of the House instantly sprung to their feet, and, regardless of parliamentary rules, applauded with cheers and clapping of hands... Spectators in the galleries, which were crowded to excess... Waved their hats and cheered loud and long...

ON THE MILITARY SIDE, THE UNION TOOK UP A "TOTAL WAR" APPROACH TO BREAK THE CONFEDERATE WILL TO FIGHT.

AFTER STRIKING THROUGH GEORGIA, SHERMAN'S MEN TURNED TO THE STATE MANY BLAMED FOR STARTING THE WAR.

...THE WHOLE ARMY IS BURNING WITH AN INSATIABLE DESIRE TO WREAK VENGEANCE UPON SOUTH CAROLINA.

BURNING OF COLUMBIA, SOUTH CAROLINA, FEBRUARY 1865.

GRANT BEGAN TO CLOSE A VISE ON RICHMOND BY LAYING SIEGE TO NEARBY PETERSBURG, VIRGINIA-- THE SOURCE OF RICHMOND'S SUPPLIES.

ALARM BELLS WERE RINGING FOR THE CONFEDERACY. ITS VERY EXISTENCE WAS HANGING BY A THREAD.

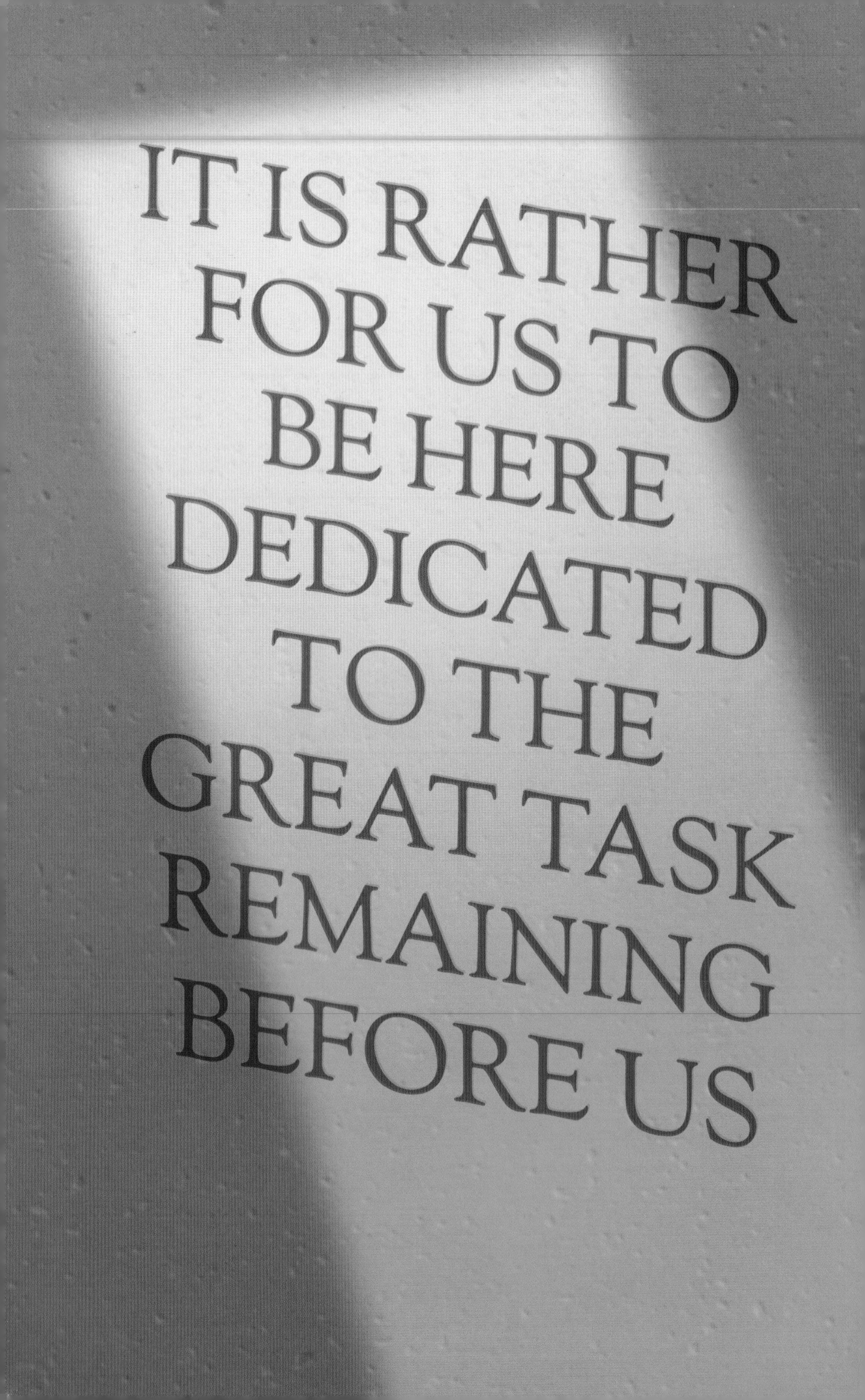
IT IS RATHER
FOR US TO
BE HERE
DEDICATED
TO THE
GREAT TASK
REMAINING
BEFORE US

RICHMOND, VIRGINIA.
APRIL 4, 1865.

SCUFF

≷GASP!≷

BLESS THE LORD! THERE HE IS! *THE GREAT MESSIAH!!*

NO, DO NOT KNEEL TO ME. FROM THIS DAY ON, YOU MUST KNEEL TO GOD ONLY.

NOW MIGHT ANY OF YOU SHOW US THE WAY TO THE LATE HEADQUARTERS OF MR. JEFFERSON DAVIS?

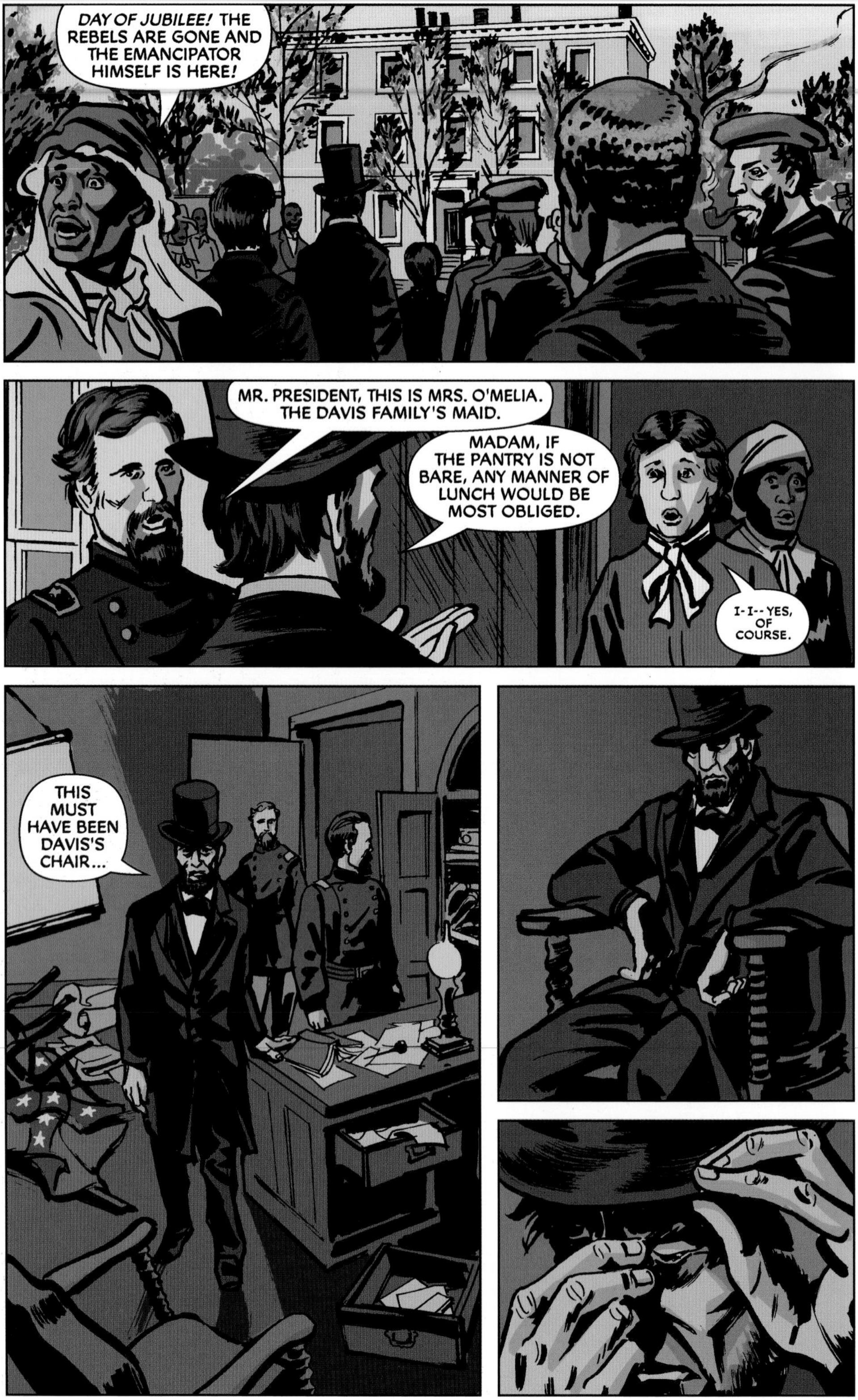
DAY OF JUBILEE! THE REBELS ARE GONE AND THE EMANCIPATOR HIMSELF IS HERE!
MR. PRESIDENT, THIS IS MRS. O'MELIA. THE DAVIS FAMILY'S MAID.
MADAM, IF THE PANTRY IS NOT BARE, ANY MANNER OF LUNCH WOULD BE MOST OBLIGED.
I-I-- YES, OF COURSE.
THIS MUST HAVE BEEN DAVIS'S CHAIR...

RICHMOND HAD AT LAST FALLEN. MOST MEMBERS OF THE CONFEDERATE GOVERNMENT HAD FLED.

BUT AS LINCOLN SAT IN DAVIS'S CHAIR, THE CONFEDERATE ASSISTANT SECRETARY OF WAR, JOHN A. CAMPBELL, CAME TO SEE HIM.

WITH SOUTHERN DEFEAT AT HAND, CAMPBELL BELIEVED HE COULD PERSUADE VIRGINIA'S LEGISLATURE TO SECEDE FROM THE CONFEDERACY AND REJOIN THE UNION. WOULD LINCOLN APPROVE?

THIS WAS THE HEART OF THE "GREAT TASK REMAINING BEFORE" LINCOLN AND HIS ALLIES.

THE FIGHTING WAS SOON OVER. LEE--AFTER A FRUITLESS ATTEMPT TO BREAK OUT OF AN ENCIRCLEMENT OF UNION TROOPS-- SAW NO USE IN FURTHER LOSS OF LIFE.

THE NEARLY STARVED ARMY OF NORTHERN VIRGINIA SURRENDERED TO GRANT ON APRIL 9, 1865.

(LATER THAT SAME MONTH, NEAR DURHAM, NORTH CAROLINA, THE FORCES OF CONFEDERATE GENERAL JOSEPH E. JOHNSTON LAID DOWN THEIR ARMS. BY MAY 1865, AFTER SUBSEQUENT SURRENDERS IN ALABAMA AND LOUISIANA, THE CONFEDERATE MILITARY WAS ESSENTIALLY DISBANDED IN FULL.)

JEFFERSON DAVIS WAS CAPTURED BY UNION SOLDIERS IN GEORGIA. THOUGH HE WAS AT FIRST IMPRISONED AND INDICTED FOR TREASON, TWO YEARS LATER HE WALKED AWAY A FREE MAN.

UNIONISTS HAD WON THE WAR. THE SOUTH WAS UNDER MILITARY OCCUPATION. BUT LINCOLN FACED ANOTHER FORMIDABLE CHALLENGE.

THE FEDERAL GOVERNMENT HAD TO PUT THE FRACTURED UNITED STATES BACK TOGETHER AGAIN.

IN OTHER WORDS, THEY NEEDED A PLAN FOR RECONSTRUCTION.

NEARLY ALL OF THE SOUTH'S MOST POPULAR, EXPERIENCED, AND INFLUENTIAL MEN HAD SIDED WITH THE CONFEDERACY. WITHOUT SWEEPING CHANGES TO WHO COULD VOTE AND HOLD OFFICE, THESE MEN WOULD LIKELY BE RETURNED TO POWER.

UNIONISTS FEARED THAT WOULD MEAN A RETURN TO DISCORD AND BLOODSHED.

LINCOLN AND HIS ALLIES NEEDED TO INFUSE THE SOUTH WITH A WHOLE NEW CLASS OF LEADERS AND CITIZENS-- ONES LOYAL TO THE UNITED STATES.

WITHOUT THIS, THE AMENDMENT TO ABOLISH SLAVERY WOULD NEVER PASS, FOR CONSTITUTIONAL AMENDMENTS BECOME LAW ONLY WHEN RATIFIED BY 3/4 OF THE STATES, AND THE OLD SOUTH'S STATUS QUO WOULD NEVER SUPPORT THIS.

REPUBLICAN PARTY LOYALISTS SAW NO WAY FORWARD BUT TO STRIP MANY SOUTHERN WHITES OF THE VOTE...

...AT LEAST TEMPORARILY.

YET LINCOLN PLANNED TO COMPLETELY PARDON ANY RANK-AND-FILE CONFEDERATE WHO WOULD PLEDGE TO "SUPPORT, PROTECT, AND DEFEND" THE UNION, THE CONSTITUTION, AND THE NEW LAWS PERTAINING TO SLAVERY.

ONCE JUST 1/10 OF THE VOTERS IN A CONFEDERATE STATE TOOK THIS OATH, LINCOLN WOULD ALLOW THEM TO FORM NEW GOVERNMENTS-- AND SEND LEGISLATORS BACK TO WASHINGTON.

10% PLAN

LINCOLN PUSHED FOR LENIENCE. HE DID NOT WANT AMERICANS TO SUFFER THE BARBARITIES THAT FAILED REBELLIONS USUALLY FACED: EXECUTIONS, EXILES, SEIZURES OF LAND AND PROPERTY.

THE TORTURE AND KILLING OF REBELS WHO OPPOSED CATHERINE THE GREAT, RUSSIA, 1775.

SOUTHERN STATE HOME RULE

10% PLAN

SLAVERY

WHITE SUPREMACY

BUT LINCOLN'S APPROACH REVOLTED OTHER WASHINGTON HEAVYWEIGHTS.

THE "RADICAL REPUBLICANS" WERE DETERMINED TO ENACT MORE PUNITIVE MEASURES FOR THE SOUTH.

THE WHOLE FABRIC OF SOUTHERN SOCIETY MUST BE CHANGED, AND NEVER CAN IT BE DONE IF THIS OPPORTUNITY IS LOST...

THADDEUS STEVENS, CONGRESSMAN FROM PENNSYLVANIA, 1865.

ONE RADICAL HELD THAT DISLOYAL SOUTHERN STATES HAD "COMMITTED SUICIDE"...

...AND NOW HAD THE STATUS OF U.S. TERRITORIES--100% SUBJECT TO CONTROL BY CONGRESS.

THE STATUS OF "SECEDED" STATES WAS INDEED A PUZZLE. IF IT HINGED ON AN UNSOUND LEGAL THEORY, *COULD SECESSION BE SAID TO HAVE REALLY HAPPENED IN THE FIRST PLACE?* LINCOLN DID VIEW THE SOUTH AS "OUT OF [ITS] PROPER PRACTICAL RELATION WITH THE UNION." BUT HE COULD NOT ACCEPT THE "STATE SUICIDE" THEORY.

YET LINCOLN AND THE RADICALS DID AGREE...

...ON ENDING SLAVERY AND EXTENDING CIVIL RIGHTS TO AFRICAN AMERICANS.

ON APRIL 11, 1865, THE PRESIDENT WENT EVEN FURTHER.

IT IS... UNSATISFACTORY TO SOME THAT THE [VOTE] IS NOT GIVEN TO THE COLORED MAN.

I WOULD MYSELF PREFER THAT [VOTING RIGHTS] WERE NOW CONFERRED ON THE VERY INTELLIGENT, AND ON THOSE WHO SERVE OUR CAUSE AS SOLDIERS.

JOHN WILKES BOOTH, A CONFEDERATE SYMPATHIZER AND ARDENT WHITE SUPREMACIST, WITNESSED LINCOLN'S CALL FOR PARTIAL BLACK ENFRANCHISEMENT.

THAT MEANS NIGGER CITIZENSHIP...

THAT IS THE LAST SPEECH HE WILL EVER MAKE.

BOOTH'S WORDS TURNED OUT TO BE TRUE. HE MADE THEM TRUE.

BOOTH HAS BEEN PAINTED AS A SOLO MADMAN. BUT HE WAS JUST PART OF A TEAM OF ASSASSINS BENT ON TOPPLING AS MUCH OF THE FEDERAL GOVERNMENT AS IT COULD.

THAT
FROM THESE
HONORED
DEAD

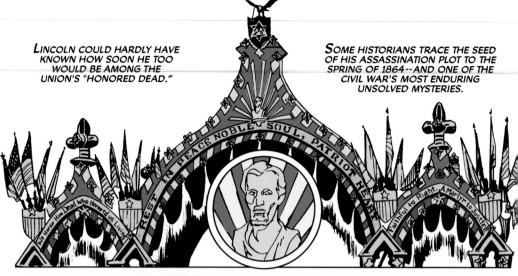

LINCOLN COULD HARDLY HAVE KNOWN HOW SOON HE TOO WOULD BE AMONG THE UNION'S "HONORED DEAD."

SOME HISTORIANS TRACE THE SEED OF HIS ASSASSINATION PLOT TO THE SPRING OF 1864--AND ONE OF THE CIVIL WAR'S MOST ENDURING UNSOLVED MYSTERIES.

IN MARCH 1864, THE UNION HATCHED A SECRET MISSION: A RAID TO FREE PRISONERS OF WAR HELD NEAR RICHMOND.

A PARTY OF THESE RAIDERS WAS AMBUSHED ON A COUNTRY ROAD. COMMANDER ULRICH DAHLGREN WAS SHOT DEAD.

PAPERS WERE FOUND ON DAHLGREN'S BODY: ORDERS TO BURN RICHMOND-- AND TO CAPTURE AND KILL JEFFERSON DAVIS AND HIS CABINET.

SUCH ACTS WOULD HAVE BEEN TANTAMOUNT TO TERRORISM, TO MURDER. CONFEDERATES QUICKLY PUBLICIZED THE DOCUMENTS.

IN THE CIVIL WAR, A BLACK FLAG MEANT MERCILESS, LAWLESS COMBAT-- OPPOSITE OF THE WHITE FLAG OF SURRENDER.

UNION LEADERS DENIED THEY WROTE THE ORDERS. DEBATE OVER THEIR AUTHENTICITY CONTINUES.

DAHLGREN HIMSELF OR HIS SUPERIOR, GENERAL HUGH JUDSON KILPATRICK (A CAVALRY COMMANDER AT GETTYSBURG), HAS BEEN SAID TO HAVE WRITTEN THEM. THEY MIGHT ALSO HAVE BEEN CONFEDERATE FORGERIES.

NEVERTHELESS, MANY OF LINCOLN'S HARSHEST CRITICS-- BOOTH AMONG THEM-- THOUGHT HE HAD ABDICATED THE "RULES OF WAR" AND NO LONGER DESERVED TREATMENT AS AN HONORABLE FOE.

Richmond Daily Dispatch
The Last Raid of the Infernals; Their Plans

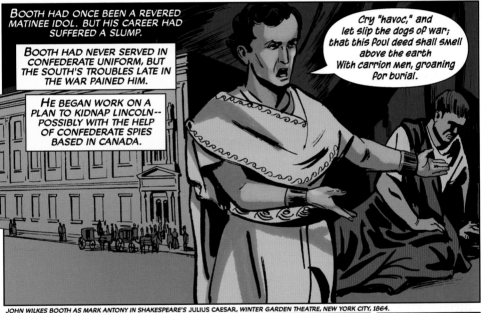

BOOTH HAD ONCE BEEN A REVERED MATINEE IDOL. BUT HIS CAREER HAD SUFFERED A SLUMP.

BOOTH HAD NEVER SERVED IN CONFEDERATE UNIFORM, BUT THE SOUTH'S TROUBLES LATE IN THE WAR PAINED HIM.

HE BEGAN WORK ON A PLAN TO KIDNAP LINCOLN-- POSSIBLY WITH THE HELP OF CONFEDERATE SPIES BASED IN CANADA.

Cry "havoc," and let slip the dogs of war; that this foul deed shall smell above the earth With carrion men, groaning for burial.

JOHN WILKES BOOTH AS MARK ANTONY IN SHAKESPEARE'S JULIUS CAESAR, WINTER GARDEN THEATRE, NEW YORK CITY, 1864.

BOOTH RECRUITED A CADRE OF MINIONS TO HELP HIM, INCLUDING...

LEWIS POWELL, A FORMER CONFEDERATE SOLDIER WOUNDED AT GETTYSBURG.

GEORGE ATZERODT, A PRUSSIAN IMMIGRANT.

JOHN SURRATT, CONFEDERATE COURIER--

--AND HIS MOTHER, MARY, AN INNKEPER.

DAVID HEROLD, A WILDERNESS GUIDE.

BUT BOOTH'S PLAN TO NAB LINCOLN AND SMUGGLE HIM TO VIRGINIA DISINTEGRATED.

DAMN IT ALL! "KING ABRAHAM AFRICANUS" CHANGED HIS PLANS.

HE WON'T BE PASSING THIS WAY AFTER ALL.

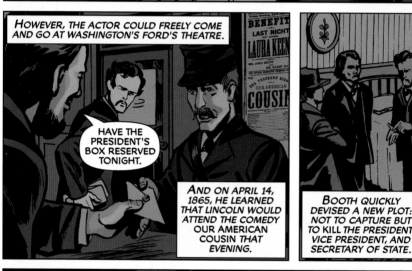

HOWEVER, THE ACTOR COULD FREELY COME AND GO AT WASHINGTON'S FORD'S THEATRE.

HAVE THE PRESIDENT'S BOX RESERVED TONIGHT.

AND ON APRIL 14, 1865, HE LEARNED THAT LINCOLN WOULD ATTEND THE COMEDY *OUR AMERICAN COUSIN* THAT EVENING.

BOOTH QUICKLY DEVISED A NEW PLOT: NOT TO CAPTURE BUT TO KILL THE PRESIDENT, VICE PRESIDENT, AND SECRETARY OF STATE.

BOOTH RETURNED TO THE THEATER AT 9:30 P.M. THAT NIGHT AND EASILY GAINED ADMISSION TO LINCOLN'S BOX.

SINCE THE ACTOR KNEW THE PLAY BEING STAGED, HE TIMED A SHOT FROM HIS DERRINGER WITH A LOUD LAUGH FROM THE AUDIENCE.

BOOTH SHOT LINCOLN ONCE IN THE BACK OF THE HEAD. THE PRESIDENT WENT INSTANTLY COMATOSE.

HE LIKELY NEVER KNEW WHO OR WHAT KILLED HIM.

ATZERODT WAS INTENDED TO KILL VICE PRESIDENT ANDREW JOHNSON. BUT HE LOST HIS NERVE AND INSTEAD GOT DRUNK.

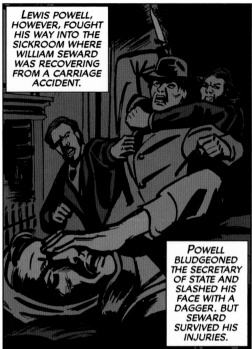

LEWIS POWELL, HOWEVER, FOUGHT HIS WAY INTO THE SICKROOM WHERE WILLIAM SEWARD WAS RECOVERING FROM A CARRIAGE ACCIDENT.

POWELL BLUDGEONED THE SECRETARY OF STATE AND SLASHED HIS FACE WITH A DAGGER. BUT SEWARD SURVIVED HIS INJURIES.

LINCOLN WAS TAKEN TO A HOME ACROSS THE STREET FROM THE THEATER. DOCTORS DID ALL THEY COULD. A CROWD GATHERED. MANY WAITED, EXPECTING TO HEAR ELOQUENT LAST WORDS FROM THE PRESIDENT.

BUT THESE NEVER CAME. LINCOLN DIED AROUND 7 A.M. THE NEXT MORNING.

PLEASE, HUSBAND!

SPEAK JUST ONE WORD TO ME!

NEWS OF THE ASSASSINATION SWEPT AROUND THE WORLD. IN THE NORTH, BUILDINGS WERE DRAPED IN BLACK. CHURCHES WERE PACKED; SCHOOLS AND OFFICES CLOSED. ANGRY MOBS SOUGHT REVENGE ON CONFEDERATE SYMPATHIZERS. FORMER SLAVES ON SOUTH CAROLINA'S HILTON HEAD ISLAND OPENLY WORRIED: "WE'RE GOING TO BE SLAVES AGAIN."

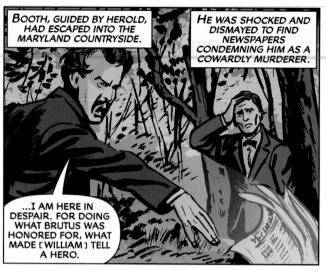

BOOTH, GUIDED BY HEROLD, HAD ESCAPED INTO THE MARYLAND COUNTRYSIDE.

HE WAS SHOCKED AND DISMAYED TO FIND NEWSPAPERS CONDEMNING HIM AS A COWARDLY MURDERER.

...I AM HERE IN DESPAIR. FOR DOING WHAT BRUTUS WAS HONORED FOR, WHAT MADE [WILLIAM] TELL A HERO.

COLONEL LAFAYETTE BAKER, A UNION DETECTIVE AND SPY, JOINED THE MANHUNT FOR BOOTH AND HIS COCONSPIRATORS.

TWELVE DAYS AFTER HE DELIVERED THE FATAL BULLET, BOOTH WAS TRACKED TO A VIRGINIA FARM.

AUTHORITIES WANTED HIM ALIVE. SO TO "SMOKE HIM OUT," CAVALRY OFFICERS SET FIRE TO THE BARN WHERE BOOTH WAS HIDING. BUT A UNION SERGEANT WITH A LIGHT TRIGGER FINGER SHOT BOOTH IN THE NECK.

CRACK!

THE ASSASSIN DIED AFTER SUNRISE.

POWELL, HEROLD, ATZERODT, AND MARY SURRATT WERE CONVICTED BY MILITARY TRIBUNAL AND HANGED TO DEATH ON JULY 7, 1865. JOHN SURRATT ESCAPED TO EUROPE. FOUR OTHERS WERE SENT TO PRISON.

BOOTH KILLED MORE THAN JUST A PRESIDENT.

HE ALSO KILLED LINCOLN'S PLANS TO BE LENIENT WITH THE SOUTH.

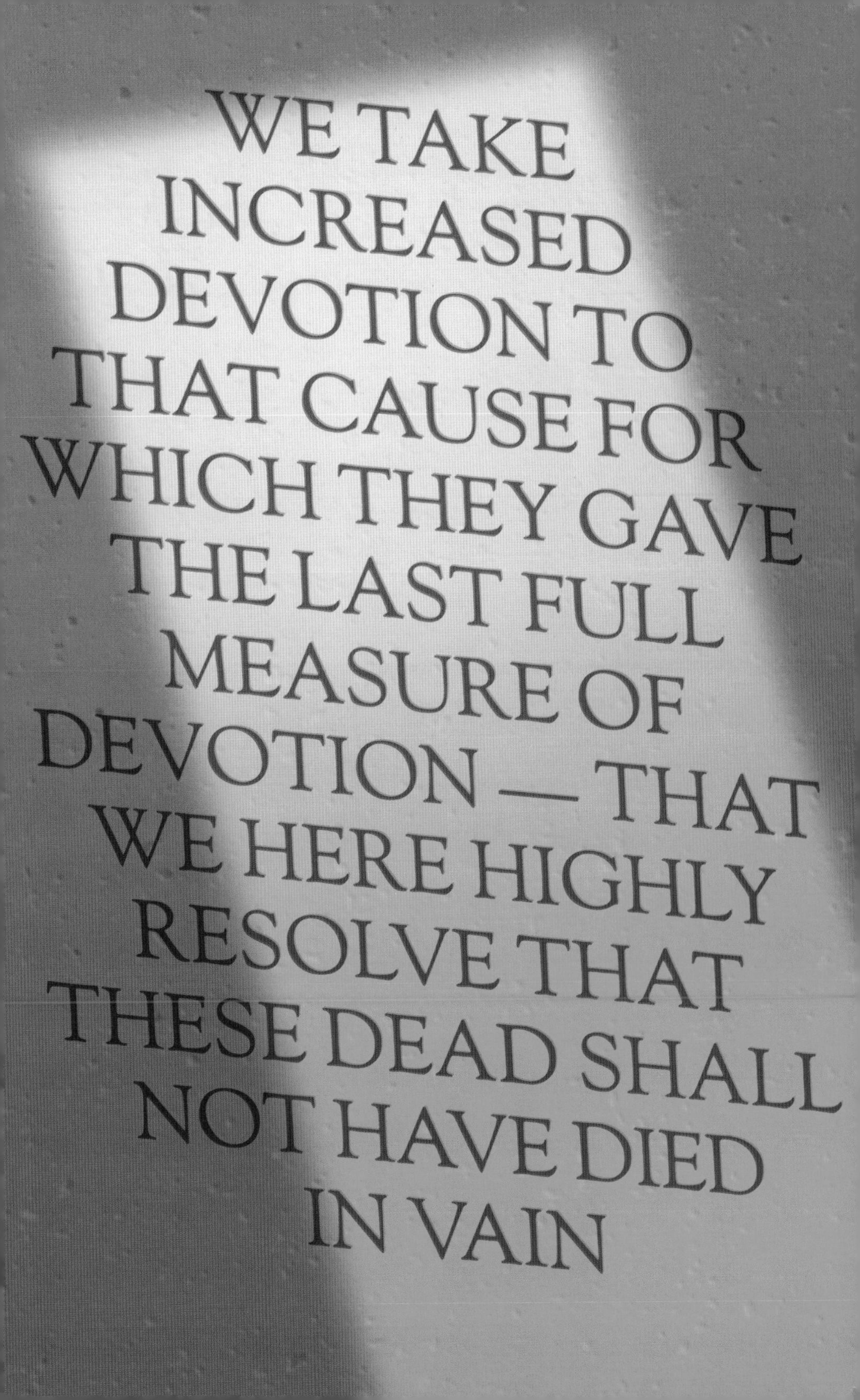
WE TAKE
INCREASED
DEVOTION TO
THAT CAUSE FOR
WHICH THEY GAVE
THE LAST FULL
MEASURE OF
DEVOTION — THAT
WE HERE HIGHLY
RESOLVE THAT
THESE DEAD SHALL
NOT HAVE DIED
IN VAIN

THE CIVIL WAR HAD CLAIMED YET ANOTHER LIFE.

LINCOLN HAD GIVEN HIS "LAST FULL MEASURE OF DEVOTION" TO HIS "CAUSE."

WHEN THE FIGHTING WAS OVER, HAD THE PRESIDENT-- AND THOSE UNION SUPPORTERS WHO HAD PERISHED AT GETTYSBURG AND SO MANY OTHER BATTLES-- "DIED IN VAIN"?

NO. THE DEPARTED SOULS COULD BE CERTAIN OF HAVING DRAMATICALLY TRANSFORMED AMERICA'S FUTURE.

LINCOLN

PRESIDENTIAL FUNERAL PROCESSION, COLUMBUS, OHIO, APRIL 29, 1865.

FOR THEY HAD PRESERVED THE UNION. AND, TO A SIGNIFICANT DEGREE, THE VICTORS OF THE CIVIL WAR HAD ALSO RECONCILED TWO OF THE FATAL CONTRADICTIONS BETWEEN THE DECLARATION OF INDEPENDENCE AND THE CONSTITUTION.

FIRST, THEY HAD INVALIDATED SECESSION "AT WILL"-- AN IDEA MANY THOUGHT IMPLICIT IN THE DECLARATION OF INDEPENDENCE.

THE FORMER CONFEDERATE STRONGHOLDS WERE REQUIRED TO WRITE NEW STATE CONSTITUTIONS. IN THEM, SECESSION HAD TO BE PLAINLY RENOUNCED.

This state shall ever remain a member of the American union, and all attempts... to dissolve the said union, shall be resisted with the whole power of the state.

CONSTITUTION OF THE STATE OF SOUTH CAROLINA, 1868.

AN 1869 SUPREME COURT CASE CLARIFIED SECESSION...

...LEAVING OPEN THE POSSIBILITY THAT STATES MAY LEGALLY SECEDE IF THE OTHERS AGREE TO PERMIT IT.

THE UNION BETWEEN TEXAS AND THE OTHER STATES WAS AS COMPLETE, AS PERPETUAL, AND AS INDISSOLUBLE AS THE UNION BETWEEN THE ORIGINAL STATES.

THERE WAS NO PLACE FOR RECONSIDERATION OR REVOCATION, EXCEPT THROUGH REVOLUTION OR THROUGH CONSENT OF THE STATES.

TEXAS V. WHITE, 1869.

A SECOND TENSION BETWEEN THE CONSTITUTION AND THE DECLARATION WAS THE PRACTICE OF CHATTEL SLAVERY-- WHOLLY INCOMPATIBLE WITH THE NOTION "ALL MEN ARE CREATED EQUAL."

BUT BY THE TIME OF LINCOLN'S DEATH, SLAVERY HAD BEEN ALL BUT ABOLISHED...

...AND NOT IN THE GRADUAL WAY LINCOLN MIGHT ONCE HAVE PREFERRED, BUT INSTEAD QUITE QUICKLY

AND BY THE END OF THE WAR, LINCOLN HAD BACKED AWAY FROM ADVOCATING "COLONIZATION" FOR BLACKS

ONLY BY ENDING SLAVERY HAD UNIONISTS BEEN ABLE TO DEFEAT THE CONFEDERACY. IT HAD BEEN BOTH A PRACTICAL STEP TO WEAKEN THE SOUTH...

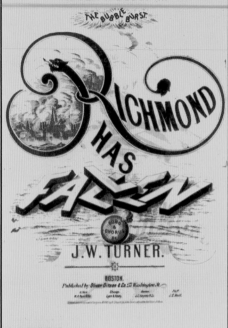

... AND ALSO A WAY OF TRANSFORMING THE CIVIL WAR INTO A MORAL CRUSADE. THIS HAD TO BE DONE TO KEEP UNION STATES TOGETHER AND WILLING TO MAKE FURTHER SACRIFICE.

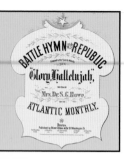

ON DECEMBER 6, 1865, THE "RECONSTRUCTED" STATE GOVERNMENT OF GEORGIA RATIFIED THE 13th AMENDMENT. ABOLITION WAS NOW THE SUPREME LAW OF THE LAND.

GEORGIA HAS, IN GOOD FAITH, ABOLISHED SLAVERY.

...THE RATIFICATION OF THIS AMENDMENT WILL... REMOVE FROM AMONG US THAT CAUSE OF BITTERNESS AND SECTIONAL STRIFE WHICH HAS WASTED OUR PROPERTY AND DELUGED OUR LAND IN BLOOD.

JAMES JOHNSON, PROVISIONAL GOVERNOR OF GEORGIA, 1865.

AFTER MORE THAN 250 YEARS, THE LAST NAIL HAD BEEN PUT IN THE COFFIN OF HUMAN BONDAGE IN AMERICA.

THE NEW SOUTHERN STATE CONSTITUTIONS ALSO PROCLAIMED HUMAN EQUALITY.

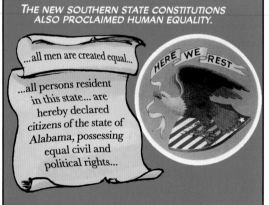

...all men are created equal...

...all persons resident in this state... are hereby declared citizens of the state of Alabama, possessing equal civil and political rights...

HERE WE REST

CONSTITUTION OF THE STATE OF ALABAMA, 1868.

BUT ANOTHER ONE OF THE DISPARITIES BETWEEN THE UNITED STATES' FOUNDING DOCUMENTS PROVED RESILIENT.

EVEN THE PRESSURES OF THE CIVIL WAR COULD NOT RECONCILE THE ENDURING DEBATE OVER FEDERAL GOVERNMENT POWER.

THE TROUBLED RECONSTRUCTION ERA IS A POTENT ILLUSTRATION OF THAT.

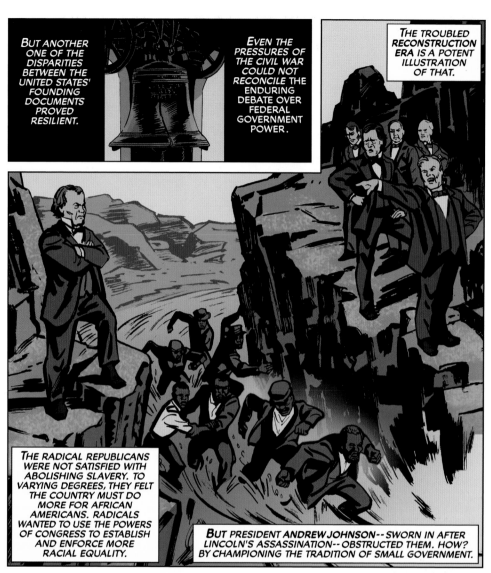

THE RADICAL REPUBLICANS WERE NOT SATISFIED WITH ABOLISHING SLAVERY. TO VARYING DEGREES, THEY FELT THE COUNTRY MUST DO MORE FOR AFRICAN AMERICANS. RADICALS WANTED TO USE THE POWERS OF CONGRESS TO ESTABLISH AND ENFORCE MORE RACIAL EQUALITY.

BUT PRESIDENT *ANDREW JOHNSON*-- SWORN IN AFTER LINCOLN'S ASSASSINATION-- OBSTRUCTED THEM. HOW? BY CHAMPIONING THE TRADITION OF SMALL GOVERNMENT.

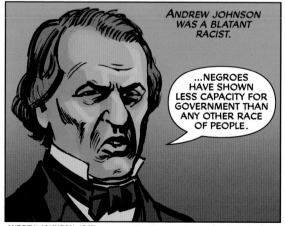

ANDREW JOHNSON WAS A BLATANT RACIST.

...NEGROES HAVE SHOWN LESS CAPACITY FOR GOVERNMENT THAN ANY OTHER RACE OF PEOPLE.

ANDREW JOHNSON, 1867.

IN THE SOUTH AND THE NORTH, THE DEEP ROOTS OF RACIAL BIGOTRY POWERFULLY COMBINED WITH SMALL GOVERNMENT IDEALS.

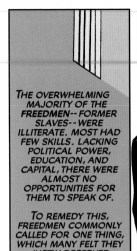

THE OVERWHELMING MAJORITY OF THE FREEDMEN-- FORMER SLAVES--WERE ILLITERATE. MOST HAD FEW SKILLS. LACKING POLITICAL POWER, EDUCATION, AND CAPITAL, THERE WERE ALMOST NO OPPORTUNITIES FOR THEM TO SPEAK OF.

TO REMEDY THIS, FREEDMEN COMMONLY CALLED FOR ONE THING, WHICH MANY FELT THEY JUSTLY DESERVED AS PAYMENT...

...FOR LIFETIMES OF UNCOMPENSATED WORK.

[FREEDOM] IS TAKING US FROM UNDER THE YOKE OF BONDAGE AND PLACING US WHERE WE COULD REAP THE FRUIT OF OUR OWN LABOR...

THE WAY WE CAN BEST TAKE CARE OF OURSELVES IS TO HAVE LAND.

SOME SOUTHERN PLANTATIONS HAD BEEN CONFISCATED. FREEDMEN WERE GRANTED PLOTS OF THEIR OWN.

IN 1865, CONGRESS ALSO ESTABLISHED THE BUREAU OF REFUGEES, FREEDMEN, AND ABANDONED LANDS. BUREAU AGENTS WORKED TO HELP FREED-MEN SECURE THEIR OWN FARMS AND BECOME SELF-RELIANT.

MINISTER GARRISON FRAZIER, 1865. (EMPHASIS ADDED)

BUT JOHNSON REVERSED THOSE GAINS.

HE EMBARKED ON A CAMPAIGN OF ISSUING PRESIDENTIAL PARDONS TO FORMER CONFEDERATES. SOON, VIRTUALLY ALL CONFISCATED LAND WAS GIVEN BACK TO WHITES. IN SOME INSTANCES, THE U.S. ARMY EVICTED THE FREEDMEN.

SOUTHERN STATES ADOPTED PUNITIVE "BLACK CODES" TO FORCE FREEDMEN BACK TO COTTON PLANTATIONS-- GENERALLY UNDER STRICT CONTRACTS WITH HORRENDOUS WORKING CONDITIONS AND LOW WAGES.

"BLACK CODES" INCLUDED TAXING AFRICAN AMERICANS IF THEY DIDN'T WORK AS FARMERS OR LABORERS AND PREVENTING THEM FROM HUNTING OR FISHING TO FEED THEMSELVES.

OUTRAGED BY JOHNSON'S CONDUCT, RADICALS "WENT FOR THE JUGULAR."

...I CHARGE ANDREW JOHNSON... WITH THE COMMISSION OF ACTS WHICH IN CONTEMPLATION OF THE CONSTITUTION, ARE HIGH CRIMES AND MISDEMEANORS, FOR WHICH, IN MY JUDGMENT, HE OUGHT TO BE IMPEACHED.

JAMES MITCHELL ASHLEY, CONGRESSMAN FROM OHIO, 1867.

CLEARLY, WITHOUT FURTHER INTERVENTION, AFRICAN AMERICANS WOULD BE SCARCELY BETTER OFF THAN THEY HAD BEEN UNDER SLAVERY.

...THIS WAR SHALL NOT CEASE UNTIL EVERY FREEDMAN AT THE SOUTH HAS THE RIGHT TO VOTE.

FREDERICK DOUGLASS, 1868.

EX-CONFEDERATE STATES-- WHERE STILL ONLY WHITES COULD VOTE-- WERE NOT LIKELY TO ADOPT BLACK SUFFRAGE ON THEIR OWN.

SO THE RADICALS-- WITH THEIR ALLY, FUTURE PRESIDENT ULYSSES S. GRANT-- PUSHED THROUGH THE 14th AND 15th AMENDMENTS TO THE CONSTITUTION.

POINTEDLY THWARTING THE DRED SCOTT DECISION, THE 14th AMENDMENT MADE ALL EX-SLAVES U.S. CITIZENS. THE 15th AMENDMENT ABOLISHED RESTRICTING WHO COULD VOTE BY "RACE, COLOR, OR PREVIOUS CONDITION OF SERVITUDE."

ONCE BLACK VOTING RIGHTS WERE IN PLACE, AFRICAN AMERICANS WERE ELECTED TO HIGH OFFICE IN SOUTHERN STATES.

HIRAM REVELS WON THE MISSISSIPPI SENATE SEAT ONCE HELD BY JEFFERSON DAVIS.

HIRAM REVELS, SENATOR FROM MISSISSIPPI.

JOSIAH WALLS, CONGRESSMAN FROM FLORIDA.

P. B. S. PINCHBACK, GOVERNOR OF LOUISIANA.

FRANCIS CARDOZO, SOUTH CAROLINA SECRETARY OF STATE.

BUT A MAJOR OFFENSIVE AGAINST THE RADICALS AND THEIR EXPANSION OF GOVERNMENT POWER ARGUABLY BEGAN TO PLAY OUT ON MAY 16, 1868.

ANDREW JOHNSON-- IMPEACHED BY THE HOUSE OF REPRESENTATIVES-- FAILED TO BE CONVICTED AND REMOVED FROM OFFICE BY THE SENATE.

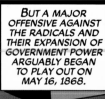

For President SEYMOUR — Vice President BLAIR

OUR MOTTO: This is a White Man's Country; Let White Men Rule.

CONSERVATISM WAS ON AN UPSWING.

EVEN PROMINENT REPUBLICAN SENATORS BROKE FROM THEIR PARTY TO ACQUIT JOHNSON. A SINGLE "NOT GUILTY" VOTE IN HIS FAVOR SAVED HIM.

VIOLENCE AGAINST REPUBLICANS AND AFRICAN AMERICANS, MOSTLY IN THE SOUTH, INTENSIFIED.

WHITE MOBS AND PARAMILITARIES LIKE THE KU KLUX KLAN CONTROLLED ELECTIONS WITH INTIMIDATION AND MURDER. THEY WERE BENT ON RESTORING THE OLD WHITE POWER STRUCTURE.

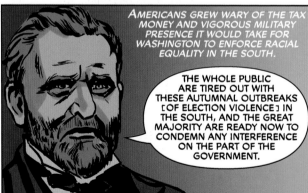

AMERICANS GREW WARY OF THE TAX MONEY AND VIGOROUS MILITARY PRESENCE IT WOULD TAKE FOR WASHINGTON TO ENFORCE RACIAL EQUALITY IN THE SOUTH.

THE WHOLE PUBLIC ARE TIRED OUT WITH THESE AUTUMNAL OUTBREAKS [OF ELECTION VIOLENCE] IN THE SOUTH, AND THE GREAT MAJORITY ARE READY NOW TO CONDEMN ANY INTERFERENCE ON THE PART OF THE GOVERNMENT.

CRAFTY NEW VOTING LAWS EXPLOITED LOOPHOLES IN THE 15th AMENDMENT. IN SOUTHERN STATES, THE INFLUENCE OF AFRICAN AMERICAN VOTERS WITHERED.

MISSISSIPPI'S BLACK VOTER REGISTRATION FELL FROM 90% IN 1868 TO 6% IN 1892.

THE NUMBER OF BLACKS IN OFFICE PLUMMETED.

ULYSSES S. GRANT, 1875.

MANY AMERICANS GREW SICK OF REMINDERS OF THE WAR.

...THE WAY OUT OF MOST OF OUR COMPLICATIONS IS IN LETTING THE PAST DROP ABSOLUTELY...

CHARLES DUDLEY WARNER, WRITER, 1887.

WITH THE 13th, 14th, AND 15th AMENDMENTS, MOST WHITES FELT ENOUGH HAD BEEN DONE FOR AFRICAN AMERICANS.

[THE NEGRO] NOW HAS ALL THAT LAW CAN CONFER...

THE ROAD TO THE NEGRO'S SOCIAL EQUALITY LIES THROUGH HIS CAPACITY FOR WORK...

CHICAGO TRIBUNE, APRIL 2, 1871.

THE "REBEL" STATES WERE READMITTED TO THE UNION. ALL FEDERAL TROOPS IN THE SOUTH WERE WITHDRAWN. IN RAPID SUCCESSION, PRO-STATES' RIGHTS POLITICIANS CAME BACK TO POWER.

RECONSTRUCTION WAS OVER. AS THE 20th CENTURY NEARED, THE GOVERNOR OF SOUTH CAROLINA BOASTED...

JIM CROW
REDEMPTION
HOME RULE

THE WHITES HAVE ABSOLUTE CONTROL OF THE STATE GOVERNMENT, AND WE INTEND AT ANY AND ALL HAZARDS TO RETAIN IT.

WE DENY, WITHOUT REGARD TO COLOR, THAT "ALL MEN ARE CREATED EQUAL"; IT IS NOT TRUE NOW, AND WAS NOT TRUE WHEN JEFFERSON WROTE IT.

BENJAMIN TILLMAN, 1890.

STILL, HOPE FOR RACIAL EQUALITY SPROUTED WITH THE FIRST NEW BUILDING TO RISE FROM THE RUINS OF CHARLESTON:

A BLACK CHURCH.

THAT THIS NATION, UNDER GOD

TWO COMMONPLACE WORDS OF THE GETTYSBURG ADDRESS ARE EASY TO OVERLOOK. BUT THEY ARE, IN FACT, LOADED WITH MEANING.

NATION

IN THE SPEECH, LINCOLN KEPT DESCRIBING THE UNITED STATES AS A "NATION." THIS WAS TO ACTIVELY EMPHASIZE HIS VISION OF THE UNION AS AN INDIVISIBLE WHOLE--NOT A LEAGUE OF SOVEREIGN STATES, AS SECESSIONISTS WOULD HAVE IT.

GOD

IN THE TIME OF THE CIVIL WAR, AMERICAN CULTURE WAS DEEPLY ROOTED IN CHRISTIANITY. IT WOULD HAVE BEEN DIFFICULT INDEED FOR LINCOLN'S WORDS TO STRIKE AT THE HEART OF HIS INTENDED AUDIENCE WITHOUT MENTIONING THE DEITY.

EVEN TODAY SOME AMERICANS CLAIM THEIR COUNTRY IS FAVORED BY GOD AS A PLACE SET ASIDE TO CREATE A MODEL CHRISTIAN SOCIETY. THIS SENTIMENT WAS MUCH MORE COMMON IN THE 1800s.

SECESSION ENRAGED MANY UNIONISTS BECAUSE, TO THEM, TO BREAK UP THE COUNTRY WAS TO UPSET GOD'S HOLY ESTABLISHMENT.

LIKEWISE, SOME SECESSIONISTS ARGUED THAT GOD INTENDED SLAVERY TO EXIST. IN THE BIBLE'S "CURSE OF HAM" STORY, THEY FOUND DIVINE MANDATE FOR BLACK SERVITUDE. AND THUS ABOLITIONISM WAS A SIN--A DEFIANCE OF GOD'S ORDER.

RELIGIOUS JUSTIFICATIONS FOR THE CIVIL WAR WERE PREACHED FROM PULPITS BOTH SOUTH AND NORTH.

CHRISTIAN UNION.

JOHN: 17: 20, 21.

Neither pray I for these alone, but for them also which shall believe on me, through their word. That they all may be one, as thou Father, art in me, and I in thee, that they also may be one in us: that the world may believe that thou hast sent me.

JESUS CHRIST.

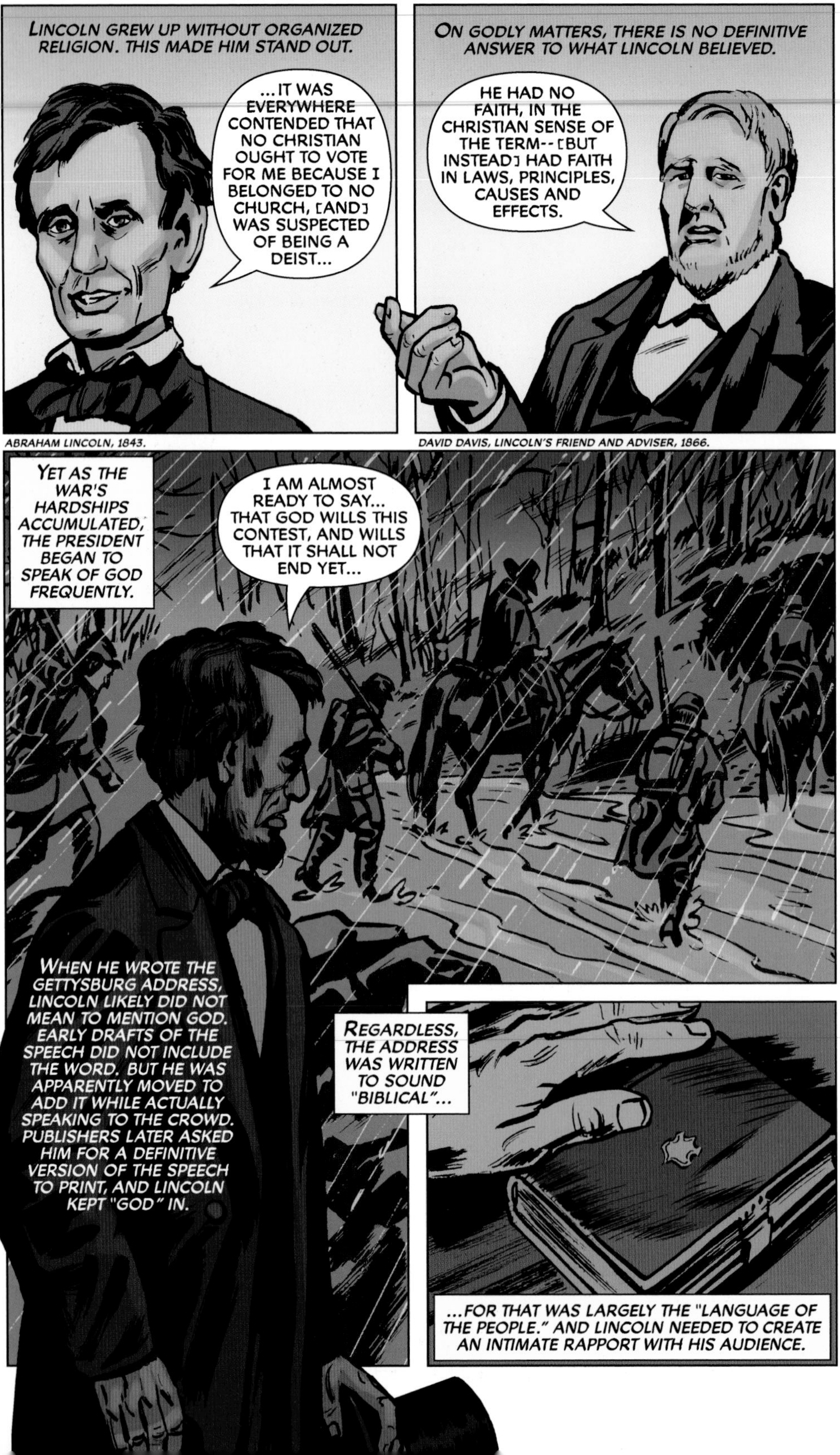
LINCOLN GREW UP WITHOUT ORGANIZED RELIGION. THIS MADE HIM STAND OUT.
...IT WAS EVERYWHERE CONTENDED THAT NO CHRISTIAN OUGHT TO VOTE FOR ME BECAUSE I BELONGED TO NO CHURCH, [AND] WAS SUSPECTED OF BEING A DEIST...
ABRAHAM LINCOLN, 1843.
ON GODLY MATTERS, THERE IS NO DEFINITIVE ANSWER TO WHAT LINCOLN BELIEVED.
HE HAD NO FAITH, IN THE CHRISTIAN SENSE OF THE TERM--[BUT INSTEAD] HAD FAITH IN LAWS, PRINCIPLES, CAUSES AND EFFECTS.
DAVID DAVIS, LINCOLN'S FRIEND AND ADVISER, 1866.
YET AS THE WAR'S HARDSHIPS ACCUMULATED, THE PRESIDENT BEGAN TO SPEAK OF GOD FREQUENTLY.
I AM ALMOST READY TO SAY... THAT GOD WILLS THIS CONTEST, AND WILLS THAT IT SHALL NOT END YET...
WHEN HE WROTE THE GETTYSBURG ADDRESS, LINCOLN LIKELY DID NOT MEAN TO MENTION GOD. EARLY DRAFTS OF THE SPEECH DID NOT INCLUDE THE WORD. BUT HE WAS APPARENTLY MOVED TO ADD IT WHILE ACTUALLY SPEAKING TO THE CROWD. PUBLISHERS LATER ASKED HIM FOR A DEFINITIVE VERSION OF THE SPEECH TO PRINT, AND LINCOLN KEPT "GOD" IN.
REGARDLESS, THE ADDRESS WAS WRITTEN TO SOUND "BIBLICAL"...
...FOR THAT WAS LARGELY THE "LANGUAGE OF THE PEOPLE." AND LINCOLN NEEDED TO CREATE AN INTIMATE RAPPORT WITH HIS AUDIENCE.

THE ADDRESS'S OPENING LINE HAS THE RING OF THE KING JAMES BIBLE'S PSALM 90:10.

FOUR SCORE AND SEVEN YEARS AGO

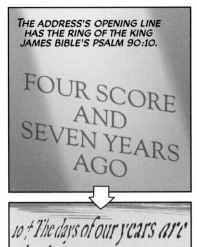

10 ¶ The days of our years are threescore years and ten;

BY AND LARGE, WHEN AFRICANS WERE ENSLAVED IN AMERICA, THEIR MASTERS TAUGHT THEM CHRISTIANITY.

HOPE FOR A BETTER AFTERLIFE HELPED SLAVES BEAR THEIR MANY BURDENS.

INDEPENDENT BLACK CHURCHES WERE ESTABLISHED. BUT IN THE SOUTH, THEY WERE LARGELY BANNED AFTER SLAVE REVOLTS IN 1822 AND 1831.

HORRID MASSACRE IN VIRGINIA

AT THE END OF THE CIVIL WAR, FREEDOM ARRIVED. THIS MEANT AFRICAN AMERICANS COULD ONCE MORE WORSHIP AS THEY PLEASED.

BLACK MINISTERS-- OFTEN LITERATE AND WISE-- WERE LOOKED TO AS LEADERS AND EDUCATORS. WHITE MISSIONARIES FROM THE NORTH ALSO CAME TO MINISTER AND TEACH THE FREEDMEN.

IN SPITE OF LYNCHINGS, ELECTION TAMPERING, AND "JIM CROW" LAWS FROM THE 1870s AND ON, THESE PEOPLE OF FAITH LIT THE WAY TOWARD FURTHER RECONCILING THE CONSTITUTION WITH THE DECLARATION OF INDEPENDENCE...

...IN A "SECOND RECONSTRUCTION," WHICH BEGAN TO TAKE HOLD EIGHTY YEARS AFTER THE FIRST.

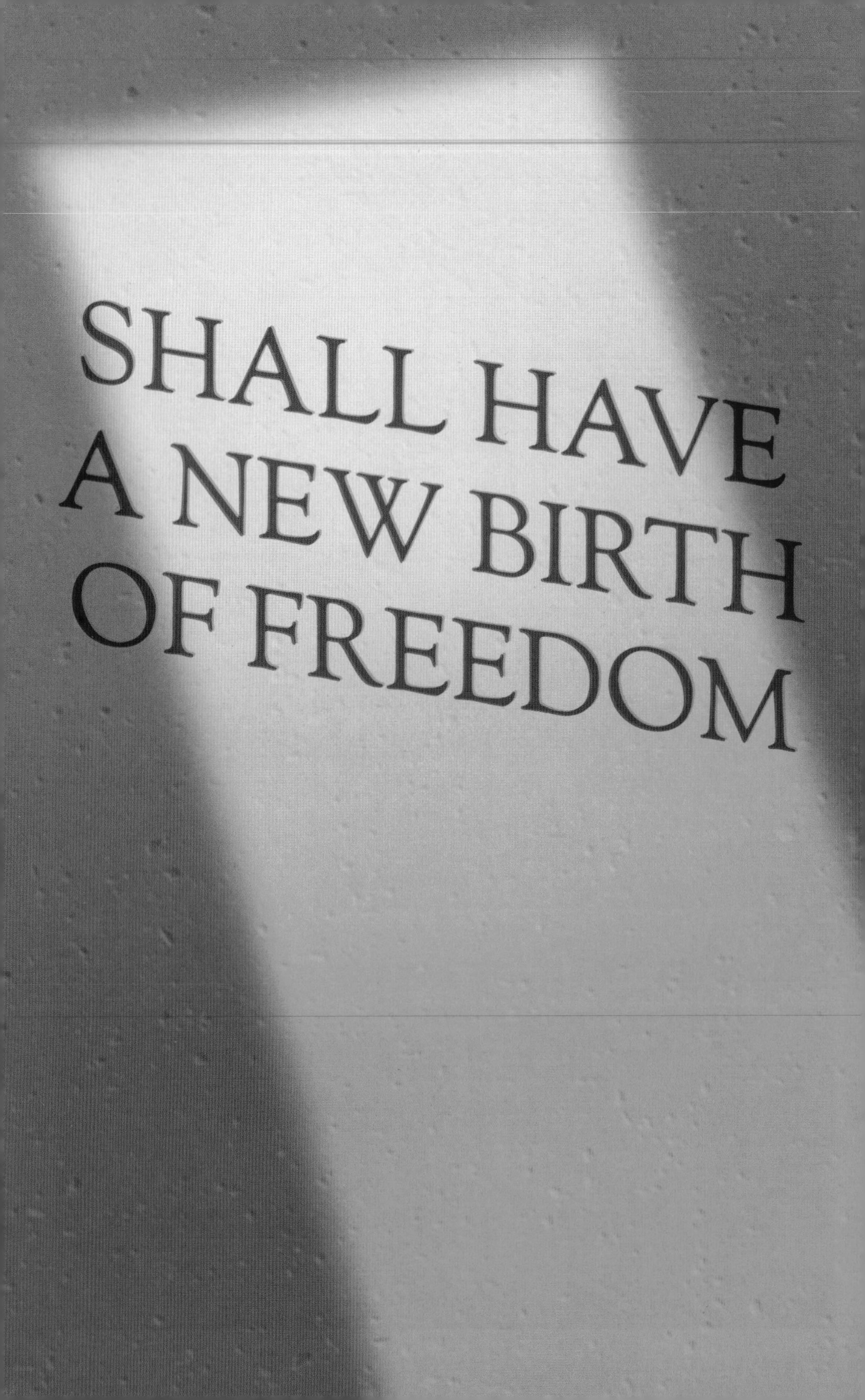
SHALL HAVE
A NEW BIRTH
OF FREEDOM

LINCOLN DARED TO HOPE THAT THE UNION COULD ACTUALLY WIN THE CIVIL WAR.

AS THE TREES ARE NOT DEAD, THOUGH THEIR FOLIAGE IS GONE...

IN THE GETTYSBURG ADDRESS, HE EXPRESSED SOMETHING EVEN MORE DARING AND UNCERTAIN: THAT VICTORY WOULD PRODUCE NOT MERELY PEACE AND REUNION BUT ALSO "A NEW BIRTH OF FREEDOM."

...OUR HEROES ARE NOT DEAD, THOUGH THEIR FORMS HAVE FALLEN.

AS LYRICAL AND GLORIOUS AS THAT PHRASE SOUNDS, WHAT EXACTLY DOES IT MEAN?

SURELY "A NEW BIRTH OF FREEDOM" MUST BE A BLANKET TERM COVERING EVERYTHING LINCOLN WANTED FOR HIS COUNTRY:

* RESTORATION OF THE UNION
* THE PRESERVATION OF AMERICA AS A SHINING EXAMPLE OF REPUBLICAN GOVERNMENT
* THE IMPROVEMENT OF AMERICA'S ECONOMY AND LIVING STANDARDS BY FEDERAL GOVERNMENT POWER, WITHOUT OBSTRUCTIONIST STATES GETTING IN THE WAY

* THE TRIUMPH OF FREE LABOR
* THE END OF SLAVERY
* THE EXTENSION OF CIVIL RIGHTS TO AFRICAN AMERICANS

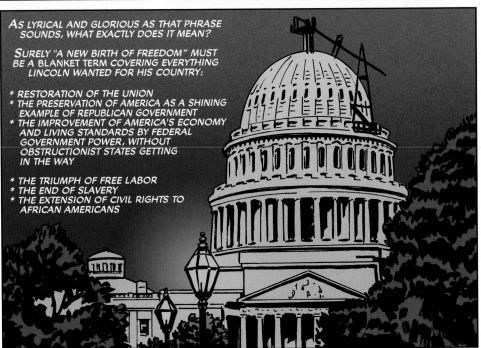

LINCOLN HAD WAGED WAR TO BRING THESE GOALS ABOUT. BUT JUST AS SOME OF THEM WERE COMING TO FRUITION, HE DIED.

HE DID NOT LIVE TO WITNESS HIS FELLOW REPUBLICANS' SPOTTY, COMPROMISED EFFORTS TO TRANSFORM THE SOUTH OVER THE NEXT 12 YEARS.

THE END OF THE REBELLION IN THE UNITED STATES. 1865.

WOULD LINCOLN HAVE THOUGHT THAT RECONSTRUCTION REALIZED HIS AMBITIONS...

...ESPECIALLY GIVEN THAT AFRICAN AMERICANS REMAINED (AT BEST) SECOND-CLASS CITIZENS FOR GENERATIONS AFTER THE WAR?

CAN ANYTHING AS SWEEPING AS A "NEW BIRTH OF FREEDOM" BE SAID TO HAVE HAPPENED AT ALL?

IT'S PROBABLY MOST ACCURATE TO SAY THAT AMERICA HAD NOT ONE BUT TWO "NEW BIRTH[S] OF FREEDOM" SEGREGATED BY RACE.

IN OTHER WORDS, THERE WAS ONE "NEW BIRTH OF FREEDOM" FOR WHITES AND ANOTHER FOR BLACKS.

PART 1: THE "NEW BIRTH OF FREEDOM" FOR WHITES

SINCE THE VERY BEGINNING, SECTIONAL RIVALRY HAD DOGGED AMERICAN POLITICS.

[southerners] are habituated to despotism by being the sovereigns of slaves: and it is only accident and interest that had made... them the temporary sons of liberty.

...the balance of power is in the [north]-eastern states, & they appear determined to keep it in that direction.

WILLIAM GORDON, DELEGATE FROM MASSACHUSETTS, 1782.

TIMOTHY BLOODWORTH, DELEGATE FROM NORTH CAROLINA, 1786.

AND FOR SO MUCH OF THE 19th CENTURY, DISCORD BETWEEN NORTH AND SOUTH MONOPOLIZED THE COUNTRY'S ENERGY AND ATTENTION.

BUT IN THE POSTWAR YEARS, FATIGUE SET IN.

THE ERA OF SECESSIONISTS, PROSLAVERY "FIRE-EATERS," ABOLITIONISTS, AND RADICAL REPUBLICANS SLIPPED AWAY. THE COUNTRY'S OVERWHELMINGLY WHITE BODY POLITIC SHOOK OFF THE FESTERING OLD HOSTILITIES AND OBSESSIONS OF FREE LABOR vs. SLAVERY, NORTH vs. SOUTH, BLACK vs. WHITE.

IN 1872, A COMMITTEE OF MEN WAS CHARGED WITH TURNING THE GETTYSBURG BATTLEFIELD INTO A HISTORIC SITE. THEY MADE A TELLING DECISION.

THERE WAS A GREAT DEAL OF MONEY FROM TOURISM TO BE MADE. AND THAT WOULD BE COMPROMISED IF SOUTHERN VISITORS FELT UNWELCOME IN GETTYSBURG. SO THE COMMITTEE AGREED TO "EXCLUDE PARTISAN AND SECTIONAL SPIRIT" FROM ALL MEMORIALS AND EXHIBITS.

THESE EXCLUSIVELY WHITE MEN DECIDED NEVER TO MENTION SLAVERY.

THE 50th ANNIVERSARY OF THE BATTLE CAME IN 1913.

TO MARK THIS, A "GREAT REUNION" WAS HELD ON THE BATTLEFIELD FOR SURVIVING VETERANS.

(SUCH "BLUE-GRAY" CONVENTIONS, WHICH WELCOMED THOSE WHO HAD FOUGHT ON BOTH SIDES, HAD ALREADY BEEN TAKING PLACE FOR DECADES.)

PRESIDENT WOODROW WILSON-- THE FIRST SOUTHERN-BORN PRESIDENT SINCE THE CIVIL WAR, WHOSE FATHER HAD OWNED SLAVES-- ADDRESSED THE CROWDS.

HOW WHOLESOME AND HEALING THE PEACE HAS BEEN! WE HAVE FOUND ONE ANOTHER AGAIN AS BROTHERS AND COMRADES IN ARMS...OUR BATTLES LONG PAST, THE QUARREL FORGOTTEN.

...EXCEPT THAT WE SHALL NOT FORGET THE SPLENDID VALOR, THE MANLY DEVOTION OF THE MEN THEN ARRAYED AGAINST ONE ANOTHER, NOW GRASPING HANDS AND SMILING INTO EACH OTHER'S EYES.

IN THIS "NEW BIRTH OF FREEDOM" FOR WHITES, THE ISSUES OF RACE WERE LARGELY BULLDOZED TO THE SIDELINES.

A MORE PALATABLE NARRATIVE OF MUTUAL GLORY AND HONOR-- HOW THE WAR HAD BEEN FOUGHT-- WIDELY REPLACED DISCUSSIONS OF WHY THE WAR HAD BEEN FOUGHT.

The Story of GETTYSBURG in Pictures

WHITES HAD TAKEN THE LESSON: FIGHTING OVER THE PLACE OF BLACKS IN AMERICAN SOCIETY WAS DIVISIVE. *IT THREW UP ROADBLOCKS TO HARMONY AND ECONOMIC GROWTH.*

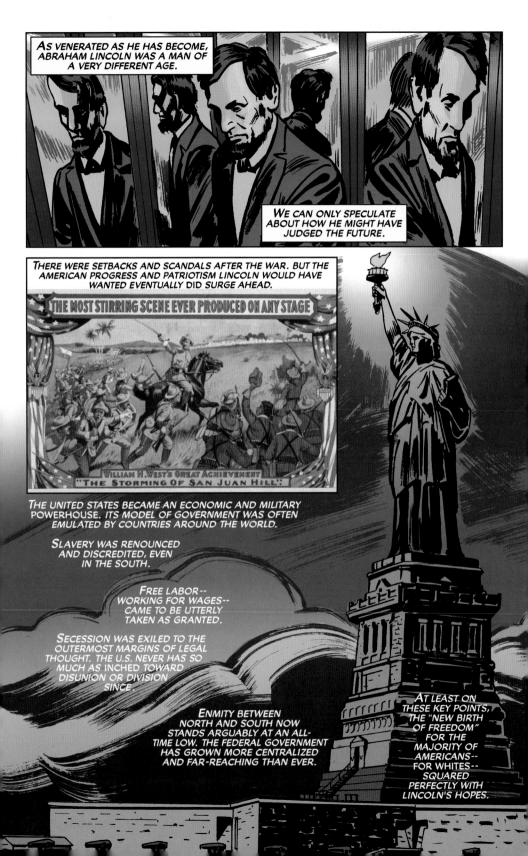

AS VENERATED AS HE HAS BECOME, ABRAHAM LINCOLN WAS A MAN OF A VERY DIFFERENT AGE.

WE CAN ONLY SPECULATE ABOUT HOW HE MIGHT HAVE JUDGED THE FUTURE.

THERE WERE SETBACKS AND SCANDALS AFTER THE WAR. BUT THE AMERICAN PROGRESS AND PATRIOTISM LINCOLN WOULD HAVE WANTED EVENTUALLY DID SURGE AHEAD.

THE MOST STIRRING SCENE EVER PRODUCED ON ANY STAGE

WILLIAM H. WEST'S GREAT ACHIEVEMENT

"THE STORMING OF SAN JUAN HILL"

THE UNITED STATES BECAME AN ECONOMIC AND MILITARY POWERHOUSE. ITS MODEL OF GOVERNMENT WAS OFTEN EMULATED BY COUNTRIES AROUND THE WORLD.

SLAVERY WAS RENOUNCED AND DISCREDITED, EVEN IN THE SOUTH.

FREE LABOR-- WORKING FOR WAGES-- CAME TO BE UTTERLY TAKEN AS GRANTED.

SECESSION WAS EXILED TO THE OUTERMOST MARGINS OF LEGAL THOUGHT. THE U.S. NEVER HAS SO MUCH AS INCHED TOWARD DISUNION OR DIVISION SINCE.

ENMITY BETWEEN NORTH AND SOUTH NOW STANDS ARGUABLY AT AN ALL-TIME LOW. THE FEDERAL GOVERNMENT HAS GROWN MORE CENTRALIZED AND FAR-REACHING THAN EVER.

AT LEAST ON THESE KEY POINTS, THE "NEW BIRTH OF FREEDOM" FOR THE MAJORITY OF AMERICANS-- FOR WHITES-- SQUARED PERFECTLY WITH LINCOLN'S HOPES.

PART 2: THE "NEW BIRTH OF FREEDOM" FOR BLACKS

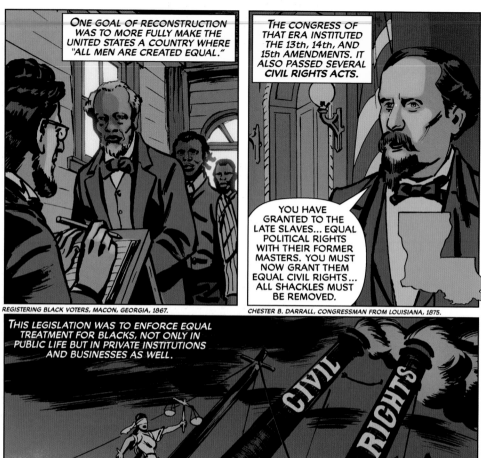

ONE GOAL OF RECONSTRUCTION WAS TO MORE FULLY MAKE THE UNITED STATES A COUNTRY WHERE "ALL MEN ARE CREATED EQUAL."

THE CONGRESS OF THAT ERA INSTITUTED THE 13th, 14th, AND 15th AMENDMENTS. IT ALSO PASSED SEVERAL *CIVIL RIGHTS ACTS.*

YOU HAVE GRANTED TO THE LATE SLAVES... EQUAL POLITICAL RIGHTS WITH THEIR FORMER MASTERS. YOU MUST NOW GRANT THEM EQUAL CIVIL RIGHTS... ALL SHACKLES MUST BE REMOVED.

REGISTERING BLACK VOTERS, MACON, GEORGIA, 1867.

CHESTER B. DARRALL, CONGRESSMAN FROM LOUISIANA, 1875.

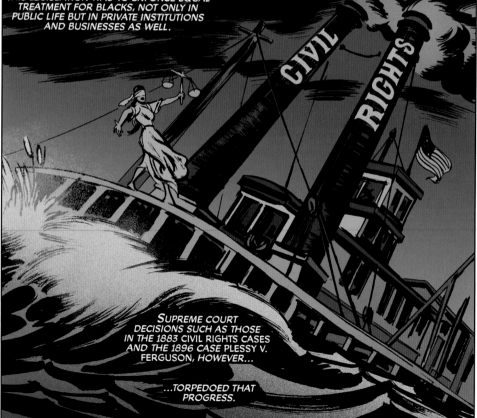

THIS LEGISLATION WAS TO ENFORCE EQUAL TREATMENT FOR BLACKS, NOT ONLY IN PUBLIC LIFE BUT IN PRIVATE INSTITUTIONS AND BUSINESSES AS WELL.

SUPREME COURT DECISIONS SUCH AS THOSE IN THE 1883 CIVIL RIGHTS CASES AND THE 1896 CASE PLESSY V. FERGUSON, HOWEVER...

...TORPEDOED THAT PROGRESS.

THE PLESSY DECISION ALLOWED FOR THE LEGAL ESTABLISHMENT OF SEPARATE BLACK AND WHITE SCHOOLS, HOSPITALS, DINING ROOMS, TRAIN CARS, DRINKING FOUNTAINS, SWIMMING POOLS, BEACHES, LAUNDRIES, THEATERS, WAITING ROOMS, RESTROOMS-- EVEN CEMETERIES.

COLORED

SUPPOSED TO BE "SEPARATE" BUT "EQUAL" IN QUALITY, TYPICALLY "COLORED" FACILITIES WERE GROSSLY INFERIOR.

"COLORED" SCHOOL, PAXVILLE, SOUTH CAROLINA, 1930s.

WHITE SCHOOL, PAXVILLE, SOUTH CAROLINA, 1930s.

THE SMALL GOVERNMENT TRADITION WAS BEHIND THE PLESSY AND CIVIL RIGHTS CASES DECISIONS.

THOUGH ON ITS FACE THE 14th AMENDMENT HAD VASTLY INCREASED WASHINGTON'S POWER OVER THE STATES...

...A CRITICAL MASS OF POST-WAR COURTS AND LAWMAKERS ALLOWED THAT POWER TO GO UNEXERCISED.

...THIS DECISION HAS INFLICTED A HEAVY CALAMITY UPON SEVEN MILLIONS OF THE PEOPLE OF THIS COUNTRY AND LEFT THEM NAKED AND DEFENSELESS AGAINST THE ACTION OF A MALIGNANT, VULGAR, AND PITILESS PREJUDICE...

FREDERICK DOUGLASS, 1883.

IT CAME TO BE ACCEPTED THAT THE FEDERAL GOVERNMENT HAD NO PLACE INTERFERING WITH RACE RELATIONS AT THE LOCAL LEVEL.

THE VAST MAJORITY OF AFRICAN AMERICANS REMAINED IN THE SOUTH AFTER THE CIVIL WAR.

SIMPLE POVERTY KEPT MOST FROM LEAVING. MANY ALSO FOUND IT HARD TO PULL AWAY FROM TIES OF FAMILY AND COMMUNITY.

SO FOR SOUTHERN BLACKS LIVING UNDER RACIAL SEGREGATION, LINCOLN'S "NEW BIRTH OF FREEDOM" WAS ESPECIALLY DENIED.

FAR FROM BEING ACTIVIST AND POWERFUL ON THEIR BEHALF, THE FEDERAL GOVERNMENT HAD PRACTICALLY ABANDONED REPRESENTING THEM.

WHILE THE U.S. HELD ITSELF UP TO THE WORLD AS A BASTION OF LIBERTY...

...THE STATUS OF ITS OWN AFRICAN AMERICAN CITIZENS MADE THE COUNTRY LOOK HYPOCRITICAL.

"Shall we be more tender with our dollars than with the Lives of our sons"

Secretary of the Treasury

Buy a United States Government Bond of the

2nd LIBERTY LOAN

of 1917

RACIAL DISCRIMINATION REMAINS A SOURCE OF EMBARRASSMENT TO THIS GOVERNMENT IN THE DAY-TO-DAY CONDUCT OF ITS FOREIGN RELATIONS... [AND] JEOPARDIZES THE EFFECTIVE MAINTENANCE OF OUR MORAL LEADER-SHIP OF THE FREE AND DEMOCRATIC NATIONS OF THE WORLD.

U.S. STATE DEPARTMENT BRIEF, 1954.

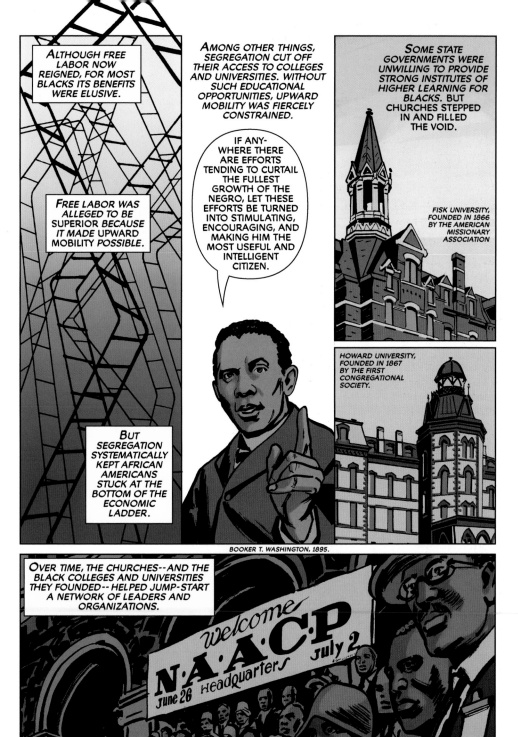

ALTHOUGH FREE LABOR NOW REIGNED, FOR MOST BLACKS ITS BENEFITS WERE ELUSIVE.

FREE LABOR WAS ALLEGED TO BE SUPERIOR *BECAUSE* IT MADE UPWARD MOBILITY *POSSIBLE.*

BUT SEGREGATION SYSTEMATICALLY KEPT AFRICAN AMERICANS STUCK AT THE BOTTOM OF THE ECONOMIC LADDER.

AMONG OTHER THINGS, SEGREGATION CUT OFF THEIR ACCESS TO COLLEGES AND UNIVERSITIES. WITHOUT SUCH EDUCATIONAL OPPORTUNITIES, UPWARD MOBILITY WAS FIERCELY CONSTRAINED.

IF ANY-WHERE THERE ARE EFFORTS TENDING TO CURTAIL THE FULLEST GROWTH OF THE NEGRO, LET THESE EFFORTS BE TURNED INTO STIMULATING, ENCOURAGING, AND MAKING HIM THE MOST USEFUL AND INTELLIGENT CITIZEN.

BOOKER T. WASHINGTON, 1895.

SOME STATE GOVERNMENTS WERE UNWILLING TO PROVIDE STRONG INSTITUTES OF HIGHER LEARNING FOR BLACKS. BUT CHURCHES STEPPED IN AND FILLED THE VOID.

FISK UNIVERSITY, FOUNDED IN 1866 BY THE AMERICAN MISSIONARY ASSOCIATION

HOWARD UNIVERSITY, FOUNDED IN 1867 BY THE FIRST CONGREGATIONAL SOCIETY.

OVER TIME, THE CHURCHES--AND THE BLACK COLLEGES AND UNIVERSITIES THEY FOUNDED-- HELPED JUMP-START A NETWORK OF LEADERS AND ORGANIZATIONS.

welcome N·A·A·C·P June 26 Headquarters July 2

WORKING INSIDE THE SYSTEM, THESE ACTIVISTS CHIPPED AWAY AT SEGREGATION.

ONE SUCH EXAMPLE CAN BE SEEN IN THE LANDMARK 1954 SUPREME COURT DECISION BROWN V. BOARD OF EDUCATION.

LAWYER THURGOOD MARSHALL (A GRADUATE OF HOWARD UNIVERSITY LAW SCHOOL) SUCCESSFULLY ARGUED THAT THE PLESSY DECISION COULD NOT JUSTLY APPLY TO EDUCATION-- AND THAT THE CONSTITUTION'S "EQUAL PROTECTION" CLAUSE EMPOWERS WASHINGTON TO STOP SEGREGATION IN STATES' PUBLIC SCHOOLS.

...NEGRO CHILDREN HAVE ROAD BLOCKS PUT UP IN THEIR MINDS AS A RESULT OF... SEGREGATION, SO THAT THE AMOUNT OF EDUCATION THAT THEY TAKE IN IS MUCH LESS THAN OTHER STUDENTS TAKE IN.

THURGOOD MARSHALL, 1952.

THROUGHOUT THE CIVIL RIGHTS ERA (1950s-1960s), HIGHLY TRAINED ACTIVISTS AND EVERYDAY PEOPLE ALIKE WORKED TO STRIKE DOWN SIMILAR UNJUST LAWS.

THEY TOOK UP THE LEGAL TOOLS THAT HAD BEEN LEFT OUT TO RUST SINCE RECONSTRUCTION: POWERS OF THE FEDERAL GOVERNMENT, ESPECIALLY THOSE RESERVED TO IT IN THE 14th AMENDMENT.

WAITING ROOM FOR WHITES ONLY BY ORDER OF POLICE DEPT.

COLORED ENTRANCE ONLY

COLORED WAITING ROOM

COLORED SERVED IN REAR

NOW!

BUT THE OFFICIALS OF THE SOUTH FOUGHT BACK. THEIR WORDS ECHOED THE SMALL GOVERNMENT TRADITION.

FRIENDS, I'M A MISSISSIPPI SEGREGATIONIST, AND I AM PROUD OF IT!

ROSS BARNETT, GOVERNOR OF MISSISSIPPI, 1962.

THERE WILL BE NO ENFORCED INTEGRATION IN VIRGINIA.

J. LINDSAY ALMOND JR., GOVERNOR OF VIRGINIA, 1958.

I DRAW THE LINE IN THE DUST AND TOSS THE GAUNTLET BEFORE THE FEET OF TYRANNY, AND I SAY SEGREGATION NOW, SEGREGATION TOMORROW, AND SEGREGATION FOREVER!

GEORGE C. WALLACE, GOVERNOR OF ALABAMA, 1963.

WHITES PUSHED BACK AGAINST RACIAL PROGRESS, WITH BOTH PEACEFUL DEMONSTRATIONS...

SAVE SEGREGATION VOTE STATES RIGHTS

...AND MOB VIOLENCE.

AS TENSIONS ROSE, HISTORY REPEATED ITSELF.

AS IN THE CIVIL WAR AND RECONSTRUCTION, WASHINGTON--TO ENFORCE FEDERAL LAW--DEPLOYED THE MILITARY ON SOUTHERN SOIL.

IN RESPONSE, VIOLENCE AND SEETHING RHETORIC FLARED UP.

MY FELLOW CITIZENS, WE ARE NOW AN OCCUPIED TERRITORY.

ORVAL FAUBUS, GOVERNOR OF ARKANSAS, 1957.

BUT THIS TIME NO NEW CIVIL WAR BROKE OUT.

WHY NOT?

PERHAPS THOSE FOUNDING DOCUMENTS' CONTRADICTIONS-- THE ONES OVER SLAVERY AND STATE SOVEREIGNTY-- HAD BEEN TOO THOROUGHLY SETTLED.

WITH SLAVERY LONG ABOLISHED, SOUTHERN PASSION OVER STATES' RIGHTS WAS INSUFFICIENT TO PLUNGE THE NATION BACK INTO DISUNION.

DECLARATION OF INDEPENDENCE

THE "NEW BIRTH OF FREEDOM" FOR BLACKS WOULD NOT BE POSTPONED ANY LONGER.

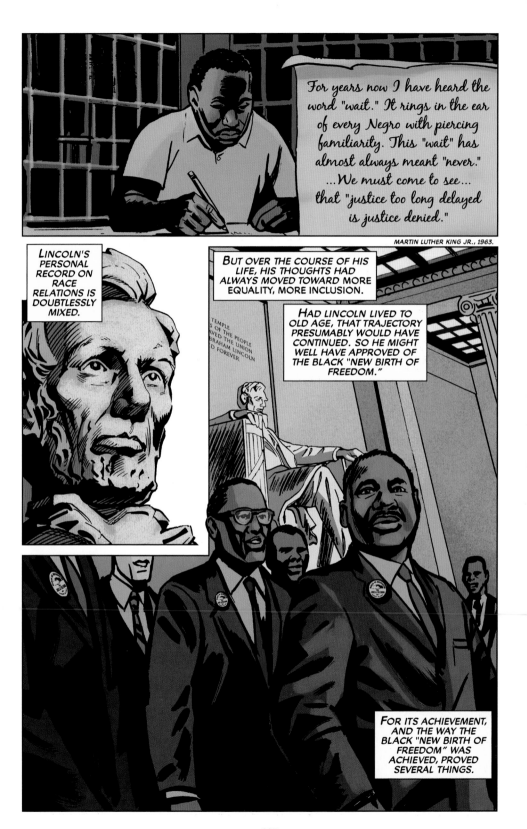

For years now I have heard the word "wait." It rings in the ear of every Negro with piercing familiarity. This "wait" has almost always meant "never." ...We must come to see... that "justice too long delayed is justice denied."

MARTIN LUTHER KING JR., 1963.

LINCOLN'S PERSONAL RECORD ON RACE RELATIONS IS DOUBTLESSLY MIXED.

BUT OVER THE COURSE OF HIS LIFE, HIS THOUGHTS HAD ALWAYS MOVED TOWARD MORE EQUALITY, MORE INCLUSION.

HAD LINCOLN LIVED TO OLD AGE, THAT TRAJECTORY PRESUMABLY WOULD HAVE CONTINUED. SO HE MIGHT WELL HAVE APPROVED OF THE BLACK "NEW BIRTH OF FREEDOM."

FOR ITS ACHIEVEMENT, AND THE WAY THE BLACK "NEW BIRTH OF FREEDOM" WAS ACHIEVED, PROVED SEVERAL THINGS.

IT PROVED THE UNION WAS STURDY ENOUGH TO WEATHER NEW STORMS.

IT PROVED THE FEDERAL GOVERNMENT COULD LEAD THE WAY AND MAKE STATES ACCEPT CHANGE.

IT PROVED FREE LABOR COULD GUIDE MORE AND MORE OUT OF POVERTY.

FINALLY, IT PROVED THE UNITED STATES COULD RESONATE MORE CLEARLY WITH THE CALL OF ITS MOST RHAPSODIC PHILOSOPHICAL MAXIM...

JOIN, or DIE.

...THAT ALL MEN ARE CREATED EQUAL.

REGARDLESS OF HOW GENUINELY THE COUNTRY'S FOUNDERS EMBRACED THAT IDEAL THEM-SELVES, THEY HELPED BRING ABOUT A WORLD WHERE THAT NOTION IS MORE WIDELY BELIEVED AND DEARLY CHERISHED THAN EVER BEFORE.

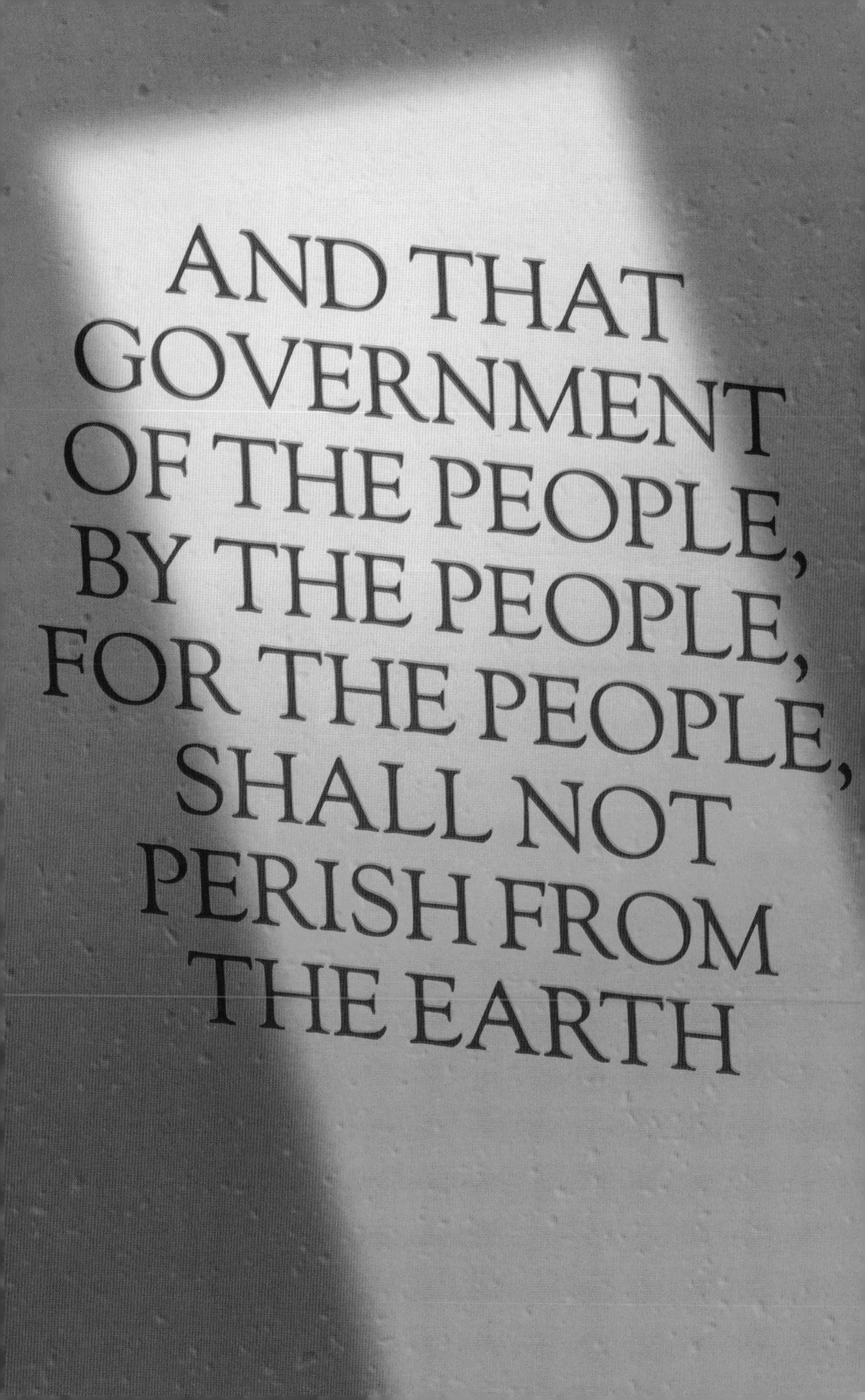
AND THAT
GOVERNMENT
OF THE PEOPLE,
BY THE PEOPLE,
FOR THE PEOPLE,
SHALL NOT
PERISH FROM
THE EARTH

THE FINAL WORDS OF THE GETTYSBURG ADDRESS MAKE A SUBTLE YET STRONG DISTINCTION. THEY CATEGORICALLY REJECT THE IDEA THAT GOVERNMENT IS OF, BY, AND FOR THE STATES-- AS SECESSIONISTS WOULD HAVE HAD IT.

THIS PASSAGE OF THE SPEECH IS ONE OF ITS MOST FAMILIAR AND REVERED. ODDLY, IT IS ALSO ONE OF THE LEAST ORIGINAL. IN FACT, NOTABLE FIGURES HAD EXPRESSED STRIKINGLY SIMILAR SENTIMENTS MANY TIMES BEFORE LINCOLN.

SO-- IS LINCOLN A PLAGIARIST?

I AM IN FAVOR OF THE DEMOCRACY... THAT SHALL GIVE US THE RULE, WHICH SHALL BE OF THE PEOPLE, BY THE PEOPLE, FOR THE PEOPLE.

CLEON, ATHENIAN STATESMAN, 420 B.C.

IT IS, SIR, THE PEOPLE'S CONSTITUTION, THE PEOPLE'S GOVERNMENT, MADE FOR THE PEOPLE, MADE BY THE PEOPLE, AND ANSWERABLE TO THE PEOPLE.

DANIEL WEBSTER, SENATOR FROM MASSACHUSETTS, 1830.

...I LOOK FORWARD TO THE TIME... WHEN THE GOVERNMENT IS OF ALL, FOR ALL, AND BY ALL...

REVEREND THEODORE PARKER, ABOLITIONIST, 1849.

ANY CHARGE OF PLAGIARISM WOULD BE OFF THE MARK.

LINCOLN WAS A LOVER OF THE LAW. AND IN HIS CAREER AS A LAWYER, HIS STOCK IN TRADE ALWAYS INVOLVED *PRECEDENT*.

LEGAL CASES ARE OFTEN WON BY REFERENCING THE WAYS SIMILAR CONTROVERSIES HAVE BEEN SETTLED IN THE PAST. IN LAW, DECISIONS CONSIDERED "SOUND" BECAUSE OF PERSUASIVE, UNDERLYING LOGIC ARE BROUGHT UP AS EXAMPLES AGAIN AND AGAIN. THEY THUS DEVELOP INTO ACCEPTED TRUTHS.

SO THE GREATER THE NUMBER OF EXAMPLES OF EMINENT THINKERS CLAIMING GOVERNMENT SHOULD BE OF, BY, AND FOR THE PEOPLE...

...THE MORE SOUND THOSE WORDS BECAME TO LINCOLN.

THE POWER OF PRECEDENT IS PRECISELY WHY, IN THE GETTYSBURG ADDRESS, LINCOLN CONSISTENTLY REFERRED BACK TO THE DECLARATION OF INDEPENDENCE. HE WAS MAKING THE ARGUMENT THAT THE CONFEDERACY'S POSITIONS ON SLAVERY, STATE SOVEREIGNTY, AND GOVERNMENT POWER WERE WRONG. LINCOLN WANTED TO GET PEOPLE TO BELIEVE THAT "OUR FATHERS" HAD ALREADY SETTLED THOSE CONTROVERSIES.

AS A CANNY POLITICIAN, LINCOLN WAS WELL AWARE THAT MANY DID NOT ACCEPT HIS VISION OF THE UNION.

BUT TO WIN OVER TO HIS SIDE AS MANY PEOPLE AS HE COULD, HE KNEW HE WAS OBLIGED TO OUTPERFORM HIS OPPONENTS IN A BATTLE OF LANGUAGE AND IDEAS-- JUST AS THE MILITARY HE COMMANDED HAD TO OUTPERFORM ITS OPPONENTS IN LITERAL *COMBAT*.

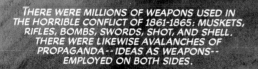

THERE WERE MILLIONS OF WEAPONS USED IN THE HORRIBLE CONFLICT OF 1861-1865: MUSKETS, RIFLES, BOMBS, SWORDS, SHOT, AND SHELL. THERE WERE LIKEWISE AVALANCHES OF PROPAGANDA--IDEAS AS WEAPONS-- EMPLOYED ON BOTH SIDES.

AND IN THAT WAY, THE GETTYSBURG ADDRESS WAS JUST ANOTHER WEAPON USED TO WIN THE CIVIL WAR. NOT ONLY THAT-- BUT TO MAKE SURE IT WOULD *STAY WON.* TO PRESERVE VICTORY FOR THE HAMILTONIAN STRAIN OF AMERICAN POLITICS.

THE HAMILTONIAN TRADITION OF STRONG GOVERNMENT WON THE CIVIL WAR. IT ALSO LIVED ON TO BECOME THE DOMINANT FORCE IN U.S. POLITICS.

OUT OF MILLIONS OF POLITICAL SPEECHES FROM YESTERYEAR, THE GETTYSBURG ADDRESS HAS STAYED ALIVE BECAUSE IT HAS PROVEN ITSELF SO EFFECTIVE IN PROMOTING A CERTAIN VISION OF THE UNION.

THE CONTRADICTIONS BETWEEN AMERICA'S FOUNDING DOCUMENTS-- THE SAME ONES THAT CAUSED THE CIVIL WAR IN THE FIRST PLACE-- HAVE CONTINUED TO WRESTLE FOR THE SOUL OF THE COUNTRY. AND THE GETTYSBURG ADDRESS HAS, LIKE A SWORD, BEEN DRAWN TIME AND AGAIN IN THE FIGHT FOR *THE IDEA* THAT AMERICANS ARE NOT MANY PEOPLES BUT ONE, AND THAT WASHINGTON-- NOT THE STATE CAPITOLS-- IS THE PEOPLE'S FOREMOST DEFENDER OF FREEDOM AND LIBERTY.

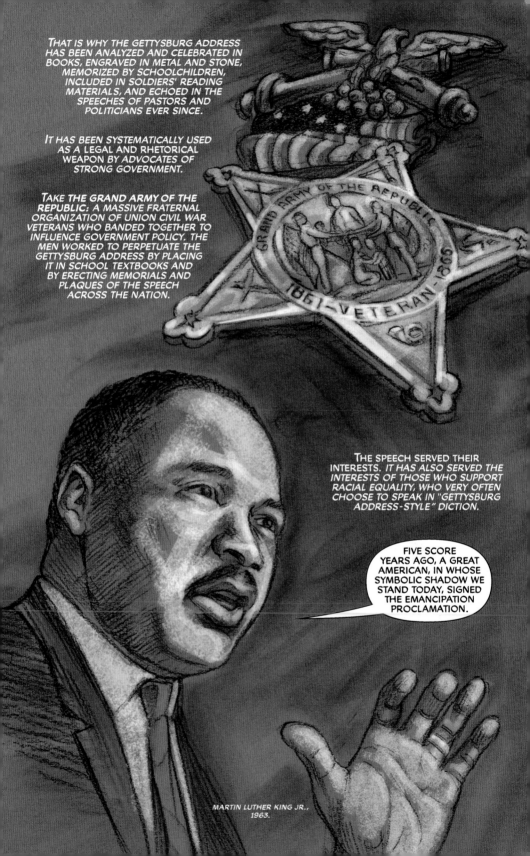

THAT IS WHY THE GETTYSBURG ADDRESS HAS BEEN ANALYZED AND CELEBRATED IN BOOKS, ENGRAVED IN METAL AND STONE, MEMORIZED BY SCHOOLCHILDREN, INCLUDED IN SOLDIERS' READING MATERIALS, AND ECHOED IN THE SPEECHES OF PASTORS AND POLITICIANS EVER SINCE.

IT HAS BEEN SYSTEMATICALLY USED AS A LEGAL AND RHETORICAL WEAPON BY ADVOCATES OF STRONG GOVERNMENT.

TAKE THE GRAND ARMY OF THE REPUBLIC: A MASSIVE FRATERNAL ORGANIZATION OF UNION CIVIL WAR VETERANS WHO BANDED TOGETHER TO INFLUENCE GOVERNMENT POLICY. THE MEN WORKED TO PERPETUATE THE GETTYSBURG ADDRESS BY PLACING IT IN SCHOOL TEXTBOOKS AND BY ERECTING MEMORIALS AND PLAQUES OF THE SPEECH ACROSS THE NATION.

THE SPEECH SERVED THEIR INTERESTS. IT HAS ALSO SERVED THE INTERESTS OF THOSE WHO SUPPORT RACIAL EQUALITY, WHO VERY OFTEN CHOOSE TO SPEAK IN "GETTYSBURG ADDRESS-STYLE" DICTION.

FIVE SCORE YEARS AGO, A GREAT AMERICAN, IN WHOSE SYMBOLIC SHADOW WE STAND TODAY, SIGNED THE EMANCIPATION PROCLAMATION.

MARTIN LUTHER KING JR., 1963.

STANDING ON THE GETTYSBURG BATTLEFIELD ON MEMORIAL DAY 1963, A WHITE SOUTHERN DEMOCRAT--THE MAN WHO WOULD SOON BECOME PRESIDENT HIMSELF--SAID...

ONE HUNDRED YEARS AGO, THE SLAVE WAS FREED.

ONE HUNDRED YEARS LATER, THE NEGRO REMAINS IN BONDAGE TO THE COLOR OF HIS SKIN...

WE AS A NATION HAVE FAILED OUR-SELVES BY NOT TRUSTING THE LAW AND BY NOT USING THE LAW TO GAIN SOONER THE ENDS OF JUSTICE WHICH LAW ALONE SERVES...

UNTIL JUSTICE IS BLIND TO COLOR, UNTIL EDUCATION IS UNAWARE OF RACE, UNTIL OPPORTUNITY IS UNCONCERNED WITH THE COLOR OF MEN'S SKINS, EMANCIPATION WILL BE A PROCLAMATION BUT NOT A FACT. TO THE EXTENT THAT THE PROCLAMATION OF EMANCIPATION IS NOT FULFILLED IN FACT, TO THAT EXTENT...

...WE SHALL HAVE FALLEN SHORT OF ASSURING FREEDOM TO THE FREE.

LYNDON B. JOHNSON, 1963.

AS CHIEF EXECUTIVE, JOHNSON SIGNED CONGRESS'S CIVIL RIGHTS ACT OF 1964, OUTLAWING RACE AND GENDER DISCRIMINATION IN THE WORKPLACE, PUBLIC SPACES, AND PRIVATE BUSINESSES. IN 1965, HE SIGNED CONGRESS'S VOTING RIGHTS ACT, STRENGTHENING BLACK SUFFRAGE.

IN 1964, CONGRESS ALSO PASSED (AND THE STATES RATIFIED) THE 24th AMENDMENT TO THE U.S. CONSTITUTION, CLOSING SEVERAL OF THE LOOPHOLES THAT SOME STATES HAD USED TO SUPPRESS AFRICAN AMERICANS FROM VOTING AND HOLDING OFFICE.

AND IN THE HALLS OF THE 1960s SUPREME COURT, CASES REAFFIRMED THE FEDERAL GOVERNMENT'S POWER TO ENFORCE CIVIL RIGHTS LAWS. THE 1967 CASE LOVING v. VIRGINIA STRUCK DOWN STATE LAWS BANNING INTERRACIAL MARRIAGES THAT HAD BEEN ON THE BOOKS SINCE THE 19th CENTURY.

THESE VICTORIES WON BATTLES.

THEY DID NOT WIN THE WAR.

THEY COULD NOT *PURGE* THE COUNTRY OF RACISM AND PREJUDICE. THEY DID NOT PURGE IT OF VIOLENCE.

BUT LIKE THE GETTYSBURG ADDRESS, THEY MADE A CASE. *THEY PUSHED AN ARGUMENT.*

SOME KIND OF FINAL VICTORY WOULD LIKELY ALWAYS BE ELUSIVE. BUT THAT WAS, AND IS, BESIDE THE POINT.

JUST AS LINCOLN SAID, THE VISION OF A GENUINELY FREE SOCIETY MUST BE...

...CONSTANTLY LOOKED TO, CONSTANTLY LABORED FOR, AND EVEN, THOUGH NEVER PERFECTLY ATTAINED, CONSTANTLY APPROXIMATED, AND THEREBY CONSTANTLY SPREADING AND DEEPENING ITS INFLUENCE, AND AUGMENTING THE HAPPINESS AND VALUE OF LIFE TO ALL PEOPLE, OF ALL COLORS, EVERYWHERE.

The END

JH:

This book is dedicated to my wife, Annie, who makes everything possible. I would also like to thank the following people for their help with
this project: our agent, Frank Scatoni; our editor, Will Hinton; produc-
tion editor Andrea Molitor; and everyone at HarperCollins. Professor
Matthew Osborn of Occidental College, Steve Kleiman, Licensed Battlefield Guide of Gettysburg Kurt Anschuetz, Peter Wall, and Mary-Rush
Yelverton. Thanks also to the staffs of the libraries and institutions that
made research for this book possible, including the Library of Congress,
the U.S. National Park Service, New York Public Library, the Hunting-
ton Library, Cornell University Library, Los Angeles Public Library, and
Cleveland Public Library. As space does not permit a proper source list
and suggestions for further reading, please see jonathanhennessey.com.

AM:

For Ruby and our boys, Alden and Henry. Coloring assistance from Ruby
McConnell and Cat Farris.

HarperCollins books may be purchased for educational, business, or sales
promotional use. For information please write: Special Markets Department,
HarperCollins Publishers, 10 East 53rd Street, New York, NY 10022.

FIRST EDITION

Library of Congress Cataloging-in-Publication Data has been applied for.

ISBN 978-0-06-196976-8

13 14 15 16 17 OV/SCP 10 9 8 7 6 5 4 3 2 1